The Complete Vegan Cookbook

The Complete Vegan Cookbook

Over 200 Tantalizing Recipes
Plus Plenty of Kitchen Wisdom for
Beginners and Experienced Cooks

SUSANN GEISKOPF-HADLER
and MINDY TOOMAY

PRIMA HEALTH

A Division of Prima Publishing

3000 Lava Ridge Court · Roseville, California 95661

(800) 632-8676 · www.primahealth.com

PRIMA HEALTH and colophon are registered trademarks of Prima Communications Inc., registered with the United States Patent and Trademark Office.

NUTRITIONAL ANALYSES

A per serving nutritional breakdown is provided for each recipe. If a range is given for an ingredient amount, the breakdown is based on the smaller number. If a range is given for servings, the breakdown is based on the larger number. If a choice of ingredients is given in an ingredient listing, the breakdown is calculated using the first choice. Nutritional content may vary depending on the specific brands or types of ingredients used. "Optional" ingredients or those for which no specific amount is stated are not included in the breakdown. Nutritional figures are rounded to the nearest whole number.

Library of Congress Cataloging-in-Publication Data
Geiskopf-Hadler, Susann.
    The complete vegan cookbook : over 200 tantalizing recipes plus plenty of kitchen wisdom for beginners and experienced cooks / Susann Geiskopf-Hadler, Mindy Toomay.
        p.   cm.
    Includes index.
    ISBN 0-7615-2951-9
    1. Vegan cookery. I. Toomay, Mindy. II. Title.
TX837 .G3798 2001
641.5'636—dc21   2001020796

01 02 03 04 DD 10 9 8 7 6 5 4 3 2 1
Printed in the United States of America

Visit us online at www.primahealth.com

We dedicate this book to creative and conscientious cooks

who season every meal with joy and mindfulness.

Why not make a daily pleasure out of a daily necessity?

—Peter Mayle, *A Year in Provence*

Contents

Acknowledgments

Every book is the sum total of countless contributions. This one is due, first and foremost, to the vision and investment of our publisher, who invited us to write the "definitive" vegan cookbook. The notion gripped and guided us as we shaped a book that would be worthy of that description. The early encouragement of our editor, Susan Silva, and the patient detail work of Shawn Vreeland, assistant project editor, were enormously valuable. The copyeditor, designer, page compositor, and proofreader worked hard to fine-tune the project, for which we are grateful. And last but never least, our friends and families contributed inspiration and support, and happily devoured the fruits of our labors. Thank you, one and all.

Introduction

Our age is the golden age of nutrition. Hundreds of modern scientists are exploring the frontiers of diet, discovering which chemical compounds in food contribute to vibrant energy and strong immunity and which ones bring on fatigue and chronic illness.

There is still a lot to learn but this much we know. Plant foods—vegetables, herbs, grains, beans, fruits, nuts, and seeds—are packed with antioxidant vitamins, blood-building minerals, and bowel-toning fiber. They are low in calories and virtually free of saturated fat and cholesterol. The research is telling us, without a doubt, that eating an abundance of foods from the vegetable kingdom leads to healthier, and maybe even longer, lives.

In light of all this, it is not very surprising that more and more people are choosing to eat plant foods exclusively, giving up all meat, dairy products, eggs, and other animal-derived foods. For many, the vegan decision goes beyond concerns about personal health. They realize that the livestock industry depletes and degrades the environment and that inhumane treatment of animals is common at large-scale "factory farms." To walk the vegan path is to consider all the consequences of how we eat and to make food choices that are both wise and compassionate.

But our purpose here is not to preach the virtues of veganism. No single eating plan is right for everyone, all the time. Cooking vegan even occasionally can be beneficial to your health and to the planet's. So we wrote this book to feed you well, to fuel your culinary imagination, and to encourage you to cook with creativity and awareness.

We offer *The Complete Vegan Cookbook* as an inspirational and practical guide, whether you are brand new to meatless cooking or have been vegan for years. Beginning cooks will glean valuable guidance from chapter 1, "Cooking Fundamentals," where we teach you how to follow a recipe and explain basic techniques and tools. A cook's best friend is a well-equipped kitchen and chapter 2 gives succinct guidelines to "Stocking the Vegan Pantry." And for those who love cooking for friends and family, chapter 3 gives some indispensable tips on menu planning, and provides some menu suggestions for everyday and special-occasion meals. If you're looking for a short course on good nutrition, spend some time with the appendix, "Nutrition Fundamentals," which covers the basics of this vast and complex science.

The heart of the book is our 200-plus recipes that demonstrate the delicious variety to be enjoyed on an animal-free diet. We hope these dishes convince you that vegan eating can be supremely satisfying, as well as health-promoting.

May this book nurture in all our readers a passion for fresh and fabulous cooking that celebrates life.

A Simple Definition

The vegan diet is made up exclusively of foods from the vegetable kingdom. It excludes all animal products: meat, poultry, fish, seafood, eggs, dairy products, and honey. Products that are processed using animal ingredients, like gelatin and standard white table sugar, are also eliminated from the vegan way of eating.

1

Cooking Fundamentals

W hether you've been cooking for years or are a novice in the kitchen, this chapter can make the time you spend there more enjoyable. If you're relatively new to cooking, read through it from time to time, until the basic terms and techniques become second nature. If you're already a skilled cook, this chapter provides a useful refresher course and can instruct you in some methods you may not have tried.

SUCCESSFUL COOKING FROM OUR RECIPES

Experienced cooks are guided by instinct and intuition as they dream up new dishes or cook old favorites from memory. But following recipes is a fun and satisfying process, too, especially when you're just starting out in the kitchen or when you want to learn something new. If you need a beginning course in following recipes, or if a refresher course might do you good, here are some tips.

- Use only the freshest, best-quality ingredients. Your finished dish will be only as good as the individual components that go into it, so don't compromise on quality.

- Read a recipe all the way through before beginning. This will allow you to perform any preliminary steps, such as bringing ingredients to room temperature. It will also give you a clear mental picture of the entire process.

- Set all your ingredients and tools out on the work surface before you begin to cook. This will save you from having to walk from one end of the kitchen to the other to look for a spice or an implement, when you should be keeping your eye on what's happening on the stove.

- For certain ingredients, quantities are approximate. When we call for a large carrot, for instance, the one you select may be smaller or larger than ours. This is nothing to worry about. When using a very specific amount is essential to the success of a dish, we provide precise measurements. Otherwise, use your own judgment.

- Seasonings are always a matter of personal taste. Naturally, we have provided recipes for dishes that taste good to us, seasoned as we like them. Some people prefer more or less of certain seasonings—such as salt or garlic. You are welcome to adjust amounts accordingly. We often customize recipes as we're cooking, and we encourage you to do the same.

- When serving hot food, warm the serving dishes and the individual plates so the food stays at the optimum temperature as long as possible. This is easily accomplished by placing the dishes near the heat source as you cook, or you may warm the oven for several minutes right before dinnertime, turn off the heat, and place the dishes there until needed.

A Dictionary of Cooking Terms

Keep in mind that "proper" technique is not essential for most home cooking. Mastering a few very simple cutting and mixing basics is all that's required for you to begin turning out delicious dishes. Your primary classroom is your own kitchen, and the more you cook, the more skilled and confident you will become.

If at some point you want advanced training, say in the classic French methods, there are many schools, books, and videos that can teach you. But don't let the lack of such training make you think you can't be a great cook! And remember: Even the most accomplished chefs are always learning from their successes and failures.

Below are explanations of the basic cooking terms used in this book, listed in alphabetical order for quick reference.

Al dente Italian term, literally meaning "to the tooth," describes pasta that is tender but still slightly chewy.

Bake To cook, covered or uncovered, in an oven.

Beat To make a mixture smooth with a brisk whipping or stirring motion, using a wooden spoon, fork, egg beater, or electric mixer.

Blanch To cook briefly in boiling water; frequently done to loosen the skin of a fruit, nut, or vegetable for easy peeling.

Blend To mix two or more ingredients until thoroughly combined.

Boil To cook in rapidly bubbling liquid.

Braise To cook slowly with a small amount of liquid in a tightly covered pan, on the stovetop or in the oven.

Broil   To cook by direct heat, usually under a flame or electric coils.

Chiffonade   French technique in which leafy herbs or other greens are stacked and rolled into a loose cylinder, then sliced crosswise into paper-thin shreds using a sharp knife.

Chill   To place in the refrigerator for a designated time.

Chop, finely   To cut into pieces about the size of a pea.

Chop, coarsely   To cut into larger, irregular pieces.

Cool   To remove from the heat and let stand at room temperature.

Dice   To cut into cubes of roughly uniform size.

Dice, finely   To cut into very small cubes of roughly uniform size.

Dissolve   To disperse a dry ingredient into a liquid, creating a solution.

Emulsified   Refers to a combination of ingredients that has been vigorously whipped together, often using a wire whisk, until they are completely blended and slightly thickened, such as vinaigrette.

En papillote   Literally "in paper," refers to a cooking method in which ingredients are baked in a tightly closed paper packet, producing a moist and aromatic dish.

Fold   To gently add ingredients in an under-and-over motion, using a wooden spoon or rubber spatula.

Fork-tender   Usually used to describe vegetables that are easily pierced with a fork, but still firm enough to retain their shape.

Fry   To cook in hot oil.

Marinate   To place food in seasoned liquid for a period of time, infusing it with the flavors of the marinade.

Mince   To cut into tiny uniform pieces.

Mix   To stir ingredients together until evenly distributed.

Pack, firmly   To place an ingredient in a measuring cup or spoon and compress with your hand or a wooden spoon.

Pack, lightly   To place an ingredient in a measuring cup or spoon without compressing.

Parboil   See Blanch.

Sauté   To lightly brown ingredients in oil or other liquid.

Simmer   To bubble gently.

Steam   To cook over boiling water in a covered pan, with the food suspended above the water.

Stir   To mix ingredients with a circular motion until well blended.

Stir-fry   To cook in a skillet or wok in a small amount of liquid over high heat, tossing the ingredients frequently.

Toss   To combine ingredients with a gentle lifting and dropping motion, usually using two implements.

Whip   To beat rapidly, incorporating air and producing volume in the ingredients.

Whisk   To beat rapidly with a wire whisk, for quick and thorough blending of ingredients (as in a salad dressing).

Zest   To remove the colored rind of citrus fruits, not including the white pith, using a grater or zester; also refers to bits of rind removed in this manner.

Simple Techniques

Blanching Vegetables and Fruits

Some recipes call for blanching (also called parboiling) to cook vegetables a bit before adding them to a recipe. This brightens their color and slightly softens their texture. Blanching is also used to loosen the skins of fruits, such as tomatoes and peaches, so they can be easily peeled.

Here's how it's done:

First, put a few quarts of water on to boil in a large stockpot. Wash the vegetables and/or fruits and leave them whole or chop them as instructed in the recipe.

For vegetables, drop them into the rapidly boiling water and cook from 30 seconds to 5 minutes, depending on their size and density. Test a piece from time to time to check for doneness; it should still be quite firm, but not as crunchy as it was when raw. When done, immediately transfer the vegetables to a colander and rinse with cold water to stop the cooking, then set aside to drain thoroughly.

For tomatoes, cut one small slit through the skin of each tomato, then carefully drop the whole tomatoes into the rapidly boiling water. Within a minute or so their skins will begin to pull away from the slit. At this point, gently transfer the tomatoes with a slotted spoon to a bowl of ice water. When cool enough to handle, remove the skins and cut out the stems. If the recipe calls for seeding the tomatoes after blanching, cut the peeled tomatoes in half crosswise and gently squeeze over the sink to remove the juicy seed pockets.

For peaches or nectarines, drop the whole fruit into the rapidly boiling water and cook about 1 minute. Immediately transfer them, gently, to a bowl of ice water. When they are cool enough to handle, peel off the skin.

Cooking Dried Beans

Cooked dried beans provide excellent protein and fiber and are an important component of the vegan eating plan. Canned beans are readily available, but the texture and flavor of freshly cooked ones are far superior.

Before cooking dried beans, sort through them to find and discard any small pebbles, dirt clods, or other foreign objects. Also discard any beans that look moldy or shriveled. Rinse the beans well to remove surface dirt, drain, and transfer them to a large stockpot.

The smaller dried legumes, such as lentils and split peas, can be cooked without presoaking and will be done in under an hour. With larger beans, however, several hours of soaking will reduce the cooking time considerably and is reputed to reduce the amount of gas they produce in the digestive tract.

To presoak, cover the beans with fresh water to a depth of about 4 inches, cover the pot, and allow the beans to soak at room temperature for several hours or overnight. If you are pressed for time, use this shortcut method: Cover the beans with water as described above, then bring the pot to a strong simmer. Immediately turn off the heat and allow the beans to soak for 1 hour.

To cook the beans, drain off the soaking liquid and add enough fresh water to submerge the beans to a depth of about 2 inches. Bring to a strong simmer over high heat, then reduce the heat to medium and simmer gently until the beans are tender but not mushy. Cooking times will vary, depending on the size, type, and age of the beans, but plan on an hour or longer. Check the pot frequently and add more water, as needed, to keep the beans fully submerged.

You may add peeled cloves of garlic, bay leaves, chili flakes, and/or kombu seaweed to the pot, if desired. The first three ingredients will add flavor; the kombu will mineralize the broth and may further reduce the "windy" nature of the beans. Many cooks believe that salting beans early in the cooking process can toughen them, so wait to add salt until the beans are almost done.

As a general rule of thumb, 1 cup of dried beans will yield 2 to 2 ½ cups of cooked beans. We usually cook beans in large batches because cooked beans kept on hand in the refrigerator add convenient nutrition and fiber to salads and soups and are easily turned into tasty spreads (see the Appetizers chapter for specific recipes). Beans also freeze well; cool the beans completely before freezing them in measured portions.

If a recipe calls for cooked and drained beans, strain off the cooking liquid, but don't throw it away. It contains a good quantity of minerals and makes a delicious and nourishing broth on its own.

Cooking Grains

Whole dried grains provide complex carbohydrates for strong and steady energy production, as well as vitamins, minerals, and fiber. They are another important part of a healthy vegan diet. Many different grains are available, each having a distinct flavor, texture, and nutrition profile. This wide variety allows us to enjoy whole grains on a daily basis without monotony.

A few grains, like millet and quinoa, are best rinsed before cooking to remove surface saponin, which gives the grain a bitter taste. Some, like buckwheat groats (kasha) and barley, are usually toasted lightly before cooking. Cooking times and specific instructions vary from grain to grain.

Despite these differences, though, the general cooking instructions are the same for all grains. They are added to rapidly boiling water (the typical ratio is 1 cup grain to 2 cups water), tightly covered, then simmered over very low heat until the grain has absorbed all the water and is plump and tender.

When the grain is done, turn off the heat and allow the pot to stand with its lid in place for at least 5 minutes or up to an hour before serving. The grain will continue to absorb the steam in the pan, ensuring a light and fluffy, rather than a mushy, texture. This cooking method is referred to as "steaming" and produces delicious and easy-to-digest grains that can be used in a multitude of ways.

Look up individual grains in the index for recipes that give specific cooking instructions. Simple directions for steaming brown and basmati rice appear on pages 289 and 299.

Leftover cooked grains can be stored in the refrigerator in a closed glass or plastic container for up to a few days. They are delicious added to miso broth, green salad, and burritos. Plain cooked grains can also make a great breakfast. Reheat the grains in a little water or eat them cold, with your favorite cereal toppings.

Reconstituting Dried Fruits and Vegetables

Dried fruits and vegetables are often reconstituted before being added to a recipe, to intensify their flavors and soften them to a chewable consistency.

Dried fruits like figs and apricots can simply be immersed in hot water, fruit juice, brandy, or wine and allowed to sit at room temperature until soft and chewable. The amount of time required will vary from fruit to fruit, but 15 to 30 minutes is the norm. Check frequently and don't let the fruit sit any longer than necessary in the liquid, as it will become mushy and flavorless.

Dried tomatoes that are not packed in oil are placed in a bowl and covered with hot water, then allowed to plump for about 15 to 30 minutes, until chewable but not mushy. When they are slightly softened, remove the tomatoes from the liquid and proceed as directed in the recipe. The soaking liquid may be reserved for a soup or sauce.

Dried mushrooms are reconstituted before use by soaking them in hot water for 30 minutes or so. When the mushrooms are tender, lift them out of the water, leaving behind any bits of soil or sand. Strain the soaking liquid and use it where liquid is needed in the dish, or save it for another recipe, such as a soup or sauce. Shiitake mushrooms should be carefully inspected for grit that may be caught in the gills under the caps.

Sea vegetables, such as hijiki and wakame, are reconstituted by soaking in warm water for about 30 minutes. They plump a great deal when soaked, so use a large bowl. When tender and plumped, lift them from the soaking water and use them as called for in a recipe. Reconstituted sea vegetables can be eaten without further cooking, simply chopped and added to a green salad or a bowl of cooked rice.

Roasting Bell Peppers

Bell peppers develop a delightful smoky sweetness when roasted. They are great in salads and sandwiches, and are called for in many recipes.

Place a whole, uncut pepper under a very hot broiler or on a hot grill and turn it every few minutes until the entire skin is charred black. Remove the blackened pepper to a paper or plastic bag, fold the bag closed, and set aside. The steam inside the bag will finish the cooking and the pepper will become quite tender. When it is cool enough to handle, remove the pepper from the bag and rub it gently with a paper or cloth towel to remove the charred skin. Discard the stem and seeds and proceed with the recipe.

This same technique can be applied to tomatoes and eggplants. Leftover roasted vegetables can be stored in a covered glass or plastic container in the refrigerator for up to a few days.

Steaming Vegetables

Steaming is the easiest and most nutritious way to prepare fresh vegetables for daily consumption. Simply chop the vegetable as directed in a recipe or according to your own preference. Place a steamer tray in a large saucepan and add about 2 inches of water. Place the pan over medium-high heat and add the vegetable to the tray. Cover the pan tightly and cook until the vegetable is fork-tender, meaning it is easily pierced with a fork but still firm enough to hold its shape.

Steaming times vary according to the type and size of the vegetable. Generally speaking, tender green vegetables will steam in 5 to 10 minutes, once the water has come to a boil. Whole artichokes, beets, and other dense vegetables may take 25 minutes or longer; add some water midway through to keep the pan from going dry. Chopping dense vegetables before steaming will hasten their cooking time.

When the vegetable is fork-tender, immediately remove it from the pan. If you simply turn off the heat and leave the lid and the vegetable in place, it will continue to cook and you may end up with vegetable mush.

Leftover steamed vegetables can be stored in a covered glass or plastic container in the refrigerator for up to a few days. They are a nice addition to green or grain salads.

Toasting Nuts and Seeds

Toasting brings out the essential flavors of nuts and seeds and gives them a pleasant crunch. Place raw, unsalted nuts or seeds in a single layer in a dry cast-iron skillet or other heavy pan over medium-high heat on the stovetop. Shake the pan or stir the contents frequently as they heat. When the nuts or seeds have darkened in color and emit a wonderful roasted aroma, they are done. Immediately transfer them to a plate or bowl so they don't continue cooking in the hot pan.

Alternatively, nuts and seeds can be toasted (or, more accurately, roasted) in a conventional or toaster oven, following the same general directions.

For special spiced nuts, you may add a small amount of oil and the sweet or savory spices of your choice. See Spicy Toasted Pumpkin Seeds (page 49) and Roasted Peanuts with Chili and Lime (page 50) for inspiration.

Toasted nuts and seeds can be stored in airtight containers in a dark, cool place for up to a few weeks, or in the freezer for longer periods.

ESSENTIAL TOOLS

Having the proper tools on hand makes any task more enjoyable—from sewing to gardening, automotive repair to home restoration. Why should cooking be any different? There are a lot of fancy gadgets on the market for cooking enthusiasts, but not all of them are absolute essentials. Here we present the items we consider to be kitchen necessities, as well as some that are less commonly used but great for certain purposes.

If you are just starting out, and the following list seems daunting, keep in mind that it isn't necessary to spend hundreds of dollars to stock your kitchen. Bowls, baking dishes, and many other cooking tools are readily available at garage sales or thrift stores. Start with the basics and build from there, guided by your cooking preferences and your pocketbook.

To begin with, you can get by with a few mixing bowls, measuring cups and spoons, one medium-sized skillet and one saucepan with a tight-fitting lid, a couple of wooden spoons, a cutting board, and one good knife. As soon as possible, invest in a blender and large stockpot for making soups and cooking pasta. Round out your assortment of knives, baking dishes, appliances, and gadgets over time.

When you're beginning to cook, your most important assets are enthusiasm and a willingness to learn. So relax, keep it simple, and have fun.

Here is a list of the kitchen tools we use most frequently.

Appliances:

Blender

Electric mixer (hand-held)

Food processor

Immersion blender

Small coffee grinder (for spices and seeds)

Toaster oven

Cookware:

Baking dishes in assorted sizes

Cast-iron skillets: 8-inch and 10-inch

Glass pie plate

Loaf pan

Muffin tin

Saucepans with lid (glass lids are preferable): 1-quart and 2-quart

Stockpots with lid: 4-quart and 8-quart

Teakettle

Wok with lid

Other essentials:

Can opener

Clean rags and sponges

Colanders in various sizes

Corkscrew

Cotton tea towels

Custard cups for holding pre-measured ingredients

Cutting boards

Garlic press

Graters

Juicing dish (manual)

Kitchen scale

Kitchen timer

Knives: 10-inch or 12-inch chef's knife, 4-inch paring knife, bread knife

Ladle

Measuring spoons

Mixing bowls

Nutcracker

Nutmeg grater or grinder

Pepper grinder

Pot holders

Rolling pin

Rubber spatulas

Salad spinner

Sharpening steel and stone

Slotted spoon

Metal spatula

Strainers in various sizes

Tongs

Whisks in assorted sizes

Wooden spoons

The Art of Measuring

Learning how to measure ingredients correctly is an important technique in recipe preparation. Once you have spent enough time in the kitchen, you will be able to "eyeball" a tablespoon of minced parsley, but until then you should use the measuring tools and techniques outlined below when you're cooking from a recipe.

The methods are different for measuring wet and dry ingredients, but one important rule applies to both: Don't pour or level off ingredients directly over the bowl you are using to mix the ingredients. Any excess will end up in the recipe, and the dish may suffer for it.

MEASURING DRY INGREDIENTS

Nesting plastic or metal measuring cups are used for dry ingredients. Dip the cup into the ingredient or scoop the dry ingredient into the cup, until it is overflowing. Then hold the full cup upright and level it off with a straight edge, such as the handle of a wooden spoon. Unless the recipe says to do so, do not shake or tap the cup to settle the contents before leveling off.

MEASURING LIQUID INGREDIENTS

Glass measuring cups are equipped with a spout and bear red marks to delineate quantities. These are specially designed for measuring liquids. Place the measuring cup on a level surface, pour in the liquid, then bend down to check the desired mark at eye level.

MEASURING SPOONS

Measuring spoons come in sets, usually ranging in capacity from ⅛ teaspoon to 1 tablespoon. You might want to own more than one set, as you will sometimes need to measure many small quantities for a single recipe. When using measuring spoons for dry ingredients, dip the spoon into the ingredient, then level off with a straight edge, such as the handle of a wooden spoon. To measure a liquid ingredient, pour it directly into the measuring spoon, filling it to the brim.

MEASURING BULK WEIGHT

A kitchen scale comes in handy when a recipe calls for an ounce or pound of an ingredient. If necessary, use the adjusting mechanism to set the scale at precisely "0" before you place the food you are weighing on it. If you are using a digital scale, follow the manufacturer's directions.

2

Stocking the Vegan Pantry

Do you sometimes stare into your refrigerator or cupboards and wonder why there's nothing to eat in there? Stocking the pantry is a simple and essential task that many well-intentioned cooks neglect. A well-stocked pantry enhances your enjoyment of cooking, whether you're following a recipe or creating a dish on the spot. A last-minute run to the store is one sure way to dampen a cook's enthusiasm.

A little preliminary planning helps immensely. Assess your supply of the staples—like beans, grains, and seasonings—and make your weekly shopping list. Then choose a couple of recipes you'd like to try, and add any needed ingredients to your list.

Set aside about two hours a week for grocery shopping. Learn the layout of your favorite grocery store and the hours of the local farmer's market to keep the pantry full of inspiration while keeping shopping time to a minimum.

This section suggests items to keep on hand in your pantry and refrigerator for quick, high-quality meal preparation.

GRAINS

Grains are the seeds of certain plants wrapped in a protective shell, along with all the nutrients required to start the growing process if the seeds are planted. Grains are an excellent source of vitamins, minerals, amino acids, and fiber. Buy your grains in moderate quantities and store them in tightly sealed jars in a cool cupboard. Add bay leaves to your grain jars to help keep the bugs out.

Flour is made by grinding whole grains. Buy organic, if possible, and look for "stone-ground" on the label. This means the grinding was done using millstones with grooves that allow air to circulate, keeping the grain cool. This practice prevents rancidity and ensures a fresh and nutty—not bitter—taste.

Although it is a processed food, pasta has a place in the healthy vegan diet. Many varieties of whole-grain pasta are available—wheat, corn, rice, and buckwheat among them. Standard semolina pasta, although made from "white" flour, is an unadulterated product that you can enjoy in moderation. Some pasta varieties include spinach, artichoke flour, or other vegetable flours, which add interesting color and flavor. Pasta has a long shelf life, but you should use it within a few months, as it will get brittle and stale over time.

Grain beverages are called for in some recipes and are convenient for topping cooked or dry cereal. They also make satisfying and healthful beverages for children and adults, plain or with flavor enhancers such as vanilla, maple syrup, and/or carob or cocoa powder.

We keep our pantries stocked with:

Barley
Basmati rice, brown and white
Buckwheat flour
Bulgur
Brown rice, long- and short-grain
Cornmeal
Kasha (buckwheat groats)
Mixed cracked grains for hot cereal
Oats, whole groats and rolled

Orzo (rice-shaped Greek semolina pasta)
Pasta, dried (various grains and shapes)
Quinoa
Rice milk and/or mixed grain beverage
Soba (Japanese buckwheat noodles)
Unbleached all-purpose flour
Whole wheat pastry flour
Wild rice

LEGUMES

Dried legumes are fiber-rich foods that also provide plenty of protein and minerals. We keep a wide variety on hand, because they are important to a healthy vegan diet. Buy legumes in moderate quantities, depending on the frequency with which you use them. Dried beans have quite a long shelf life, but they can get old and stale if kept for too long, just like other dried foods.

When cooking beans, we make extra and freeze them in measured amounts for future use. For spur-of-the moment inspiration, we also keep different varieties of canned cooked beans on hand.

We keep our pantries stocked with:

Adzuki beans	Lentils (brown, red, and
Black beans	French/green varieties)
Cannellini beans	Mung beans
Garbanzo beans	Split peas
Kidney beans	

FRESH VEGETABLES, FRUITS, AND HERBS

Everyone's diet should include an abundance of seasonal fresh vegetables, fruits, and herbs, preferably organically grown. They bring wonderful colors, textures, aromas, and flavors into the daily diet, along with vitamins, minerals, and fiber. Shop for a few days' worth of produce at a time and eat it quickly, as many nutrients diminish with age. And try not to get stuck in a broccoli and carrot rut. These are important foods that can be eaten frequently, but the vegetable kingdom holds so many great new discoveries. Remember: For the best nutrition, it's important to include a wide variety of fresh foods in the diet.

The rule of thumb when selecting vegetables of all types is to look for deep, uniform color (no yellowing or bruising) and a crisp, not limp, texture. The rules for fruit are a little more complex, since ripeness can be tricky to evaluate in a melon, pear, or avocado. Here again, good color and texture are important indicators of quality.

Fresh herbs can be picked right off the plant and tossed into the cooking pot. Since they are easy to grow, we plant our favorites just outside the kitchen so they are always only a few steps away. If you don't grow your own, purchase fresh herbs as you need them and store them loosely wrapped in plastic in the refrigerator. When selecting leafy fresh herbs at the market, look for robust leaves and a fresh aroma.

The local farmer's market is a great place to find just-picked produce. See if your community has one, and make it a regular stop on your weekly shopping rounds. We frequently buy the following fresh produce, when in season, and store it as noted. This is only a partial list, proof that we love vegetables!

Stored at Room Temperature

Vegetables: Onions, shallots, garlic, potatoes, sweet potatoes, winter squash

Fruits: Apples, pears, avocados, bananas, mangoes, pineapples, papayas, citrus fruits, melons

Stored in the Refrigerator

Vegetables: Carrots, celery, green beans, salad greens, steaming greens, broccoli, cabbage, cauliflower, beets, rutabagas, green onions, ginger, chilies, parsley, cilantro, basil, eggplant, zucchini and other summer squashes, artichokes, asparagus, shelling and edible pod peas

Fruits: Ripe strawberries, blueberries, figs

DRIED FRUITS

Drying foods is the oldest and most practical way to extend the bounty of the season. Only the moisture is removed during the drying process; most of the nutrients and flavor remain. Dried fruits are rich in minerals—especially iron, copper, and potassium—and in fiber. Remember, however, that in dried fruits, the sugars and calories become concentrated, so eat them in moderation.

Natural food stores are excellent places to find a wide selection of dried fruits. An organic, unsulfured variety is best from a health standpoint, although some people prefer the brighter color of sulfur-treated fruit. Store dried fruits in airtight containers, such as glass jars with tight-fitting lids, in a cool, dark place.

We keep our pantries stocked with:

Dried apricots	Prunes
Dried cranberries	Raisins, dark and golden
Dried figs	Sun-dried tomatoes
Dried mangos	

SEA VEGETABLES

Seaweeds, more affectionately called sea vegetables, have been enjoyed as food for centuries and can add great taste, variety, and nutrition to the vegan diet. Sea vegetables are an easy-to-digest source of important minerals—including potassium, calcium, magnesium, iron, and iodine—as well as vitamins and amino acids. They also deliver healthy fiber to the digestive tract. Most people can eat seaweeds in abundance and experience only positive effects; however, people with hyperthyroidism should minimize iodine-rich foods in their diets, including sea veggies.

Kombu, usually sold in thick strips, is traditionally used to make a flavorful broth and is a good addition to the bean cooking pot (see page 7). Wakame and hijiki can be served raw in salads after reconstituting, and are delicious stir-fried or cooked in soups. Nori sheets are most often used as sushi wrappers, but can also be snipped into soups. The nutritious red algae called dulse is available in flakes or "granules" and makes a great table condiment. All these varieties and more are sold in dried form at Asian markets and natural-food stores.

We keep our pantries stocked with:

Dulse	Nori
Hijiki	Wakame
Kombu (kelp)	

SOY FOODS

In the wake of recent research suggesting that some components found in the soybean can help regulate estrogen production—thereby offering protection against hormone-linked cancers—it seems every newspaper and magazine trumpeted the news. The media asserted en masse that soy foods should be a regular part of the diet, especially for women in their perimenopausal years.

In vegetarian circles, the value of soy foods isn't news. Tofu, tempeh, and other soy products have been an important protein source in meatless diets for decades. If these delicious, versatile, protein-rich foods also inhibit cancer and stabilize hormone function, so much the better.

But there is another side to the soy story that has been less widely reported. Soy is a common allergen, sometimes a hidden one. Common symptoms include digestion difficulty, sinus congestion, or headaches after a soy-heavy meal. If you have any reason to suspect you might be allergic, you would be wise to eliminate soy products from your diet for about a week to see if your symptoms diminish.

And there's another downside to soy: Recent research indicates that consumption of nonfermented soy foods may suppress thyroid function. Those with diagnosed or suspected hypothyroidism should probably avoid soy and read up on these findings. Fermented soy products, like tempeh and miso, apparently do not have this effect and are probably safe in moderation.

Concerns about protein digestion and mineral absorption have also surfaced in connection with nonfermented soy foods. Paradoxically, the same components and qualities of the soybean that may be problematic for some people are decidedly health promoting for others. Self-awareness and moderate consumption can mitigate any possible adverse effects.

Most people can enjoy soy foods regularly, in moderate amounts, and reap their health benefits without worry. We recommend you read labels carefully, and select only those products made from organically grown soybeans.

We keep our pantries stocked with:

Miso, light and dark varieties	Tempeh
Soy milk	Tofu
Tamari soy sauce	

NUTS AND SEEDS

Nuts are an excellent source of protein, B vitamins, phosphorus, iron, and calcium. Because of the high oil content of most types of nuts, we use them rather sparingly—as crunchy and flavorful additions to other foods or as a healthy snack, just a few at a time. Nuts still in their shells will last for months when stored in a cool, dry place. Shelled nuts should be stored in airtight containers in the refrigerator or freezer for day-to-day use.

Seeds are full of flavor, nutrients, and essential fatty acids. Select seeds carefully—rancidity is a common problem. If you can find a bulk supplier, you can smell and taste before you buy. A fishy smell or bitter taste indicates rancidity.

When buying nut and seed butters, compare labels. The best butters contain nothing but the nut or seed itself. A small amount of salt is an acceptable additive, but sweeteners and preservatives are not. Oil separation is a natural occurrence—when you are ready to use the butter, simply stir the contents of the jar to blend the oil back in. Store nut and seed butters in the refrigerator, as they spoil quickly when exposed to light, warmth, and air.

We keep our pantries stocked with:

Almonds	Pumpkin seeds
Almond butter	Sesame butter (tahini)
Flaxseeds	Sesame seeds
Peanut butter	Sunflower seeds
Pecans	Walnuts
Pine nuts	

OILS

Oils are composed of fatty acids, which play an important role in any healthy diet. High-quality seed and vegetable oils, eaten in moderation, are healthy fats to include in the diet. Lard, shortening, and hydrogenated margarine, on the other hand, may adversely affect health. Hydrogenation—the process used to solidify liquid fats—subjects oil to high heat, intense pressure, and chemical adulteration. Since heat and air are prominent causes of rancidity, hydrogenated oils bear little resemblance, in nutrition or taste, to the fresh oil from which they are made. Lecithin, a vital participant in fat metabolism, is destroyed in the hydrogenation process, as are vitamins A, B, E, and K.

Ask at your health food store about reputable oil brands, and buy oils in small quantities. The best seed oils are often "cold-pressed," and the labels will indicate this. Store all oils tightly sealed in a cool, dark place. Our preferred everyday cooking oils—canola and olive—do not require refrigeration, but they should be stored in airtight containers in a cool, dark place. Organic oils are becoming readily available and we highly recommend you seek them out.

Specialty oils like avocado, flax, and walnut add distinctive flavors to foods when used raw, as in salad dressings. Keep these delicate oils refrigerated. Infused oils are also good pantry additions, since a small amount packs a delicious wallop.

We keep our pantries stocked with:

Avocado oil	Sesame oil
Canola oil	Sunflower oil
Dark (toasted) sesame oil	Toasted sesame oil
Flaxseed oil	Walnut oil
Olive oil	

DRIED HERBS AND SPICES

Magic in the kitchen happens when you combine just the right herbs and spices with even the most basic ingredients. Depending on the dish, we use these seasonings either fresh or dried, ground or whole. Fresh herbs are discussed under "Fresh Vegetables, Fruits, and Herbs" on page 18.

In general, dried herbs impart a stronger flavor than their fresh counterparts. They can withstand long cooking times, whereas fresh herbs are usually added toward the end of the preparation so their lively colors, aromas, and flavors can shine through.

Of the dried herbs and spices, the ground varieties are more perishable than the dried leaf form. We like to purchase our herbs from a bulk supplier in small quantities. This way, we continuously restock our pantries, ensuring that the herbs are always at their optimum level of freshness and flavor. Natural food stores often carry a selection of both culinary and medicinal herbs in bulk.

When adding a dried leafy herb to a dish, crush it quickly between your palms to release the aroma and flavor. Some recipes will call for whole spices to be ground with a mortar and pestle or toasted before use. See the Simple Techniques section of this book for toasting directions (page 10).

We keep our pantries stocked with:

Dried Herbs and Spices	
Allspice, whole berries and ground	Ginger, ground
Basil	Herbes de Provence (see page 310)
Bay leaf	Italian Seasoning (see page 310)
Caraway seeds	
Cardamom, pods and ground	Oregano
Chili flakes, dried red	Nutmeg, whole
Chili powder	Paprika, mild
Chinese Five-Spice Powder (see page 311)	Pepper, black and cayenne
Cinnamon, sticks and ground	Rosemary
Cloves, whole and ground	Sage
Coriander, seeds and ground	Sea salt
Cumin, seeds and ground	Sweet Spice Blend (see page 311)
Curry Blend (see page 311)	Tarragon
Dill	Thyme
Garlic, granulated	Turmeric

VINEGARS

Vinegar is a useful food to keep on hand, for flavoring as well as health purposes. The naturally fermented vinegars, such as those made from brown rice and apple cider, provide enzymes and healthy bacteria that stimulate digestion in people with a sluggish system. Used in salad dressings, vinegar not only brightens up the flavor of vegetables, but also refreshes the palate and aids digestion. Some nutrition consultants suggest that eating vinegar or other high-acid foods with dense carbohydrates like grains and pasta can be problematic for some people. If you experience gas, heartburn, or other ill effects after eating spaghetti with tomato sauce, for example, perhaps you should minimize high-acid foods in your diet.

We keep our pantries stocked with:

Apple cider vinegar	Red wine vinegar
Balsamic vinegar	Umeboshi plum vinegar
Brown rice vinegar	White wine vinegar
Raspberry vinegar	

SWEETENERS

Most of us enjoy something sweet from time to time. One theory holds that since mother's milk is sweet, this is the first flavor we learn to distinguish as babies. It's not surprising then, that we associate sweetness with love and comfort throughout our lives and crave sweet foods.

Unfortunately, sweeteners can overload us with simple carbohydrates, stressing the insulin production process and contributing to a host of health problems. All sweeteners, therefore, should be consumed infrequently and in moderation.

For that occasional sweet indulgence, we most commonly use sweeteners that offer trace minerals and vitamins rather than completely empty calories. Granulated sugar has its place as an occasional ingredient, but we seek out the organic brands that aren't processed using bonemeal or harsh chemicals. As always, reading labels will help you determine the most healthful choices.

Although honey offers some nutrient value, it is produced by bees, and bees are destroyed during its harvest. Honey is therefore avoided in the vegan diet.

We keep our pantries stocked with:

Blackstrap molasses	Organic granulated sugar
Brown rice syrup	Turbinado sugar
Maple syrup	

WINES AND SPIRITS

In moderation, fermented grape and grain beverages can have their place in a healthy diet. We find many culinary uses for white and red wines, dry sherry, rum, brandy—even beer, occasionally. The sweet Japanese rice wine called mirin shows up in a number of our recipes. It is available at Asian specialty shops and some well-stocked supermarkets.

Wines and spirits add interesting flavor to a dish without adding fat. The amounts used are small, and alcohol is destroyed by cooking, so the amount that ends up in the finished dish is negligible.

We keep our pantries stocked with:

Brandy	Rum
Dry sherry	Vermouth
Marsala	White wines, such as Chardon-
Mirin	nay and Sauvignon Blanc
Port	
Red wines, such as Merlot and	
Cabernet Sauvignon	

CONDIMENTS AND OTHER SEASONING STAPLES

Used as recipe ingredients or table condiments, these staples are convenient flavor enhancers for many cooked and raw foods, and they keep well. Sample different brands to discover your favorites.

We keep our pantries stocked with:

Capers	Pickled jalapeños
Catsup	Prepared horseradish
Mango chutney	Salsa
Mustards, various kinds	Tofu mayonnaise

CONVENIENCE FOODS

We all want to be happy cooks, not kitchen slaves, so in addition to keeping the basic raw ingredients on hand, it is useful to stock up on certain "convenience" foods. The following items can help you pull a meal together quickly or provide a quick snack when your energy is low.

We keep our pantries stocked with:

Beans, canned (black, garbanzo, kidney)	Rice, rye, and whole wheat crackers
Fruit preserves	Tomatoes, canned (diced, sauce, whole)
Granola and other high-fiber dry cereals	Tomato paste, in a tube
Olives, green and black varieties	Tortillas and chapatis
Pickles, sweet and sour	Whole-grain bread

3

Menus for Entertaining and Everyday Meals

A few minutes spent carefully planning a menu and organizing recipe requirements will help you have a relaxed and enjoyable experience. We look to the seasons for menu planning inspiration—whether for a festive celebration or weeknight fare. Let the market's freshest produce as well as the temperature outdoors motivate you.

When designing a menu, make a point of thinking in new ways. Seek a harmonious balance of tastes, colors, and textures in the meal, and choose recipes accordingly. Potatoes and rice aren't the only carbohydrate choices, and salads don't have to be mostly lettuce. Apply your attention and creativity to everyday meals, and both you and the people you feed will wake up to the pleasures of the table.

When cooking for a special occasion, let the time of year, the occasion, and the guest list guide your menu. The first storm of the season might inspire you to heat up the oven and prepare a wonderful casserole dish or lead you to prepare a hearty stew. Sometimes an international theme will be the catalyst for the menu. Whatever inspires you, choose a central theme or a special dish to be the foundation of the meal.

Consider your own style and pace in the kitchen, as well as the time you have available for preparing a meal. An unfamiliar recipe generally takes a bit longer to prepare, so when trying a new dish, use tried-and-true recipes for the rest of the meal.

When possible, prepare part of the meal ahead of time, leaving only the items that require your full attention for the last moment.

Depending on the setting, invite your guests to stir the risotto, whisk up the salad dressing, or simply pour a glass of wine and keep you company. Asking friends to help can free you to focus on the overall picture, and gives them a sense of contribution.

And don't neglect the visual presentation of your creations. The simplest touch, such as a fresh flower garnish, can make a meal seem special. First and foremost, we eat for nourishment—but to be sensually delighted by what is on our plates makes a meal truly memorable.

The following menu plans are organized by season to encourage the use of fresh produce. We hope they inspire you to get creative and have fun, whether you're cooking a weeknight meal for the family or a special occasion feast.

Spring

Although there is still a chill in the air, the sprouting of new greenery and the opening of flowers convince us that spring has arrived. The days lengthen as the vernal equinox approaches, and our appetites diminish a bit as warmer weather arrives. The coarser, cool-season fruits and vegetables are still available and constitute the bulk of our diets, but early strawberries and the season's first asparagus delight our senses with their vibrant colors and delicate flavors. A spring birthday or Easter celebration may be the cause for a special menu.

Chasing Away the Chill
Split Pea Soup with Sweet Potato and Mexican Seasonings, page 113
Mushroom and Soy Cheese Quesadillas, page 245
Leafy salad with vinaigrette

First Taste of Spring
Lemony Fava Bean Pesto with Crostini, page 45
Linguine with Asparagus, Walnuts, and Fresh Herbs, page 146
Radishes and carrot sticks
Fabulous Fruit Crisp with Creamy Topping, page 285

Easter Buffet Extravaganza
Caramelized Onion and Tempeh Spread, page 38
Fresh crusty bread
Fresh Peas and Shallots with Provencal Herbs, page 128
Bulgur and Red Lentil Pilaf with Kale and Olives, page 167
Beets with Potato Garlic Sauce, page 136
Leafy salad with vinaigrette
Chocolate-Cinnamon Walnut Cake, page 283

Summer

In the heat of summer, cooking becomes a lower priority for most of us, but our increased summer activities call for special attention to nutrition. Fresh fruits and vegetables are in abundance at this time—many to be enjoyed raw or with minimum preparation. For cooking, we call the grill into service as an outdoor kitchen. The 4th of July brings the traditional celebration that launches summer, and throughout this benevolent season we look for any excuse to have friends and family over to eat.

Mediterranean Moment
Garlic-Marinated Green Olives, page 48
Roasted Peppers in Spicy Marinade, page 52
Cannellini Bean Spread with Balsamic and Oregano, page 44
Tomato, Bread, and Basil Salad, page 74
Sesame bread sticks

Cool Asian Breeze
Pressed Tofu with Savory Toppings, page 55
Edamame in the pods (see page 155)
Rice, Red Pepper, and Bean Sprouts with Ginger Peanut Dressing,
	page 79
Rice crackers

Tex-Mex Grill
Grilled Sweet Pepper, Summer Squash, and Tempeh Fajitas, page 229
Serrano Chili Rice, page 174
Leafy salad with vinaigrette

Autumn

After months of carefree activity in the summer sun, we tend to spend more time at home in the fall. Those of us who have gardens are busy harvesting and putting up the last of summer's bounty. The gold and orange colors of autumn leaves are mirrored in the vegetables and flowers that appear at the market. We begin to crave hearty soups, stews, and casseroles. With the onset of cooler evenings, the kitchen stove again becomes the heart of our homes. Halloween suggests pumpkin soup, and Thanksgiving reminds us how good oven roasted root vegetables taste.

Early Autumn Supper

Grilled Butternut Squash Soup with Shiitake Mushrooms, page 100

Green Bean Salad with Asian Seasonings, page 72

Dried Apricot and Coconut Pudding, page 281

South of the Border Casual

Spicy Toasted Pumpkin Seeds, page 49

Chips and salsa

Corn, Pineapple, and Jicama Salad with Tomatillos and Rum, page 87

Eggplant Enchiladas with Almond Mole, page 216

Autumn Elegance

Baby Spinach with Pears, Toasted Walnuts, and Cumin Vinaigrette,
    page 67

Zucchini Stuffed with Mushroom Quinoa in Tomato Coulis, page 208

Steamed carrots

Grilled Fruit with Rum Glaze and Sweet Soy Cashew Topping, page 290

WINTER

When it's stormy outside, it's a pleasure to linger in a warm and cozy kitchen. Winter is the perfect time for baking, as friends and family bask in the warmth and wonderful aromas. The temptation to eat a cookie hot out of the oven overpowers us. Winter is a time to huddle together, sip warm soup, share stories around a fire, and enjoy a delicious hearty meal. With Christmas and the New Year, we have lots of occasions to prepare sumptuous feasts.

Family Fireside Supper

Barley and Mushroom Pilaf with Toasted Pecans, page 173

Green Beans with Orange Allspice Glaze, page 132

Carrot sticks

Oatmeal Raisin Cookies with Fresh Nutmeg, page 279

Raja's Feast

Mulligatawny, page 96

Pita Crisps, page 304

Cauliflower in Coriander Cashew Sauce, page 134

Steamed Basmati Rice, page 299

Mango chutney and cultured soy "yogurt" as condiments

Comfort Food for Friends

Classic Lentil, Tomato, and Potato Stew, page 114

Fresh crusty bread

Leafy salad with vinaigrette

Arborio Rice Pudding with Pears, page 280

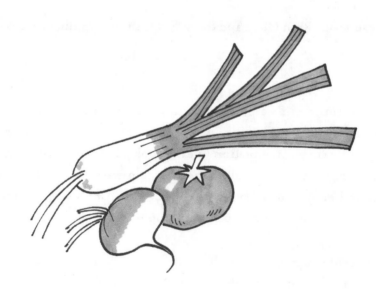

4

Appetizers

Caramelized Onion and Tempeh Spread

Sesame-Eggplant Spread

Caponata

Spiced Garbanzo and Carrot Spread with Mint

Kidney Bean Dip with Chili and Lime

Cannellini Bean Spread with Balsamic and Oregano

Lemony Fava Bean Pesto with Crostini

Artichoke and Roasted Pepper Relish

Black Olive Tapenade with Capers

Garlic-Marinated Green Olives

Spicy Toasted Pumpkin Seeds

Roasted Peanuts with Chili and Lime

Pearl Onions Pickled in Balsamic Vinegar

Roasted Peppers in Spicy Marinade

Mushrooms with Cumin and Sherry Vinegar

Fresh Fava Beans in Basil Marinade

Pressed Tofu with Savory Toppings

Grape Leaves Stuffed with Rice and Herbs

Tofu-Stuffed Squash Blossoms

Crostini with Tomatoes, Basil, Garlic, and Capers

Appetizers is a catchphrase for all "small bites"—foods that can be speared with a toothpick, spread on a cracker, or eaten in just a few forkfuls. They are tasty morsels that appease the appetite while we're waiting for the main meal.

As this chapter demonstrates, appetizers can be as simple as a bowl of spiced pumpkin seeds or as elaborate as a stuffed and sautéed squash blossom. The occasion itself and the remainder of the menu can help you determine the number and type of appetizers to serve. Generally speaking, composed appetizers are well suited to an elegant gathering, while simple snacks like olives, nuts, and spread-it-yourself hummus are perfect for the casual get-together. If the menu is laden with rich dishes, keep the appetizers on the light side.

Marinated foods, dips, spreads, and salsas are all simple to prepare and can be made several hours—even a day—ahead of time. Foods held overnight should be refrigerated, but the flavors will be best if you return them to room temperature before serving. Leftovers can be stored in a tightly closed container in the refrigerator and enjoyed as a healthy snack over the course of a few days.

Any combination of recipes in this chapter can be combined to create a finger food buffet, where "appetizers" become the whole meal. Prepare several spreads or dips, two to three composed appetizers, and set out some marinated vegetables and toasted nuts or seeds. This is a very easy and enjoyable way to entertain, as all of the work is done ahead of time. Use your prettiest serving dishes and arrange everything in a pleasing manner before the guests arrive, then you're free to simply enjoy their company.

Caramelized Onion and Tempeh Spread

YIELD: 20 appetizer servings

This spread is a delicious appetizer and a great sandwich filling when layered with lettuce and red onion slices. Serve at room temperature with crisp crackers or baguette slices.

EACH SERVING PROVIDES

54 calories, 3 g protein, 3 g fat, 1 g dietary fiber, 4 g carbohydrates, 105 mg sodium, 0 mg cholesterol

3 tablespoons olive oil

3 medium yellow onions, diced

3 cloves garlic, minced

8 ounces soy tempeh, cubed

¼ cup dry sherry

2 tablespoons soy sauce

2 tablespoons minced fresh rosemary

Heat the oil in a large heavy-bottomed skillet over medium-high heat. Stir in the onions and garlic. Reduce the heat to medium-low, and sauté until very soft and well-browned, about 20 minutes, stirring frequently. Add the tempeh, sherry, soy sauce, and rosemary. Continue to cook for about 5 minutes, stirring almost constantly. Remove from the heat and allow to cool.

Purée the mixture in a food processor to a thick, homogeneous consistency. Spoon into a serving bowl, cover, and refrigerate for at least one hour or up to 3 days before serving.

Sesame-Eggplant Spread

YIELD: 16 appetizer servings

1 tablespoon plus 1 teaspoon extra-virgin olive oil

2 pounds eggplant (about 2 medium)

2 tablespoons sesame tahini, raw or toasted

1 tablespoon fresh-squeezed lemon juice

2 cloves garlic, minced

½ teaspoon salt

½ teaspoon ground cumin

A pinch cayenne pepper

This creamy, garlicky eggplant spread can become addictive. Make it in the late summer, when eggplants are at their very best. Serve it on your favorite bread or cracker, or stuff it into pocket bread with raw or steamed veggies.

EACH SERVING PROVIDES
*37 calories, 1 g protein, 2 g fat,
2 g dietary fiber, 4 g carbohydrates,
70 mg sodium, 0 mg cholesterol*

Preheat the broiler and rub a baking sheet with 1 teaspoon of the oil. Cut the eggplants in half lengthwise, and place them cut side down on the baking sheet. Broil 6 inches from the heat source for 20 minutes; the skin should be blackened and crisp and the eggplants perfectly soft. Turn them over and broil 5 minutes longer to lightly brown the tops. Put the eggplants on a plate, and set aside to cool.

When the eggplants are cool enough to handle, discard any liquid that has collected on the plate. Scrape the eggplant pulp out of the charred skin into a bowl, being careful to include the thick layer of eggplant that tends to stick to the skin. It is fine if a few bits of charred skin end up in the bowl with the eggplant.

Add the remaining 1 tablespoon oil, tahini, lemon juice, garlic, salt, cumin, and cayenne to the bowl and stir vigorously with a fork until well combined. Serve immediately or allow the flavors to blend for a few hours at room temperature or up to two days in the refrigerator. Return to room temperature before serving.

Caponata

YIELD: 18 appetizer servings

Versions of this famous dish have been made for centuries. The ingredients are readily available almost everywhere, especially in the summertime. We like to serve caponata on a bed of colorful greens with Crostini (page 301). This recipe makes a lot—enough for a crowd. Any leftovers will stay fresh for a few days if stored in a covered jar in the refrigerator.

EACH SERVING PROVIDES
*78 calories, 2 g protein, 4 g fat,
3 g dietary fiber, 9 g carbohydrates,
437 mg sodium, 0 mg cholesterol*

1½ pounds fresh pear tomatoes, blanched, peeled, and seeded (see NOTE)

3 pounds eggplant (about 3 medium)

1 tablespoon salt

¼ cup extra-virgin olive oil

1 medium yellow onion, finely diced

2 medium ribs celery, finely diced

2 cloves garlic, minced

¼ teaspoon dried red chili flakes

1 can (7¾-ounces) water-packed pitted green olives

2 tablespoons capers, drained

¼ cup minced fresh Italian parsley

¼ cup fresh-squeezed lemon juice

Blanch, peel, and seed the tomatoes (see page 5). Chop the tomatoes and set them aside in a bowl. Wash and dry the eggplants and trim off and discard the stem ends. Without peeling, chop the eggplant into ¾-inch cubes. Place the cubes in a colander and sprinkle with the salt. Set aside in the sink or over a bowl and allow to drain for 1 hour. Rinse briefly to remove excess salt, then dry thoroughly with a clean tea towel or paper towels.

Heat the oil in a large, heavy-bottomed skillet over medium heat. Add the onion, celery, garlic, and chili flakes. Sauté for about 5 minutes, stirring frequently. Add the tomatoes and bring the mixture to a simmer over medium-high heat. Reduce the heat to low, cover, and simmer 10 minutes. Stir in the olives and capers and cook 20 to 25 minutes, until the eggplant is tender but not mushy. Stir in the parsley and lemon juice until well combined. Serve at room temperature.

NOTE: You may substitute one can (14½ ounces) whole pear tomatoes, drained and chopped.

Salsa Party!

Salsa has come of age. Gone are the days when your only choice at the supermarket was watery bottled tomato salsa with hardly any punch. Now, salsa comes in many colors and textures, and the heat ratings range from slightly zippy to scorching.

If you're a fan of south-of-the-border flavor, this is a very encouraging trend. But if you really love salsa, you'll enjoy making your own. You can set your own standards for garlic and jalapeño; include diced mango, papaya, or pineapple; and try out different herb flavors. You'll end up with a salsa so fresh and delicious, you'll want to sit down and eat it with a spoon!

To share the fun with friends, why not throw a salsa party? You provide one or two interesting salsas, black beans and Mexican rice, hot tortillas and sliced avocados. Ask your guests to bring a special store-bought or homemade salsa and their palate-cooling beverage of choice—maybe Mexican beer.

Whatever the season, a salsa party is a festive gathering. Get out your brightest tablecloths and napkins, and put on some Latin-inspired music. Then line up all the ingredients on a buffet table and invite everybody to dig in—filling tortillas with beans, rice, and whatever salsa strikes their fancy. It's a surefire crowd pleaser.

Here are some salsa recipes to fire up your imagination. The directions are the same for all of them: Combine the ingredients in a bowl and set aside at room temperature for an hour or so to allow the flavors to blend and blossom. Stir again just before serving.

TOMATOES, CORN, AND CILANTRO SALSA

1 ¼ pounds fresh pear tomatoes, diced (about 7 medium)

1 can (4 ounces) diced mild green chilies

¾ cup fresh corn kernels (about 2 small ears)

½ cup minced fresh cilantro

1 tablespoon apple cider vinegar

2 cloves garlic, minced

1 teaspoon chili powder

½ teaspoon ground cumin

¼ teaspoon salt

TOMATOES, TOMATILLOS, AND ZUCCHINI SALSA

1 pound fresh pear tomatoes (about 6 medium), diced

½ pound fresh tomatillos (about 6 medium), peeled and diced

1 medium red onion, diced

1 tablespoon fresh-squeezed lime juice

1 teaspoon dried oregano

¼ teaspoon salt

MANGO, JICAMA, AND MINT SALSA

1 medium mango, peeled, seeded, and diced

½ cup peeled and diced jicama

2 tablespoons minced fresh mint

1 tablespoon fresh-squeezed lemon juice

1 serrano chili, seeded and minced

A pinch of salt

Spiced Garbanzo and Carrot Spread with Mint

YIELD: 20 appetizer servings

This version of traditional hummus is lightened up by replacing some of the beans with cooked carrots. It has a nice fluffy texture that is good on both crisp crackers or chewy bread. Its degree of spiciness will depend on the curry powder you use; adjust the amount according to your own taste. You can make this ahead of time and store it in the refrigerator for up to a few days.

EACH SERVING PROVIDES

*41 calories, 2 g protein, 1 g fat,
1 g dietary fiber, 7 g carbohydrates,
108 mg sodium, 0 mg cholesterol*

2 cups diced carrots (about 2 medium)

1 ¾ cups (one 15-ounce can) cooked and drained garbanzo beans

3 tablespoons fresh-squeezed lemon juice

2 tablespoons sesame tahini, raw or toasted

2 tablespoons vegetable stock or water

1 ½ teaspoons curry powder

2 cloves garlic, minced

½ teaspoon salt

2 tablespoons minced fresh mint

Place a steamer rack in a saucepan and add about 2 inches of water to the pan. Place the carrots on the rack and steam over medium-high heat until very tender, about 8 minutes. In a blender or food processor, combine the cooked carrots, garbanzo beans, lemon juice, tahini, stock, curry powder, garlic, and salt. Purée until fairly smooth. Transfer to a serving bowl and stir in the mint. Serve immediately or store in the refrigerator for up to a few days.

Kidney Bean Dip with Chili and Lime

YIELD: 24 appetizer servings

2 medium fresh jalapeño chilies

4 cups cooked and drained pinto beans

¼ cup tomato juice

2 tablespoons canola oil

2 tablespoons fresh-squeezed lime juice

2 cloves garlic, minced

1 teaspoon dried oregano

½ teaspoon ground cumin

½ teaspoon salt

¼ cup minced fresh cilantro

Remove the stem of the chilies and cut them in half lengthwise. Scrape out and discard the seeds for a milder flavor. Coarsely chop the jalapeños and combine them in a food processor with the beans, tomato juice, oil, lime juice, garlic, oregano, cumin, and salt. Blend until fairly smooth, then add the cilantro and pulse to combine. Transfer to a serving bowl, cover, and refrigerate until serving.

Almost Instant

This dip is also delicious when prepared with kidney or black beans. Make it several hours in advance so the flavors can blend, then serve it with pita or tortilla chips and your choice of assorted fresh vegetable. Store any leftovers in the refrigerator for an instant snack.

EACH SERVING PROVIDES

*49 calories, 2 g protein, 1 g fat,
3 g dietary fiber, 8 g carbohydrates,
54 mg sodium, 0 mg cholesterol*

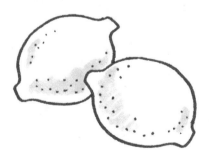

Cannellini Bean Spread with Balsamic and Oregano

YIELD: 10 appetizer servings

Almost Instant

This spread can be served with rustic country bread or chips. It will keep well in the refrigerator for several days, to be enjoyed as a healthy snack.

EACH SERVING PROVIDES

54 calories, 3 g protein, 2 g fat, 2 g dietary fiber, 8 g carbohydrates, 175 mg sodium, 0 mg cholesterol

2 cups cooked and drained cannellini beans

2 tablespoons vegetable stock or water

1 tablespoon extra-virgin olive oil

1 tablespoon balsamic vinegar

1 teaspoon dried oregano

¼ teaspoon salt

Several grinds black pepper

Place the beans in a food processor along with the stock, oil, vinegar, basil, salt, and pepper. Purée. If the mixture seems too thick, add an additional tablespoon or two of water to achieve the right consistency. Transfer to a serving bowl, cover, and refrigerate until serving.

Lemony Fava Bean Pesto with Crostini

YIELD: 12 appetizer servings

3 pounds fresh fava beans, in pods
    (about 2 cups, shelled)

3 tablespoons vegetable stock or
    water

3 tablespoons extra-virgin olive oil

3 tablespoons fresh-squeezed
    lemon juice

2 shallots, minced

1 tablespoon minced fresh rosemary

1 teaspoon crushed fennel seed

¼ teaspoon salt

Several grinds black pepper

1 recipe Crostini (page 301)

¼ cup finely minced parsley

½ to 1 teaspoon organic granulated
    sugar, if needed (see NOTE)

This pesto is one way to enjoy the distinctive nutty taste of fava beans. Shelling, blanching, and peeling them takes a bit of patience, but the rest is a snap.

EACH SERVING PROVIDES
*155 calories, 5 g protein, 5 g fat,
3 g dietary fiber, 24 g carbohydrates,
290 mg sodium, 0 mg cholesterol*

Bring several cups of water to a boil. Shell the beans, discarding the pods, and add them to the boiling water. Return the water to a boil and blanch the beans for 30 seconds to 2 minutes, depending on their size, until their skins have visibly loosened. Transfer to a colander, and rinse well with cold water to stop the cooking.

When the beans are cool enough to handle, pop them out of their skins. Discard the skins and place the beans in a blender or food processor. Add the stock, olive oil, lemon juice, shallots, rosemary, fennel seed, salt, and pepper. Purée.

Spread a scant tablespoon of the mixture on each crostini slice, arrange on a platter, sprinkle the minced parsley on top, and serve.

NOTE: Older favas can taste a bit bitter. The sugar here is to be used only if you think it's needed to balance out the flavors.

Artichoke and Roasted Pepper Relish

YIELD: 12 appetizer servings

Serve this Mediterranean treat on Crostini (page 301). *If you have trouble finding artichoke bottoms you may substitute artichoke hearts, preferably the unmarinated kind.*

EACH SERVING PROVIDES

34 calories, 1 g protein, 1 g fat,
1 g dietary fiber, 5 g carbohydrates,
221 mg sodium, 0 mg cholesterol

1 can (14 ounces) artichoke
  bottoms, drained, finely diced
1 large red bell pepper, roasted and
  finely diced (see page 9)
½ pound fresh pear tomatoes
  (about 3 medium), finely diced
2 tablespoons minced fresh mint
2 tablespoons capers, drained

4 green onions, minced
1 tablespoon extra-virgin olive oil
1 tablespoon fresh-squeezed
  lemon juice
¼ teaspoon salt
Several grinds black pepper

Combine all ingredients, including any juice that is released by the tomatoes, in a pretty serving bowl. Set aside at room temperature for a few hours before serving to allow the flavors to blend and intensify.

Black Olive Tapenade with Capers

YIELD: 12 appetizer servings

1 cup pitted black olives, coarsely chopped

2 tablespoons tomato juice

2 tablespoons capers, drained

2 tablespoons dry sherry

1 tablespoon extra-virgin olive oil

1 tablespoon Dijon mustard

2 cloves garlic, chopped

½ teaspoon dried red chili flakes

Place all the ingredients in a small food processor, and pulse until fairly smooth. Serve immediately or allow to age and mellow in the refrigerator for up to two weeks.

Almost Instant

For this spread, we recommend using a combination of Greek calamatas and other specialty olives. It will take about ½ pound of olives with pits to yield 1 cup of pitted olives. Serve with a sliced baguette or crisp Crostini (page 301), and offer a bowl of pistachios and cut-up raw veggies to complete the appetizer course.

EACH SERVING PROVIDES
*69 calories, 1 g protein, 7 g fat,
0 g dietary fiber, 2 g carbohydrates,
641 mg sodium, 0 mg cholesterol*

Garlic–Marinated Green Olives

YIELD: 12 appetizer servings

Prepare these olives in advance and use them over the course of a month. The olives called for here are tree-ripened green olives with pits. They are commonly sold in cans, packed in water.

EACH SERVING PROVIDES

*37 calories, 0 g protein, 4 g fat,
1 g dietary fiber, 1 g carbohydrates,
477 mg sodium, 0 mg cholesterol*

1 can (12 ounces) water-packed
    unpitted green olives
8 cloves garlic

¼ cup extra-virgin olive oil
2 tablespoons sherry vinegar

Drain the olives and place them in a glass jar that has a tight-fitting lid. Peel the garlic cloves and lightly crush them with the broad side of a knife, then add them to the jar. Add the oil and vinegar, place the lid on the jar, and turn the jar to coat the olives. The marinade will not completely cover the olives, so turn the jar a few times a day, whenever you think of it. Marinate in the refrigerator for at least 2 to 3 days for best results, then bring the olives to room temperature before serving. Leftover olives may continue to marinate in the refrigerator for up to a month.

Spicy Toasted Pumpkin Seeds

YIELD: 12 appetizer servings

1 ½ teaspoons olive oil

½ teaspoon ground cumin

½ teaspoon chili powder

¼ teaspoon granulated garlic

2 cups raw unsalted pumpkin seeds

Heat the oil in a large heavy-bottomed skillet over medium heat. Stir in the cumin, chili powder, and garlic, and cook the spices for 30 seconds or so. Add the pumpkin seeds and stir or shake the pan constantly until they have all popped and turned golden brown, about 8 minutes. Serve warm or at room temperature.

Almost Instant

Pumpkin seeds are a popular ingredient in traditional Mexican cooking. Here they make a finger-licking snack. Leftover seeds may be stored at room temperature for several weeks in an airtight container.

EACH SERVING PROVIDES

53 calories, 2 g protein, 3 g fat,
0 g dietary fiber, 6 g carbohydrates,
3 mg sodium, 0 mg cholesterol

PUMPKIN SEEDS

Raw green pumpkin seeds, sold at natural food markets, are high in amino acids and minerals, and are lower in fat than most other nuts and seeds. Because of their impressive zinc content, pumpkin seeds are considered beneficial for the prostate gland. They are delicious raw, but toasting them plain in a dry pan or with oil and spices turns them into an irresistible crunchy snack.

Roasted Peanuts with Chili and Lime

YIELD: 12 appetizer servings

A bowl of nuts is always a welcome appetizer. These peanuts are crunchy, lightly salted, and just a little bit spicy, which means they awaken the appetite gently. Serve them anytime, alone or as part of an appetizer buffet.

EACH SERVING PROVIDES
*147 calories, 6 g protein, 12 g fat,
2 g dietary fiber, 6 g carbohydrates,
48 mg sodium, 0 mg cholesterol*

2 cups shelled raw unsalted peanuts
1 tablespoon fresh-squeezed lime juice
1 teaspoon chili powder
¼ teaspoon salt

Preheat the oven to 400 degrees F. Bring 4 cups of water to a boil in a small saucepan. Drop the peanuts into the water and boil them for 2 minutes. Transfer them to a colander and rinse with cold water. Drain the peanuts well, then remove and discard the skins. Spread the peanuts out on a dry baking sheet.

Place them in the oven and roast for 15 to 20 minutes, until lightly browned, shaking or stirring the nuts once midway through the cooking time so they roast evenly. Transfer the hot peanuts to a bowl and toss with the lime juice, then with the chili powder and salt. Serve warm or at room temperature.

Pearl Onions Pickled in Balsamic Vinegar

YIELD: 12 appetizer servings

1½ pounds small pearl or boiling onions

¼ cup salt

2 cups white wine vinegar

½ cup balsamic vinegar

1 tablespoon brown rice syrup

2 tablespoons olive oil

3 medium bay leaves

1 teaspoon dried oregano

½ teaspoon whole cloves

Scant ⅛ teaspoon dried red chili flakes

½ teaspoon whole black peppercorns

This recipe will make at least 12 appetizer servings; however, not all of the onions need to be eaten immediately. They keep very well in the refrigerator for several weeks and improve with age. This is an excellent recipe to double or triple and put up in quart jars, following standard canning procedures.

EACH SERVING PROVIDES
*26 calories, 1 g protein, 0 g fat,
1 g dietary fiber, 5 g carbohydrates,
1066 mg sodium, 0 mg cholesterol*

Blanch the onions for about a minute (see page 5). Trim a very small amount off the tip end of each onion and peel. Place the onions in a deep glass bowl or a small crock. Bring 4 cups of water to a boil and add the salt, stirring until dissolved. Remove this solution from the heat, allow to cool slightly, then pour over the onions. Cover the onions with a plate small enough to fit inside the bowl, directly on top of the onions. Put a weight, such as a can of tomatoes, on the plate to keep the onions completely submerged in the brine. Allow to cure at room temperature for 48 hours.

Drain the onions in a colander and rinse them with cold water to remove most of the salt. Place the onions in a bowl or pack into quart jars.

Pour the vinegars into a non-aluminum saucepan, and add the brown rice syrup, olive oil, bay leaves, oregano, whole cloves, chili flakes, and peppercorns. Bring to a boil over high heat, then reduce the heat and simmer for 5 minutes. Pour the vinegar mixture over the onions, cover, and cool to room temperature before storing in the refrigerator. Allow the onions to marinate for at least a day before serving.

Roasted Peppers in Spicy Marinade

YIELD: 8 appetizer servings

Almost Instant

Here is a strongly spiced appetizer based on Tunisian "mushwiya." It combines wonderfully with the Spiced Garbanzo and Carrot Spread (page 42) to prepare the palate for any exotic entrée. You may use peppers of any color, but red and yellow ones yield the prettiest color and sweetest flavor.

EACH SERVING PROVIDES
*49 calories, 1 g protein, 4 g fat,
1 g dietary fiber, 4 g carbohydrates,
117 mg sodium, 0 mg cholesterol*

4 canned pear tomatoes, finely chopped

2 tablespoons extra-virgin olive oil

1 tablespoon fresh-squeezed lemon juice

2 cloves garlic, minced

1 teaspoon ground cumin

1/4 teaspoon salt

1/8 teaspoon cayenne pepper

4 medium fresh bell peppers, roasted, peeled, and seeded (see page 9)

Combine the tomatoes, olive oil, lemon juice, garlic, cumin, salt, and cayenne in a serving dish. Stir until well blended. Dice the peppers into 1/2-inch pieces. Toss the peppers with the tomato mixture. Serve immediately or set aside at room temperature for a few hours before serving, so the flavors can blend and intensify.

OLIVE OIL

Olive oil has been called the world's healthiest fat. Dozens of studies have demonstrated that olive oil can lower blood pressure, prevent strokes, and lower the levels of LDL (bad) cholesterol without lowering HDL (good) levels. Fortunately, olive oil isn't just good for us, it's also delicious!

"Extra-virgin" olive oil comes from the first pressing of top-quality unripe olives and provides the best flavor and health benefits. Its great taste and aroma are best appreciated when raw, so add it to salad dressings or drizzle it on soups just before serving. "Virgin" and "pure" olive oils are more economical lower grades that can be used for cooking.

Mushrooms with Cumin and Sherry Vinegar

YIELD: 8 appetizer servings

1 pound small button mushrooms

1 tablespoon olive oil

2 tablespoons sherry vinegar

2 cloves garlic, minced

½ teaspoon ground cumin

Brush or wipe any loose dirt from the mushrooms, then trim off the tough tips of the stems. Leave the mushrooms whole.

Place the oil and vinegar in a large sauté pan or skillet over medium heat. Add the garlic and cook for 1 minute, then stir in the cumin and mushrooms. Cover the skillet and cook for 20 minutes, removing the lid to stir occasionally. Remove the lid, increase the heat to medium-high, and cook for 2 to 3 minutes, until almost all of the liquid has evaporated. Serve hot or at room temperature.

Almost Instant

Picture yourself and several friends at a public house in Spain, sipping a glass of wine from the Riojo Valley as you enjoy a plate of "tapas"— appetizers, Spanish style. These mushrooms are especially succulent.

EACH SERVING PROVIDES
*34 calories, 1 g protein, 2 g fat,
1 g dietary fiber, 3 g carbohydrates,
2 mg sodium, 0 mg cholesterol*

Fresh Fava Beans in Basil Marinade

YIELD: 12 appetizer servings

Look for fresh fava beans in an Italian grocery store or at the local farmer's market. When lightly cooked, they almost melt in your mouth. They are especially delicious combined with Mediterranean flavors, as they are here.

EACH SERVING PROVIDES

*57 calories, 2 g protein, 5 g fat,
1 g dietary fiber, 4 g carbohydrates,
59 mg sodium, 0 mg cholesterol*

3 pounds fresh fava beans, in pods
 (about 2 cups, shelled)

¼ cup extra-virgin olive oil

3 tablespoons fresh-squeezed
 lemon juice

1 clove garlic, minced

¼ teaspoon salt

A few grinds black pepper

¼ cup minced fresh basil leaves

Bring several cups of water to a boil. Shell the beans, discarding the pods, and add them to the boiling water. Return the water to a boil and blanch the beans 30 seconds to 2 minutes, depending on their size, until the skins have loosened. Transfer the beans to a colander and rinse well with cold water to stop the cooking. When the beans are cool enough to handle, pop each one out of its skin. Discard the skins and place the beans in a serving bowl.

Whisk together the oil, lemon juice, garlic, salt, and pepper until emulsified, about 1 minute. Pour this mixture over the beans, then add the basil and toss to combine. Allow to marinate at room temperature for about an hour before serving. This dish may be kept overnight in the refrigerator, but return it to room temperature before serving.

Pressed Tofu with Savory Toppings

YIELD: 6 appetizer servings

1 pound firm tofu

1 tablespoon soy sauce

⅓ cup grated daikon or red radish

3 green onions, minced

1 tablespoon grated fresh ginger

1½ teaspoons brown sesame seeds, toasted (see page 10)

On a large platter or cutting board, place a clean tea towel that has been folded in half. Remove the tofu from its package and, if necessary, slice it into slabs that are about 1½-inches thick. Place the slabs on the folded tea towel and cover with another clean folded tea towel. Place a board or baking sheet on the towel-wrapped tofu and place something heavy on top, such as a large can of tomatoes. You want enough weight to gently press some of the water out of the tofu, but not so much weight that the tofu will be flattened. Allow the tofu to rest at room temperature for about 10 minutes.

When the tofu is ready, unwrap it, and cut the slabs into pieces that are about 1½ inches × 1 inch × 2 inches. Arrange them in a pretty pattern on a flat serving dish. Drizzle the soy sauce evenly over the tofu, then distribute the radish, green onions, ginger, and sesame seeds evenly over it. Serve immediately, providing each guest with a small individual serving plate and chopsticks (or forks) for picking up the tofu.

Almost Instant

This raw tofu dish of Japanese origin is traditionally served cold at the beginning of a meal, to refresh the senses and awaken the appetite. The pressed tofu develops a wonderful custard-like texture.

EACH SERVING PROVIDES
*78 calories, 7 g protein, 6 g fat,
0 g dietary fiber, 2 g carbohydrates,
175 mg sodium, 0 mg cholesterol*

Grape Leaves Stuffed with Rice and Herbs

YIELD: 12 appetizer servings

2 cups uncooked long-grain brown rice

¾ teaspoon salt, plus a pinch

1 pound eggplant (about 1 medium)

¼ cup plus ½ teaspoon olive oil

1 medium yellow onion, diced

2 tablespoons fresh-squeezed lemon juice

1 ½ teaspoons dried dill weed

1 tablespoon plus 1 ½ teaspoons dried oregano

4 cloves garlic, minced

Several grinds black pepper

1 jar (8 ounces) prepared grape leaves

1 can (28 ounces) whole pear tomatoes

Bring 4 cups of water to a boil in a large saucepan. Add the rice and a pinch of salt, stir, and return to a boil over high heat. Cover, reduce heat to very low, and simmer 45 minutes. Remove from the heat and allow the pan to stand for 5 minutes without disturbing the lid.

Meanwhile, peel and finely dice the eggplant. Heat ¼ cup of the oil in a large skillet over medium-low heat and add the onion, eggplant, lemon juice, dill, 1 ½ teaspoons of the oregano, and 3 cloves of the garlic. Stir until well combined, then add 1 ¼ cups hot water, ½ teaspoon of the salt, and a few grinds of pepper. Simmer over low heat, uncovered, for about 40 minutes, stirring frequently, until the eggplant is very tender and the liquid has nearly evaporated. (More water can be added, 2 tablespoons at a time, if the mixture dries out before the eggplant is finished cooking.) Transfer the eggplant mixture to a large bowl and stir in the cooked rice until everything is well combined.

Rinse the grape leaves, being careful not to tear them, and place them in a colander to drain.

Preheat the oven to 350 degrees F. In a large saucepan, combine the tomatoes and their juice, the remaining 1 tablespoon of oregano, 1 clove of garlic, and ¼ teaspoon salt, along with a few grinds of pepper. Cook over medium heat for 15 minutes, mashing the tomatoes into a thick sauce with the back of a wooden spoon as they cook. Set aside.

Use the remaining ½ teaspoon oil to grease a large baking dish. Place a spoonful of the eggplant mixture near the stem end of each grape leaf and roll it up, starting at the stem end and folding the sides in as you roll to create a tightly closed bundle. Place the stuffed leaves snugly in the baking dish, seam side down. Pour the tomato sauce evenly over them, cover, and bake for 20 minutes. Serve hot or at room temperature.

Tofu–Stuffed Squash Blossoms

YIELD: 10 appetizer servings

These morsels are a seasonal treat, as fresh squash blossoms from your garden or the farmer's market are not always available. They are best made the same day you harvest, or purchase, the blossoms.

EACH SERVING PROVIDES

198 calories, 6 g protein, 9 g fat,
1 g dietary fiber, 23 g carbohydrates,
460 mg sodium, 0 mg cholesterol

The filling

1 pound firm tofu

¼ cup minced cilantro,
   loosely packed

1 ¼ teaspoons ground cumin

1 ¼ teaspoons granulated garlic

¾ teaspoon salt

½ teaspoon minced jalapeño chili

20 squash blossoms, stems trimmed
   to about 1-inch

¼ cup canola oil (approximate),
   for frying

The batter

1 box (10 ounces) egg-free tempura
   batter

½ teaspoon chili powder

½ teaspoon granulated garlic

½ teaspoon ground cumin

½ teaspoon salt

½ teaspoon mild paprika

Crumble the tofu into a strainer and allow it to drain for about an hour. Gently squeeze it occasionally as it drains, to remove as much water as possible.

To make the filling, place the drained tofu in a food processor and add the cilantro, cumin, granulated garlic, salt, and jalapeño. Process until smooth and creamy. Transfer to a pastry bag, if available, or a bowl and set aside in the refrigerator until you are ready to fill and cook the blossoms.

Prepare the tempura batter according to package directions, adding the chili powder, granulated garlic, cumin, salt, and paprika. Set aside.

Inspect the squash blossoms carefully for dirt and insects. Rinse them gently and pat dry with a clean tea towel or paper towels. Hold each blossom in your hand and fill it with $\frac{1}{20}$ (about a tablespoon) of the tofu mixture, using the pastry bag or a long-handled narrow spoon. To close the bundles, gently twist the blossom tops. Place the filled blossoms side by side on a tray or platter that has a raised edge.

Pour the batter over the blossoms on the tray, turning them to coat evenly.

Heat about 2 tablespoons of the oil in a large heavy-bottomed skillet over medium heat. Test the oil by dropping a tiny bit of the batter into it; if it immediately sizzles and foams, the oil is ready. Place as many blossoms as will fit into the hot oil. Fry for about 2 minutes, then turn and cook on the other side until golden, about 2 minutes longer. Transfer to a plate lined with paper towels to drain off some of the excess oil. Cook the remaining blossoms in the same manner, adding additional oil as needed.

Serve hot or at room temperature.

Crostini with Tomatoes, Basil, Garlic, and Capers

YIELD: 8 appetizer servings

There is one absolute pre-requisite for this dish: perfectly ripe tomatoes. You may adjust the amount of garlic to suit yourself—several large cloves would not be too much for a true garlic lover.

EACH SERVING PROVIDES
*210 calories, 6 g protein, 5 g fat,
3 g dietary fiber, 34 g carbohydrates,
572 mg sodium, 0 mg cholesterol*

1 ½ pounds fresh pear tomatoes
(about 9 medium)

½ cup minced fresh basil leaves

3 cloves garlic, minced

2 tablespoons capers, drained

2 tablespoons extra-virgin olive oil

2 teaspoons fresh-squeezed lemon
juice

¼ teaspoon salt

Several grinds black pepper

1 recipe Crostini (page 301)

Cut the tomatoes in half crosswise and squeeze out and discard the juicy seed pockets. Cut out the stems and discard them. Finely dice the tomatoes and place them in a bowl. Add the basil, garlic, capers, olive oil, lemon juice, salt, and pepper. Stir to combine well, then set aside at room temperature for an hour or two before serving, so the flavors can blend and intensify.

Top the crostini slices with spoonfuls of the tomato mixture and arrange them on a platter. Serve immediately so the crostini doesn't get soggy. Alternatively, place the tomato mixture in a bowl and the crostini in a cloth-lined basket, and invite diners to serve themselves.

5

Salads

Asparagus and Roasted Red Pepper with Apples, Jicama,
and Lime

Tomato, Zucchini, and Jicama Salad with Fresh Dill
Vinaigrette

Radish and Cucumber Salad with Fresh Mint

Spinach with Pears, Toasted Walnuts, and Cumin
Vinaigrette

Yellow Beet and Arugula Salad with Dried Cranberries

Curried Tofu Salad with Cashews and Red Bell Pepper

Napa Cabbage Salad with Crunchy Chinese Noodles

Green Bean Salad with Asian Seasonings

Asian Cabbage, Carrot, and Baked Tofu Slaw

Tomato, Bread, and Basil Salad

Potato, Cucumber, and Red Bell Pepper Salad with Chive
Dressing

Curried Cauliflower, Garbanzo, and Tomato Salad

French Lentil Salad with Fresh Basil and Mint

Barley Salad with Green Olives, Tomatoes, and Sage
Vinaigrette

Rice, Red Pepper, and Bean Sprouts with Ginger Peanut
Dressing

Bulgur, Tomatoes, and Mushrooms with Tarragon
Dressing

Confetti Quinoa Salad with Fresh Herbs

Roasted Peppers and Couscous with Capers, Lime, and
Thyme

Macaroni Salad with Cucumbers and Dill Dressing

Mexicali Pasta Salad

Broccoli Salad with Mandarin Oranges and Toasted
Walnuts

Corn, Pineapple, and Jicama Salad with Tomatillos and Rum

Tropical Fruit Salad with Coconut

The word "salad" comes from the Latin salar, meaning to salt. History tells us that in ages past, vegetables were frequently preserved in salt, a precious ingredient that provided flavor and important nutrients, as well as inhibiting spoilage. It is logical to assume that the earliest salads were this type of preparation, hence the name.

Today, the term "salad" can refer to any combination of ingredients served chilled or at room temperature. Salads are almost always seasoned with an acid such as vinegar or lemon juice, which provides a pleasant tart taste and stimulates digestion. Another nutrition note: Raw foods, which appear in most salads, are an important source of enzymes, as well as vitamins, minerals, and fiber. It's clear that eating at least one salad a day can provide important health advantages.

There is no set rule about whether to serve salad at the beginning or the end of a meal, so suit yourself. Some believe a leafy, tart salad is a perfect first course, since it gently awakens the palate and the stomach. Others prefer their green salad at the end of the meal, for a refreshing finish. A hearty salad—one made with grains, pasta, or beans—can be a meal unto itself and makes a fine lunch or supper entrée, especially during the warm summer months.

The recipes in this section intermingle an abundance of colors, textures, and flavors—inspired by the seasons—to delight your senses and expand your salad savvy.

Asparagus and Roasted Red Pepper with Apples, Jicama, and Lime

YIELD: 6 side-dish servings

Almost Instant

Simple to prepare and beautiful on the table, this unusual salad combination of fruit and vege-tables would be welcome at any Southwest-inspired feast.

EACH SERVING PROVIDES
*56 calories, 3 g protein, 0 g fat,
4 g dietary fiber, 13 g carbohydrates,
105 mg sodium, 0 mg cholesterol*

1 large red bell pepper, roasted, peeled, and seeded (see page 9)

1 ½ pounds fresh asparagus

2 tablespoons fresh-squeezed lime juice

2 tablespoons fresh-squeezed lemon juice

1 medium crisp apple

½ pound jicama

1 teaspoon chili powder

¼ teaspoon salt

A few grinds black pepper

Cut the pepper into thin 1-inch strips. Set aside. Rinse the aspara-gus spears and snap off the tough stem ends. Cut into 2-inch pieces and place on a steamer rack in a saucepan that has a tight-fitting lid. Add about 2 inches of water, cover, and cook over medium-high heat about 4 to 6 minutes, until the asparagus is barely fork-tender. Rinse immediately with cold water to stop the cooking and drain well, then toss with the red pepper strips. Set aside.

Combine the lime and lemon juices in a medium bowl. Wash the apple, cut out and discard the core, and slice the fruit into thin wedges. As you go, place the slices in the juice bowl and toss to coat. Peel the jicama and cut it into 2-inch "sticks." Add to the apple and toss again. Lift the apple and jicama out of the bowl, leaving the juices behind. Arrange them around the edge of a serving platter. Mound the asparagus and bell pepper mixture in the center.

In a small bowl, combine the chili powder, salt, and pepper. Use your fingers to sprinkle this mixture evenly over everything on the platter and garnish with lemon and lime wedges, if desired. Serve at room temperature.

Tomato, Zucchini, and Jicama Salad with Fresh Dill Vinaigrette

YIELD: 8 side-dish servings

1 pound small zucchini (about 5)

½ pound jicama

1 pound small fresh pear tomatoes, quartered lengthwise

½ medium red onion, thinly sliced

3 tablespoons extra-virgin olive oil

2 tablespoons red wine vinegar

1 clove garlic, minced

½ teaspoon salt

Several grinds black pepper

3 tablespoons minced fresh dill

2 tablespoons minced fresh parsley

Cut off and discard the ends of the zucchinis and slice them crosswise into ¼-inch slices. Peel the jicama and cut it into thin matchsticks. In a large serving bowl, combine the zucchini, jicama, tomatoes, and red onion. Set aside.

In a small bowl, whisk together the olive oil, vinegar, garlic, salt, and pepper until emulsified, about 1 minute. Add the dill and parsley and whisk to combine. Pour over the vegetables and toss to coat. Serve immediately, or cover and chill for several hours, returning to room temperature before serving.

Almost Instant

Summertime is the perfect season to prepare this crunchy salad. You can find the ingredients farm-fresh at your local market.

EACH SERVING PROVIDES
*86 calories, 2 g protein, 6 g fat,
3 g dietary fiber, 9 g carbohydrates,
142 mg sodium, 0 mg cholesterol*

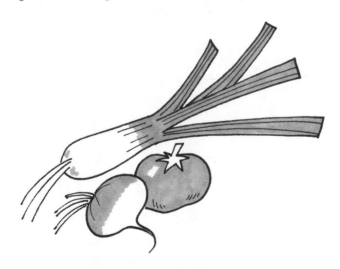

Radish and Cucumber Salad with Fresh Mint

YIELD: 4 side-dish servings

The success of this dish depends on perfectly fresh radishes, cucumbers, and tomatoes. Buy them at a farmer's market in late summer and you can't miss.

EACH SERVING PROVIDES

66 calories, 1 g protein, 4 g fat,
2 g dietary fiber, 8 g carbohydrates,
155 mg sodium, 0 mg cholesterol

2 tablespoons plain soy milk

1 tablespoon apple cider vinegar

1 tablespoon extra-virgin olive oil

1 clove garlic, minced

½ teaspoon organic granulated sugar

¼ teaspoon salt

A few grinds black pepper

1 ½ cups thinly sliced red radishes

1 ½ cups thinly sliced English cucumber

2 medium fresh pear tomatoes

¼ cup minced fresh mint

Whisk together the soy milk, vinegar, oil, garlic, sugar, salt, and pepper. Combine the radishes and cucumbers in a bowl. Cut the tomatoes in half crosswise and squeeze them gently over the sink to remove the juicy seed pockets. Finely dice the tomatoes and add them to the other vegetables in the bowl. Toss with the dressing and mint, and serve immediately, at room temperature.

Spinach with Pears, Toasted Walnuts, and Cumin Vinaigrette

YIELD: 4 side-dish servings

2 tablespoons apple cider vinegar

2 tablespoons fresh-squeezed orange juice

2 tablespoons extra-virgin olive oil

1 tablespoon maple syrup

¼ teaspoon ground cumin

¼ teaspoon salt

Several grinds black pepper

2 tablespoons minced shallot

1 medium pear, unpeeled

1 tablespoon fresh-squeezed lemon juice

6 cups washed and dried baby spinach leaves, lightly packed

¼ cup walnut pieces, toasted (see page 10)

Whisk together the vinegar, orange juice, olive oil, maple syrup, cumin, salt, and pepper until emulsified, about 1 minute. Stir in the minced shallot and set aside.

Wash and dry the pear and cut it in half from base to tip. Cut each half in half again lengthwise and slice out the core sections. Cut the pear wedges lengthwise into ¼-inch slices and toss the slices with the lemon juice.

Toss the spinach with the dressing, reserving 2 tablespoons. Arrange the dressed greens on 4 individual serving dishes. Fan out one-quarter of the pear slices on each bed of greens. Drizzle evenly with the remaining dressing, scatter some toasted walnuts on each serving, and garnish with calendula or nasturtium petals if available. Serve immediately.

Almost Instant

Bosc pears have a hint of crispness and are especially good in this salad. However, you may use any variety of pear for this dish; just make sure it is not overly ripe and mushy. Calendula or nasturtium petals would make a lovely edible garnish.

EACH SERVING PROVIDES
174 calories, 4 g protein, 12 g fat, 4 g dietary fiber, 16 g carbohydrates, 201 mg sodium, 0 mg cholesterol

Yellow Beet and Arugula Salad with Dried Cranberries

YIELD: 4 side-dish servings

2 medium yellow beets (about ¾ pound)

¼ cup dried cranberries

6 cups washed and dried arugula leaves, lightly packed

2 tablespoons balsamic vinegar

1 teaspoon organic granulated sugar

¼ teaspoon salt

Several grinds black pepper

3 tablespoons extra-virgin olive oil

Scrub the beets lightly and cook them in rapidly boiling water until a sharp knife can be easily inserted clear through their centers, about 30 minutes. Drain and set aside to cool for 30 minutes or so.

Just before serving, pour ¼ cup boiling water over the cranberries and allow them to plump for just 1 minute. Drain and set aside.

If the arugula leaves are tiny, leave them whole; otherwise, chop the leaves coarsely. Distribute the arugula between four serving plates. Peel the beets and cut them in half, then thinly slice the halves to make wedges. Arrange the beet wedges on the beds of arugula, then scatter the plumped cranberries on top.

Whisk together the vinegar, sugar, salt, and pepper, then add the olive oil and whisk until emulsified, about 1 minute. Spoon the dressing over the salads and serve at room temperature.

Vinaigrette Virtuosity

Once you master the simple art of vinaigrette dressing, your refrigerator will no longer be cluttered with expensive prepared salad dressings. It takes only a few minutes to whisk up a fresh vinaigrette at the beginning of meal preparation. Set it aside at room temperature and the flavors will blend and ripen while you cook the rest of the meal.

Think of the basic vinaigrette technique as a blank slate awaiting your creative touch. The seasoning possibilities are practically unlimited. As a rule of thumb, it is best to tie the vinaigrette flavors to the rest of the meal, as well as to the greens you are serving. With bitter greens like arugula, for instance, a touch of sweetness in the dressing is always welcome. If you are cooking a Mediterranean entrée, Italian herbs in the dressing will match up perfectly.

Use the best-quality oil for salad dressings. A superb extra-virgin olive oil is worth the price—it will be so fruity and flavorful that only a little can make a truly memorable salad. Another important element of a great salad dressing is fine vinegar. There are many varieties of vinegar available in supermarkets and gourmet markets. Sample around to discover your favorites and keep a few different varieties on hand.

To make a basic vinaigrette that will lightly dress 6 cups of greens for 4 generous salad servings, vigorously whisk together about 3 tablespoons of oil, 2 tablespoons of vinegar or lemon juice, a pinch of salt, and several grinds of pepper. Whisk the mixture long enough so that the ingredients become emulsified, meaning they are completely blended and slightly thickened. Simply multiply the ingredients if you want to make enough vinaigrette to keep on hand in the refrigerator. From this quick and easy starting point, you can explore any number of flavor directions. Below are some of the combinations we frequently enjoy on mixed greens. Use the quantities just mentioned as a guide.

- Extra-virgin olive oil, raspberry vinegar, minced shallots, salt, and pepper
- Extra-virgin olive oil, white wine vinegar, fresh snipped tarragon, salt, and pepper
- Extra-virgin olive oil, fresh-squeezed lemon juice, splash of balsamic vinegar, minced garlic, salt, and pepper
- Extra-virgin olive oil, apple cider vinegar, Dijon mustard, tomato paste, and a touch of maple syrup
- Light sesame oil, a bit of dark sesame oil, unseasoned rice vinegar, and soy sauce
- Canola oil, lime juice, ground cumin, chili powder, and salt
- Canola oil, curry powder, a touch of maple syrup, and salt
- Flaxseed oil, apple cider vinegar, soy sauce, and a pinch of cayenne

Curried Tofu Salad with Cashews and Red Bell Pepper

YIELD: 6 side-dish servings

Almost Instant

Enjoy this tofu mixture as a salad served on butter lettuce leaves, or as a sandwich spread to use on whole grain bread. The curry flavor will vary depending on the type of premixed curry powder you use. Our homemade Curry Blend (page 311) is nicely balanced.

EACH SERVING PROVIDES

*155 calories, 8 g protein, 14 g fat,
1 g dietary fiber, 3 g carbohydrates,
58 mg sodium, 0 mg cholesterol*

1 pound firm tofu

¼ cup soy mayonnaise

½ teaspoon curry powder

½ medium red bell pepper, minced

1 rib celery, minced

3 tablespoons minced fresh cilantro

¼ cup finely chopped salted cashews

On a large platter or cutting board, place a clean tea towel that has been folded in half. Remove the tofu from its package and, if necessary, slice it into slabs that are about 1 ½ inches thick. Place the slabs on the folded tea towel and cover with another clean folded tea towel. Place a board or baking sheet flat on the towel-wrapped tofu and place something heavy on top, such as a large can of tomatoes. You want enough weight to gently press some of the water out of the tofu, but not so much weight that the tofu will be flattened. Allow the tofu to rest at room temperature for about 10 minutes.

Crumble the pressed tofu into a bowl. Stir in the mayonnaise and curry powder, mashing slightly as you do to create a fairly smooth consistency. Stir in the bell pepper, celery, and cilantro. Serve as a salad on lettuce leaves, topping with the cashews, or stir the cashews into the tofu mixture and use as a sandwich filling.

Napa Cabbage Salad with Crunchy Chinese Noodles

YIELD: 6 main-dish servings

¼ cup unseasoned rice vinegar

2 tablespoons dark sesame oil

2 tablespoons canola oil

2 tablespoons mirin

2 tablespoons soy sauce

¼ teaspoon chili powder

¼ teaspoon salt

6 ounces dried ramen-style noodles

1 ½ pounds Napa cabbage (about 1 medium), shredded

4 cups mung bean sprouts (about ½ pound)

1 medium red bell pepper, thinly sliced

3 ounces unsalted cashews

This is a wonderful summertime lunch or dinner entrée. Make the salad at least 6 hours before serving, so the noodles have time to absorb the dressing. We frequently use a coiled noodle from the Asian market sold as "Chinese noodles" for this dish, but any ramen-type noodle from the natural food store can be substituted.

In a small bowl whisk together the vinegar, sesame oil, canola oil, mirin, 1 tablespoon of the soy sauce, chili powder, and salt until emulsified, about 1 minute. Set aside.

Use your hands to break up the cake of dried noodles into several pieces. Combine the cabbage, noodles, sprouts, and bell pepper in a very large bowl. Pour the dressing over this mixture and toss to combine. Cover and refrigerate for 6 to 8 hours.

Meanwhile, place the cashews in a dry, heavy-bottomed skillet over medium heat. Shake the pan frequently as the cashews toast. Soon they will be golden brown, emitting a wonderful roasted aroma. Immediately transfer them to a small bowl and pour the remaining 1 tablespoon soy sauce over them. Toss to coat and set aside at room temperature.

When the salad has marinated for the designated time, it will have condensed considerably. Toss it with the cashews, then mound it on chilled individual plates and serve.

EACH SERVING PROVIDES
*356 calories, 9 g protein, 23 g fat,
6 g dietary fiber, 33 g carbohydrates,
761 mg sodium, 0 mg cholesterol*

Green Bean Salad with Asian Seasonings

YIELD: 4 side-dish servings

Almost Instant

This simple dish turns green beans into something extra-ordinary. It is a perfect side-dish for any Asian-inspired main course.

EACH SERVING PROVIDES

*103 calories, 3 g protein, 5 g fat,
4 g dietary fiber, 13 g carbohydrates,
180 mg sodium, 0 mg cholesterol*

2 tablespoons unseasoned rice
   vinegar

1 tablespoon olive oil

1 tablespoon mirin or dry sherry

1 tablespoon fresh-squeezed orange
   juice

2 teaspoons soy sauce

1 teaspoon dark sesame oil

1 clove garlic, minced

3 tablespoons grated red onion

1 pound fresh green beans

1 teaspoon sesame seeds, toasted
   (see page 10)

Whisk together the vinegar, olive oil, mirin, orange juice, soy sauce, sesame oil, and garlic until emulsified, about 1 minute. Stir in the onion and set aside at room temperature so the flavors can blend.

Snap off and discard the stem ends of the beans and string them, if necessary. Leave the beans whole. Place a steamer rack in a saucepan and add about 2 inches of water to the pan. Place the beans on the rack and steam over medium-high heat until they are fork-tender; about 8 minutes. Immediately drain the beans in a colander and rinse them with cold water to stop the cooking. Drain very well. Toss the beans with the dressing and serve warm or at room temperature, sprinkled with the sesame seeds.

Asian Cabbage, Carrot, and Baked Tofu Slaw

YIELD: 4 side-dish servings

Dressing

2 tablespoons fresh-squeezed
   orange juice

2 tablespoons unseasoned
   rice vinegar

1 tablespoon dark sesame oil

1 tablespoon rice syrup

1 tablespoon soy sauce

Salad

3 ½ ounces Baked Tofu (page 308)

1 cup shredded green cabbage

1 cup shredded red cabbage

1 cup shredded carrots

1 teaspoon sesame seeds, toasted
   (see page 10)

3 green onions, minced

This tasty combination is a light and refreshing lunch offering, perhaps as an accompaniment to your favorite sushi (see pages 248–249).

EACH SERVING PROVIDES
106 calories, 4 g protein, 7 g fat, 2 g dietary fiber, 10 g carbohydrates, 387 mg sodium, 0 mg cholesterol

Whisk together the orange juice, vinegar, sesame oil, rice syrup, and soy sauce. Set aside. Cut the tofu into thin matchsticks.

Combine the green and red cabbage, carrots, and tofu in a bowl, then toss with the dressing, sesame seeds, and green onions. Serve chilled or at room temperature.

CARROTS

Vitamin A, derived from beta carotene, was first identified in carrots more than 150 years ago, and carrots continue to be the best dietary source for this important antioxidant. So potent is the humble carrot as a tumor inhibitor that the National Cancer Institute is currently sponsoring several large-scale studies, using the beneficial carrot compound in capsule form. Carrots also contain soluble fiber that can help lower cholesterol levels. Since carrots contain substantial amounts of natural sugars, they are a satisfying snack when eaten raw and a welcome addition to sautés and soups. Apples are nutritious and delicious, but a carrot a day may be even more effective at keeping the doctor away!

Tomato, Bread, and Basil Salad

YIELD: 6 main-dish servings

This version of Tuscan "panza-nella" is a late summer classic because that's tomato harvest time, and you must use great, vine-ripened tomatoes for this dish. The bread you select is also important. Choose a chewy, rustic loaf, not the typical supermarket "French" bread. Having met these two require-ments, you're in for a real treat.

EACH SERVING PROVIDES
*327 calories, 8 g protein, 12 g fat,
4 g dietary fiber, 47 g carbohydrates,
761 mg sodium, 0 mg cholesterol*

1-pound loaf chewy, rustic bread
¼ cup red wine vinegar
2 cloves garlic, minced
¼ teaspoon salt
Several grinds black pepper
¼ cup extra-virgin olive oil
1 medium cucumber

1 pound fresh pear tomatoes
¼ cup diced red onion
¼ cup fresh basil leaves, firmly packed
2 tablespoons capers, drained
6 large butter lettuce leaves

Preheat the oven to 350 degrees F. Cut the bread into ¾-inch cubes and arrange the cubes in a single layer on a baking sheet. Toast in the oven until lightly browned and crisp on the outside, but still soft inside, about 8 to 10 minutes. Set aside to cool completely.

Meanwhile, whisk together the vinegar, garlic, salt, and pepper, then add the oil and whisk until emulsified, about 1 minute. Set the dressing aside.

If the cucumber is waxed or if the skin tastes bitter, peel it. Cut the cucumber in half lengthwise and use a spoon to scrape out and discard the seeds. Cut the cucumber halves crosswise into ¼-inch slices, and set them aside in a large bowl.

Cut the tomatoes in half crosswise and squeeze them gently over the sink to empty out the juicy seed pockets. Cut out and discard the stem ends, then dice the tomatoes and add them to the cucumber. Add the onion, basil, capers, and dressing and toss to combine. (This much can be done ahead of time and held at room temperature for up to several hours.)

Just before serving, add the bread cubes to the tomato mixture and toss to distribute evenly. Place a lettuce leaf on each plate and mound a portion of the salad into it. Serve at room temperature.

Potato, Cucumber, and Red Bell Pepper Salad with Chive Dressing

YIELD: 12 side-dish servings

3 pounds white boiling potatoes, scrubbed and diced

1 large cucumber

¾ cup soy mayonnaise

1 tablespoon Dijon mustard

½ teaspoon salt

¼ teaspoon black pepper

½ cup minced chives (about 1 bunch)

4 green onions, minced

1 large red bell pepper, diced

This potato salad isn't the usual too-rich type; instead, the vegetables are lightly coated in a flavorful chive sauce. Make this dish ahead of time and take it to your next potluck.

EACH SERVING PROVIDES
237 calories, 3 g protein, 10 g fat, 3 g dietary fiber, 24 g carbohydrates, 206 mg sodium, 0 mg cholesterol

Place the diced potatoes in a large pot and cover them with plenty of water. Cover the pot and bring to a boil over high heat. Remove the lid, gently stir, then continue to cook over medium-high heat for about 8 to 10 minutes, until the potatoes are fork-tender, but not falling apart. Transfer them to a colander and rinse with cold water to stop the cooking. Set aside to drain.

If the cucumber is waxed or if the skin tastes bitter, peel it. Cut the cucumber in half lengthwise and use a spoon to scrape out and discard the seeds. Dice the cucumber and set it aside in a large bowl. In a small bowl, whisk together the mayonnaise, mustard, salt, pepper, and chives.

Add the potatoes, onion, and bell pepper to the cucumber in the bowl. Pour the dressing over the mixture and toss gently until well combined. Chill before serving.

Curried Cauliflower, Garbanzo, and Tomato Salad

YIELD: 6 side-dish servings

This dish makes a wonderful potluck contribution or summer buffet offering. It is filling and nourishing enough to be served as a main course salad for four. Store any leftovers in the refrigerator in a tightly closed container and enjoy them over the course of a few days— the flavor actually improves with time.

EACH SERVING PROVIDES
*122 calories, 4 g protein, 6 g fat,
4 g dietary fiber, 14 g carbohydrates,
147 mg sodium, 0 mg cholesterol*

2 tablespoons extra-virgin olive oil

2 tablespoons fresh-squeezed lemon juice

2 tablespoons fresh-squeezed orange juice

2 teaspoons soy sauce

1 teaspoon curry powder

1 teaspoon ground cumin

Several grinds black pepper

½ pound cherry tomatoes

1 pound fresh cauliflower, chopped into bite-sized pieces

1½ cups cooked and drained garbanzo beans

⅓ cup finely diced red onion

⅓ cup minced fresh cilantro

1 head butter lettuce

In a large serving bowl, whisk together the olive oil, lemon juice, orange juice, soy sauce, curry powder, cumin, and pepper until emulsified, about 1 minute. Set aside.

Discard the stems of the cherry tomatoes and halve or quarter them lengthwise, depending on their size, to create bite-sized pieces. Toss the tomatoes with the dressing, cover the bowl with a clean tea towel, and set aside at room temperature.

Place a steamer tray in a large saucepan and add about 2 inches of water to the pan. Place the cauliflower on the tray and steam until fork-tender, about 5 to 7 minutes. Immediately transfer it to a colander and rinse with cold water to stop the cooking. Drain the cauliflower thoroughly and combine it with the tomato mixture. Add the garbanzo beans, red onion, and cilantro and toss to combine well. This much can be done well ahead of time; hold the mixture at room temperature for several hours or in the refrigerator overnight.

When you are ready to serve the salad, wash and dry the butter lettuce and tear it into bite-sized pieces. Toss with the vegetable and bean mixture and serve at room temperaure.

French Lentil Salad with Fresh Basil and Mint

YIELD: 6 side-dish servings

1 cup uncooked French lentils

1 medium red bell pepper, finely diced

½ cup finely diced yellow onion

½ cup fresh basil leaves, chiffonade (see page 4)

½ cup fresh mint, chiffonade (see page 4)

¼ cup extra-virgin olive oil

2 tablespoons red wine vinegar

2 cloves garlic, minced

¼ teaspoon salt

Several grinds black pepper

French lentils, also sold as green or "du Puy" lentils, are smaller and darker than the standard brown variety and hold their shape better when cooked. Here, they are the foundation for a colorful and delicious salad. We recommend using basil-flavored red wine vinegar for this recipe if you have some on hand.

EACH SERVING PROVIDES
206 calories, 10 g protein, 10 g fat, 11 g dietary fiber, 23 g carbohydrates, 105 mg sodium, 0 mg cholesterol

Wash and sort the lentils, discarding any foreign objects you may find. Place them in a saucepan and cover them with 4 cups of water. Bring to a boil over high heat, then reduce the heat to medium-high and simmer rapidly for 12 to 14 minutes, until the lentils are tender but not mushy. Drain thoroughly in a colander, rinsing well with cold water to stop the cooking, then transfer the lentils to a large bowl and set aside to cool for at least 30 minutes.

Add the bell pepper, onion, basil, and mint to the cooled lentils and toss to combine. In a small bowl, whisk together the oil, vinegar, garlic, salt, and pepper until emulsified, about 1 minute. Pour this dressing over the lentils and toss to combine. Set aside at room temperature for up to a few hours so the flavors can blend, or refrigerate for up to a day, but bring to room temperature before serving.

Barley Salad with Green Olives, Tomatoes, and Sage Vinaigrette

YIELD: 6 side-dish servings

The type of barley we recommend here is the pearl barley sold in natural food stores, usually in bulk. It bears little resemblance to the white "pearls" typically sold in supermarkets. Natural pearl barley retains some of the bran and is therefore darker in color; nuttier in flavor; and higher in vitamins, minerals, and fiber. The barley may be cooked and the dressing made a day or two ahead of time. Combine them just before going out on a picnic or to a summer potluck.

EACH SERVING PROVIDES
*195 calories, 4 g protein, 8 g fat,
6 g dietary fiber, 29 g carbohydrates,
295 mg sodium, 0 mg cholesterol*

¼ cup vegetable stock

3 tablespoons extra-virgin olive oil

3 tablespoons white wine vinegar

1 tablespoon tomato paste

1 teaspoon Dijon mustard

2 cloves garlic, minced

½ teaspoon salt

Several grinds black pepper

2 tablespoons minced fresh sage leaves

1 cup pearl barley

½ cup finely chopped pimiento-stuffed olives

1½ cups diced fresh or canned tomatoes, with juice

Whisk together the stock, olive oil, vinegar, tomato paste, mustard, garlic, ¼ teaspoon of the salt, and black pepper until emulsified, about 1 minute. Stir in the sage and set aside at room temperature so the flavors can blend while you cook and cool the barley.

Heat a heavy-bottomed saucepan over medium heat. Add the barley and toast, stirring constantly, until the grains begin to turn a darker shade of tan, about 3 minutes. Watch closely; if the barley gets too dark, it will be ruined. Add 2½ cups of water and the remaining ¼ teaspoon salt and bring to a rolling boil. Cover, reduce heat to low, and cook for 45 minutes. Turn off the heat and let stand, with the lid in place, for 10 minutes or so, then transfer to a glass or ceramic bowl and set aside to cool.

Toss the cooled barley with the olives and tomatoes, then add the dressing and toss again. Serve at room temperature.

Rice, Red Pepper, and Bean Sprouts with Ginger Peanut Dressing

YIELD: 4 main-dish servings

¼ cup smooth or crunchy peanut butter

2 tablespoons cider vinegar

1 tablespoon soy sauce

2 teaspoons freshly grated ginger

1 teaspoon organic granulated sugar

⅛ teaspoon cayenne pepper

2 cups cooked brown rice, cold

1 medium carrot, grated

1 small red bell pepper, finely diced

3 green onions, thinly sliced

4 large red or green lettuce leaves

1 cup fresh mung bean sprouts, rinsed and drained

Thin the peanut butter by adding ⅓ cup of water a little at a time, whisking until smoothly incorporated after each addition. When all of the water has been added, whisk in the vinegar, soy sauce, ginger, sugar, and cayenne pepper.

Toss the cold rice with the carrot, bell pepper, green onions, and peanut dressing until everything is well distributed. Arrange a lettuce leaf on each of 4 individual serving plates. Fill the lettuce leaves with the rice mixture and garnish with the bean sprouts.

Almost Instant

This yummy salad makes a hearty and nourishing lunch or warm weather supper. A bowl of simple miso soup would make a nice accompaniment. This dressing is one you'll call on often—it's good with other cooked grains, pasta, and many cooked vegetables.

EACH SERVING PROVIDES
229 calories, 8 g protein, 9 g fat,
4 g dietary fiber, 32 g carbohydrates,
345 mg sodium, 0 mg cholesterol

Bulgur, Tomatoes, and Mushrooms with Tarragon Dressing

YIELD: 6 side-dish servings

Almost Instant

You will find yourself making this dish frequently during the warm summer months, when cherry tomatoes are in season. Fresh tarragon is a wonderful herb that's easy to grow in a pot on a sunny porch if you don't have the garden space. When you grow your own, it's always on hand for spontaneous inspiration.

EACH SERVING PROVIDES

*157 calories, 3 g protein, 7 g fat,
5 g dietary fiber, 21 g carbohydrates,
110 mg sodium, 0 mg cholesterol*

1 cup uncooked bulgur wheat

3 cloves garlic, minced

½ pound yellow or red cherry tomatoes

4 green onions, minced

3 tablespoons extra-virgin olive oil

2 tablespoons white wine vinegar

¼ teaspoon salt

Several grinds black pepper

¼ cup minced fresh Italian parsley

2 tablespoons minced fresh tarragon

Bring 2 cups of water to a boil in a medium-sized saucepan. Add the bulgur and garlic, return to a boil, reduce the heat to very low, cover, and simmer for 15 minutes. Turn off the heat. Without disturbing the lid, allow the pot to stand for 5 minutes. Transfer the bulgur to a large bowl, fluffing with a fork to separate the grains, and allow to cool to room temperature.

Cut the cherry tomatoes in halves or quarters, depending on their size, to create bite-sized pieces. Add the tomatoes and green onions to the cooled bulgur, tossing gently to combine.

Whisk together the olive oil, vinegar, salt, pepper, parsley, and tarragon until emulsified, about 1 minute. Pour over the bulgur mixture, toss, and serve.

Confetti Quinoa Salad with Fresh Herbs

YIELD: 6 side-dish servings

1 ¼ cups uncooked quinoa

1 medium carrot, grated

1 celery stalk, finely diced

4 red radishes, thinly sliced

½ cup finely diced red cabbage

3 tablespoons fresh-squeezed
    lemon juice

2 tablespoons extra-virgin olive oil

2 tablespoons vegetable stock

1 tablespoon tomato paste

2 cloves garlic, minced

1 teaspoon mild paprika

½ teaspoon salt

½ teaspoon organic granulated
    sugar

½ cup minced mixed fresh herbs

2 tablespoons sunflower seeds,
    toasted and chopped

This is a great way to bring the good nutrition of quinoa into your diet—as pretty as it is flavorful. Chop everything finely so it distributes well among the tiny grains. Any combination of fresh herbs—such as parsley, basil, mint, chives, tarragon, and thyme—can be used here, whatever is in season and strikes your fancy.

EACH SERVING PROVIDES
*209 calories, 6 g protein, 9 g fat,
3 g dietary fiber, 29 g carbohydrates,
236 mg sodium, 0 mg cholesterol*

Fill a large bowl with cold water and add the quinoa. Stir around with your fingers for a few moments, then drain through a fine mesh strainer. Hold the strainer under the tap and continue rinsing the quinoa with cold water for another minute or so, then set it aside to drain.

Bring 2 ½ cups of water to a boil and add the quinoa. Bring the water back to a boil, cover, reduce the heat to very low, and cook 20 minutes. Turn off the heat and allow the pot to stand for 10 minutes, without disturbing the lid, then transfer the quinoa to a plate or board to cool.

Toss the carrot, celery, radishes, and cabbage together in a large bowl with 1 tablespoon of the lemon juice. Set aside.

In a small bowl, whisk together the remaining 2 tablespoons lemon juice, the olive oil, stock, tomato paste, garlic, paprika, salt, and sugar until emulsified, about 1 minute. Stir in the fresh herbs and set aside.

When the quinoa has come to room temperature, add it to the vegetables and toss to distribute everything evenly. Add the dressing and sunflower seeds and toss again. Serve immediately.

Roasted Peppers and Couscous with Capers, Lime, and Thyme

YIELD: 8 side-dish servings

This stunning dish deserves a place of honor at a summer buffet dinner. Any color bell pepper can be used, although we especially enjoy the sweetness of the red and yellow varieties.

EACH SERVING PROVIDES

205 calories, 5 g protein, 7 g fat,

3 g dietary fiber, 31 g carbohydrates,

269 mg sodium, 0 mg cholesterol

3 tablespoons plus 2 teaspoons extra-virgin olive oil

½ teaspoon granulated garlic

¾ teaspoon dried thyme

⅛ teaspoon plus ¼ teaspoon salt

A pinch cayenne pepper

1½ cups dried couscous

2 tablespoons plus 1 teaspoon fresh-squeezed lime juice

1 tablespoon balsamic vinegar

2 tablespoons capers, not drained

2 teaspoons brown rice syrup

3 cloves garlic, minced

Several grinds black pepper

2 large bell peppers

½ cup minced fresh Italian parsley

3 green onions, minced

1 large tomato, diced

Bring 2¼ cups water to a boil in a medium saucepan, along with 2 teaspoons of the olive oil, the granulated garlic, ¼ teaspoon of the thyme, ⅛ teaspoon of the salt, and the cayenne. When it is boiling rapidly, pour in the couscous and stir. Immediately remove the pan from the heat, cover, and allow to stand 10 minutes without disturbing the lid. Transfer to a large bowl and use a fork to gently fluff the couscous and break up any large clumps. Allow to cool to room temperature.

Meanwhile, make the dressing by combining the remaining 3 tablespoons olive oil, lime juice, balsamic vinegar, capers, brown rice syrup, garlic, remaining ½ teaspoon thyme, remaining ¼ teaspoon salt, and the black pepper in a small food processor or the blender. Process to a smooth sauce consistency.

Preheat the oven to 400 degrees F. Rinse and dry the peppers. Cut the peppers in half from stem end to bottom, remove and discard the seeds, stem, and white membranes, and cut each piece in half crosswise. Use your fingers or a brush to lightly coat the insides of the pepper pieces with a small amount of the dressing. Place cut side up in a single layer in a glass baking dish and bake for about 30 minutes, until the peppers are tender.

When the couscous has cooled to room temperature, toss it with the parsley, onions, and tomato, reserving a tablespoon or so of the parsley for garnish. Toss with the remaining dressing until well combined. Arrange the peppers around the edge of a large platter and mound the couscous mixture in the center. Garnish with the reserved parsley and the lemon wedges. Serve immediately, or refrigerate for a few hours, but bring back to room temperature before serving.

CAYENNE PEPPER

Capsaicin, the active ingredient in hot peppers, has a stimulating effect on digestion and has been shown to lower blood levels of cholesterol and triglycerides. The hotter the pepper, the more capsaicin it contains, so regularly consuming cayenne pepper is a good way to reap these benefits. Besides being called for in many recipes, cayenne makes a good table condiment. During cold and flu season, a little cayenne stirred into hot lemonade that has been sweetened with a little maple syrup will chase away the chill.

Macaroni Salad with Cucumbers and Dill Dressing

YIELD: 12 side-dish servings

8 ounces dried elbow macaroni

1 large cucumber

½ medium red onion, diced

½ cup soy mayonnaise

2 tablespoons extra-virgin olive oil

1 tablespoon red wine vinegar

1 tablespoon Dijon mustard

½ teaspoon granulated garlic

¼ teaspoon salt

⅓ cup finely diced sweet pickles

2 tablespoons minced fresh dill

Bring several quarts of water to a boil, add the macaroni, and cook until al dente, about 10 minutes. Quickly cool by draining in a colander and rinsing for a few moments with cold tap water. Drain very well, then transfer to a large bowl.

If the cucumber is waxed or if the skin tastes bitter, peel it. Cut the cucumber in half lengthwise and use a spoon to scrape out and discard the seeds. Dice the cucumber and add it to the macaroni, along with the onion.

Whisk together the mayonnaise, olive oil, vinegar, mustard, garlic, and salt. Stir in the pickles and fresh dill. Pour over the macaroni, toss well, cover, and chill until serving time, at least an hour or up to a day.

Mexicali Pasta Salad

YIELD: 6 main-dish servings

½ pound fresh green beans

½ medium red bell pepper

7 ounces dried whole wheat
pasta spirals

½ cup finely diced red onion

¼ cup fresh-squeezed orange juice

¼ cup fresh-squeezed lime juice

3 tablespoons extra-virgin olive oil

1 tablespoon tomato paste

1 teaspoon ground cumin

1 teaspoon chili powder

1 teaspoon dried oregano

¾ teaspoon salt

⅛ teaspoon cayenne pepper

1½ cups cooked and drained black
beans

1 cup peeled, seeded, and diced
cucumber

15 cherry tomatoes, halved

¼ cup chopped fresh cilantro

¼ cup pumpkin seeds, toasted (see
page 10) and chopped

*We like to use whole wheat pasta
for this hearty dish. The other
strong flavors stand up well to
the pasta's earthy taste. If you
prefer regular semolina pasta, or
a non-wheat variety, feel free to
substitute it, adjusting the cooking time according to package
directions.*

EACH SERVING PROVIDES
*294 calories, 11 g protein, 9 g fat,
7 g dietary fiber, 47 g carbohydrates,
303 mg sodium, 0 mg cholesterol*

Snap off the stem ends of the beans, string them if necessary, and cut
them crosswise at a slant into 1-inch pieces. Set aside. Discard the
stem, seeds, and white membrane of the pepper and chop it into
¼-inch pieces. Set aside separately.

Bring several quarts of water to a rolling boil and stir in the
pasta. Bring the water back to a rolling boil and cook, stirring occasionally, for 7 minutes. Add the green beans, bring the water
back to a rolling boil, and cook 2 to 4 minutes longer, until the
pasta is tender but not mushy. Transfer to a colander, rinse under
cold water, and drain thoroughly.

Meanwhile, whisk together the orange juice, lime juice, olive
oil, tomato paste, cumin, chili powder, oregano, salt, and cayenne
until emulsified, about 1 minute.

Toss in a bowl with the red bell pepper, cucumber, black beans,
cherry tomatoes, onion, and dressing. Garnish with the cilantro and
pumpkin seeds and serve at room temperature.

Broccoli Salad with Mandarin Oranges and Toasted Walnuts

YIELD: 6 side-dish servings

Almost Instant

Make this composed salad on a chilly winter day. It satisfies the taste buds and brightens up the table with some of the season's best produce.

EACH SERVING PROVIDES

207 calories, 5 g protein, 17 g fat,
4 g dietary fiber, 13 g carbohydrates,
36 mg sodium, 0 mg cholesterol

1 ½ pounds fresh broccoli

2 fresh mandarin oranges
  or tangerines

⅓ cup extra-virgin olive oil

¼ cup raspberry vinegar

1 clove garlic, minced

½ teaspoon dried oregano

A dash fresh nutmeg

6 red lettuce leaves

⅓ cup walnut pieces, toasted (see
  page 10)

Cut off and discard the tough stem ends of the broccoli and peel the remaining stalks if they have very thick, tough skin. Cut the broccoli lengthwise into roughly even spears. Place the spears on a steamer rack in a saucepan that has a tight-fitting lid. Add about 2 inches of water, cover, and steam over medium-high heat about 6 minutes, until bright green and barely fork-tender. Rinse well under cold water to stop the cooking. Drain well and transfer to a large, shallow bowl.

Peel the oranges and remove the sections of fruit from the membrane. Add them to the broccoli in the bowl.

Whisk together the oil, vinegar, garlic, oregano, and nutmeg until emulsified, about 1 minute. Pour over the broccoli and oranges, toss gently, then set aside at room temperature until serving time, up to 2 hours.

Just before serving, line six salad plates with the lettuce leaves. Arrange equal amounts of broccoli spears and orange wedges atop the lettuce. Drizzle the dressing that remains in the bowl evenly over the 6 servings. Top with the toasted walnuts and serve.

Corn, Pineapple, and Jicama Salad with Tomatillos and Rum

YIELD: 8 side-dish servings

1 cup peeled and diced jicama

1 cup peeled and diced pineapple

1 tablespoon fresh-squeezed lemon juice

2 cups fresh or frozen corn kernels (see NOTE)

1 can (12 ounces) water-packed tomatillos

¼ cup minced red onion

3 tablespoons fresh-squeezed lime juice

1 tablespoon extra-virgin olive oil

1 tablespoon mirin

1 tablespoon dark rum

1 tablespoon minced fresh cilantro

⅛ teaspoon salt

A pinch cayenne pepper

Delicious, refreshing, and easy to make, this salad is the perfect accompaniment to a summertime grilled meal. It's also a popular potluck offering. Fresh pineapple is best in this dish, but drained canned pineapple may be substituted. Buy a brand that has no added sugar.

EACH SERVING PROVIDES
101 calories, 3 g protein, 2 g fat, 4 g dietary fiber, 17 g carbohydrates, 248 mg sodium, 0 mg cholesterol

Toss the jicama and pineapple in a bowl with the lemon juice. If using fresh corn, bring about 4 cups of water to a boil and add the corn kernels. As soon as the water returns to a boil, transfer the corn to a colander and rinse it under cold water. Drain thoroughly. Add the corn to the jicama and pineapple.

Drain the tomatillos and chop them coarsely. Add the tomatillos and onion to the salad mixture and toss to evenly distribute. Whisk together the lime juice, olive oil, mirin, rum, cilantro, salt, and cayenne until emulsified, about 1 minute. Toss with the salad ingredients until well combined. Chill for at least ½ hour, or up to several hours, before serving.

NOTE: If using fresh corn, you will need about 4 medium ears to yield 2 cups corn kernels.

Tropical Fruit Salad with Coconut

YIELD: 4 main-dish servings

This salad cools and refreshes, making it the perfect summer brunch or lunch offering, accompanied by muffins, if you wish. The recipe makes a lot, but it will stay fresh and tasty for a couple of days if stored in a tightly closed container in the refrigerator. Fresh pineapple is best here, but drained canned pineapple may be substituted. Buy a brand that has no added sugar.

EACH SERVING PROVIDES
*202 calories, 2 g protein, 5 g fat,
6 g dietary fiber, 41 g carbohydrates,
10 mg sodium, 0 mg cholesterol*

2 cups peeled and diced pineapple

1 large papaya, peeled, seeded, and diced

3 medium kiwis, peeled and diced

2 whole dates, seeded and finely chopped

1 large banana, thinly sliced

2 tablespoons coconut milk

1 tablespoon fresh-squeezed lime juice

¼ cup flaked coconut

In a large bowl, gently toss the fruit with the coconut milk and lime juice until everything is well distributed. If you don't plan to serve the salad immediately, chill it at this stage for up to a few hours. Place the coconut in a dry, heavy-bottomed skillet over medium heat. Toast the coconut for a few minutes, stirring constantly, until it is light tan in color. Immediately remove it from the pan. Just before serving, garnish the salad with the toasted coconut.

6

Soups and Stews

Avocado-Tomato Bisque

Creamy Broccoli Soup with Dill and Mustard

Curried Carrot and Leek Soup

Mulligatawny

Potato and Garlic Soup with Fresh Thyme

Southwest Corn, Chard, and Potato Soup

Summer Squash and Apricot Soup with Fresh Basil
and Pine Nuts

Grilled Butternut Squash Soup with Fresh Shiitake
Mushrooms

Pumpkin-Rice Soup with Sage and Allspice

Caramelized Red Onion Soup

Spinach Soup with Oregano and Calamata Olives

Beet Borscht with Lemon and Dill

Tofu, Rice, and Seaweed Soup with Garlic and Peas

Chinese Hot-and-Sour Soup

Fresh Bean Stew with Corn and Acorn Squash

Cranberry Bean Minestrone with Sage and Marjoram

Mung Bean and Zucchini Soup with Ginger

Provençal Bean and Vegetable Stew

Split Pea Soup with Sweet Potato and Mexican
Seasonings

Classic Lentil, Tomato, and Potato Stew

Curried Barley, Shiitake, and Broccoli Stew

Making good soup is a simple and satisfying art, involving all our senses. Whether smooth and rich or studded with a variety of shapes and colors, soup has a universal comfort-food appeal. No wonder. Soup is deeply nourishing, easy to digest and has a warming effect in cold weather.

Lovers of classic creamed soups will delight in our vegan versions, enriched with soy or rice milk. As a general rule, a creamed or puréed soup can be an elegant way to begin a multi-course feast. On the more substantial side, a thick stew, packed with beans and/or grains and a colorful array of vegetables, makes a satisfying meal in a bowl. Serve a crusty bread for sopping up the hot broth, and nothing will be lacking.

It might come as a surprise that many of our soups carry the Almost Instant designation. A common myth claims that soups are supposed to simmer on the stove for long hours, and some cooks avoid making soup because they don't have that kind of patience. Well, here's some good news: A delicious depth of flavor can be achieved in soups quickly when we call on the magic of vegetable stock, instead of using plain water. You will learn how easy it is to keep fresh vegetable stock on hand by reading "Investing in Stock" on page 94.

Our recipes are meant not only to nourish but to inspire. We hope you will begin to experiment on your own, simmering favorite ingredients in stock or water until their flavors are magically transformed into an aromatic and delicious potion to share with family and friends.

Avocado–Tomato Bisque

YIELD: 8 first-course servings

This velvety soup, which can be served either warm or chilled, makes a stunning first course for a Mexican–inspired dinner party. It is essential that you use perfectly ripe avocados, which yield slightly to gentle pressure when squeezed. Hard, unyielding avocados can be brought home from the market a few days before you want to make the soup. They will continue to ripen on a warm kitchen counter and will be ready when you are. Epazote is a common Mexican herb available at a well-stocked supermarket and Mexican specialty shops.

EACH SERVING PROVIDES
*95 calories, 2 g protein, 8 g fat,
3 g dietary fiber, 6 g carbohydrates,
214 mg sodium, 0 mg cholesterol*

1 medium fresh serrano chili

2 ½ cups vegetable stock

1 cup drained and chopped canned tomatoes

½ medium white onion, chopped

¼ cup fresh epazote leaves, chopped

2 medium ripe Hass avocados (1 pound)

2 tablespoons fresh-squeezed lime juice

½ teaspoon salt

½ teaspoon chili powder

¼ cup minced fresh cilantro leaves

Discard the stem of the chili and scrape out the seeds for a milder dish. Finely mince the serrano chili. Combine the stock, tomatoes, onion, epazote, and chili in a medium saucepan. Bring to a strong simmer over high heat, then reduce the heat to medium-low and simmer gently for 20 minutes. Transfer half of the mixture to a blender.

Cut open one of the avocados, and remove the pit. Use a large metal spoon to scrape the avocado flesh out of the skin and add it to the blender. Add 1 tablespoon of the lime juice and ¼ teaspoon of the salt and blend until smooth. Transfer this purée to a large bowl. Repeat the process with the remaining stock mixture, avocado, 1 tablespoon lime juice, and ¼ teaspoon salt, and add the resulting purée to the bowl.

Ladle the soup into individual shallow serving bowls. Sprinkle the chili powder over the top and distribute the minced cilantro leaves among the bowls. Allow the soup to stand at room temperature until it cools to lukewarm. Alternatively, chill the soup for several hours, then remove it from the refrigerator and top it with the garnishes about 10 minutes before serving time.

Creamy Broccoli Soup with Dill and Mustard

YIELD: 4 first-course servings

1 pound fresh broccoli

2 tablespoons extra-virgin olive oil

4 cloves garlic, minced

¼ teaspoon dill seed

2 cups vegetable stock

1 teaspoon dried dill weed

1 bay leaf

¼ teaspoon salt

3 cups plain soy milk

2 tablespoons arrowroot powder

2 tablespoons Dijon mustard

Several grinds black pepper

Almost Instant

Creamy in texture, with a complex flavor, this puréed broccoli soup is sure to become a favorite.

EACH SERVING PROVIDES
195 calories, 8 g protein, 10 g fat, 4 g dietary fiber, 23 g carbohydrates, 456 mg sodium, 0 mg cholesterol

Trim off and discard the tough stem ends of the broccoli. Peel the remaining stalks if they are particularly thick-skinned. Coarsely chop the stalks and flower heads. Set aside. Heat the oil over medium heat. Add the garlic and dill seed and sauté for a minute or two, then add the broccoli, vegetable stock, dill weed, bay leaf, and salt. Simmer over high heat, reduce the heat to medium, cover, and cook until the broccoli is very tender, about 10 minutes. Remove the bay leaf and purée the mixture with an immersion blender or transfer to a blender jar and purée in several batches. Return the soup to the pot over medium-low heat. Add the soy milk, stirring to combine.

Put 3 tablespoons of cold water in a small jar that has a tight-fitting lid. Add the arrowroot powder and shake to dissolve. Stir this into the soup, along with the mustard and pepper. Heat until the soup is barely bubbling, then serve.

Investing in Stock

As homemade ingredients go, vegetable stock is a wise investment. It is simple to prepare and can enliven sauces and stir-fries, as well as soups, with its complex goodness. Only oil rivals stock as a flavor enhancer, and stock has the distinct advantage of being almost free of calories.

A simple cup of broth, perhaps with a bit of miso stirred in, is a great restorative when you're feeling run-down. The minerals in the vegetables become concentrated in the cooking liquid, providing a warming infusion of nutrients that are easy to assimilate.

Set aside an hour over the weekend and try your hand at the ancient task of stock-making. Then you can enjoy the returns on your "stock investment" all week long.

THE BASIC TECHNIQUE

Follow these simple steps, using whatever seasonal produce you have on hand. The three ingredients we recommend including in every batch are potatoes, onions, and mushrooms, which lend a special depth of flavor to the liquid. If you collect the week's trimmings in a plastic bag in the refrigerator, it will give you a great start on your weekend batch of stock.

Step One

Collect on your work surface a large variety of vegetables, preferably organically grown. Use fresh potatoes, not green or sprouting ones, and scrub them well—but don't peel them. Dried-out mushrooms and vegetable trimmings like spinach stems, celery tops, and pea pods are great for stock. Other good ingredients include broccoli stems, carrots, green beans, zucchini, bell peppers, and turnips.

Step Two

Clean and chop the vegetables to measure about 16 cups. Place the vegetables in a large stockpot and add a few cloves of unpeeled garlic, 2 big bay leaves, a teaspoon of whole black peppercorns, and a small bunch of rinsed fresh parsley.

Step Three

Cover the ingredients with about 20 cups of cold water, enough so the vegetables are well submerged. Bring to a simmer over medium-high heat, reduce the heat to medium, and simmer uncovered, for 30 to 40 minutes, stirring occasionally.

Step Four

Turn off the heat and let the mixture steep for an additional 30 minutes. Strain and store the stock in a clean glass jar or pitcher in the refrigerator. It will stay fresh for up to a week. To store stock for longer periods, freeze it in 2-cup quantities and thaw as needed.

Curried Carrot and Leek Soup

YIELD: 4 main-dish servings

2 pounds leeks (about 2 large)

2 tablespoons olive oil

2 pounds carrots (about 6 large)

1 teaspoon curry powder

4 cups vegetable stock

1½ cups plain rice or soy milk

¼ cup minced fresh Italian parsley

½ teaspoon salt

4 lemon wedges

This soup fills the kitchen with the wonderful aroma of curry spices. Since bottled curry powder comes in different degrees of "heat," add more or less than the recipe calls for to suit your own taste.

EACH SERVING PROVIDES
255 calories, 4 g protein, 9 g fat,
9 g dietary fiber, 44 g carbohydrates,
399 mg sodium, 0 mg cholesterol

Remove and discard the tough upper greens and the root ends of the leeks. Slice the pale part of the leeks in half lengthwise and rinse under cold water to remove any dirt that is caught in the layers. Pat dry, then cut into thin slices. Heat the olive oil in a stockpot over medium heat and add the leeks. Sauté, stirring frequently, for 10 minutes.

Meanwhile, scrub the carrots and slice them into ½-inch rounds. When the leeks are ready, stir in the curry powder, then add the carrots and stock. Cover the pot, increase the heat to high, and bring to a boil. Reduce the heat to medium and simmer for about 25 minutes, stirring frequently, until the carrots are tender. Purée the soup with an immersion blender or transfer it to a blender or food processor in small batches and purée. Return to the stockpot over medium-high heat and add the milk, parsley, and salt. Heat through, then serve with lemon wedges.

Mulligatawny

YIELD: 6 first-course servings

The strange name of this soup, translated from the Hindi, means "pepper water." The British thought it an appropriate title for the fiery lentil purée they encountered in India. This version isn't all that hot. If you are a pepper devotee, feel free to increase the amount to suit your taste.

EACH SERVING PROVIDES
*148 calories, 6 g protein, 6 g fat,
7 g dietary fiber, 18 g carbohydrates,
363 mg sodium, 0 mg cholesterol*

2 tablespoons vegetable stock

1 tablespoon olive oil

1/2 medium yellow onion, diced

2 cloves garlic, minced

1 cup diced zucchini (about 1 medium)

1 cup chopped fresh fennel bulb

1 large carrot, diced

1 rib celery, diced

1 teaspoon black or yellow mustard seeds

1 teaspoon ground coriander

1/2 teaspoon ground cumin

1/8 teaspoon ground cinnamon

12 black peppercorns, crushed (or 1/8 teaspoon ground)

1 cup diced fresh or canned tomatoes, with juice

1/2 cup red or brown lentils

2 teaspoons grated fresh ginger

1/2 cup coconut milk

1 tablespoon fresh-squeezed lime juice

3/4 teaspoon salt

Heat the stock and oil in a large stockpot over medium heat. Add the onion and garlic and sauté for 2 minutes, then add the zucchini, fennel, carrot, celery, mustard seeds, coriander, cumin, cinnamon, and pepper, and sauté 3 minutes longer.

Add 5 cups of water and the tomatoes, lentils, and ginger and bring to a strong simmer over medium-high heat. Reduce the heat to medium-low, cover, and simmer 30 minutes. Purée the soup with an immersion blender or transfer to a blender jar in small batches and purée. Return the purée to the pan. Add the coconut milk, lime juice, and salt and heat through. Serve hot.

Potato and Garlic Soup with Fresh Thyme

YIELD: 4 main-dish servings

1 tablespoon olive oil

1 tablespoon dry sherry

1 medium yellow onion, chopped

2 pounds russet potatoes (4 large)

5 cups vegetable stock

6 cloves garlic, whole

2 large bay leaves

1 tablespoon fresh thyme leaves

½ teaspoon salt

Several grinds black pepper

2 tablespoons minced fresh parsley

This thick and creamy dairy-free soup is a variation of Provençal "aiïgo bouido." The flavor of the fresh thyme pulls it all together.

EACH SERVING PROVIDES
224 calories, 5 g protein, 4 g fat, 8 g dietary fiber, 42 g carbohydrates, 307 mg sodium, 0 mg cholesterol

Heat the oil and sherry in a stockpot over medium heat. Add the onion and sauté, stirring occasionally, for 7 minutes. Meanwhile, peel the potatoes and chop them into ½-inch cubes. Add the potatoes, stock, garlic, and bay leaves to the stockpot. Increase the heat to medium-high and bring to a boil, then stir, cover, reduce the heat to medium-low, and simmer for 25 to 30 minutes, until the potatoes are tender and falling apart. Add the thyme during the last 5 minutes of cooking.

Remove and discard the bay leaves. Use an immersion blender to purée the soup or transfer it to a blender jar, one third at a time, and blend for several seconds, until fairly smooth. Return the purée to the pot, add the salt and pepper, and heat until steaming, about a minute or two. Serve in warmed bowls, garnished with the parsley.

Southwest Corn, Chard, and Potato Soup

YIELD: 6 main-dish servings

Here's a simple and delicious warming soup for early autumn, when excellent corn, chard, and tomatoes are readily available.

EACH SERVING PROVIDES

*149 calories, 4 g protein, 6 g fat,
4 g dietary fiber, 24 g carbohydrates,
485 mg sodium, 0 mg cholesterol*

6 cups cleaned and chopped chard leaves (about 1 bunch)

8 cups plus 2 tablespoons vegetable stock

2 tablespoons olive oil

1 large onion, diced

3 cloves garlic, minced

1 cup diced fresh or canned tomatoes, with juice

1 cup finely diced red potato (about 1 medium)

2 teaspoons chili powder

2 teaspoons dried oregano

1 teaspoon dried thyme

1 teaspoon salt

Several grinds black pepper

2 cups fresh or frozen corn kernels (see NOTE)

¼ cup whole cilantro leaves (for garnish)

Cut out and discard the stems of the chard, then wash and finely chop the leaves to measure about 6 cups. Set aside.

In a large pot, heat 2 tablespoons of the stock with the olive oil over medium heat. When it is steaming, add the onion and garlic and stir and sauté for 3 minutes. Add the remaining 8 cups of stock, the tomatoes, potatoes, chili powder, oregano, thyme, salt, and pepper, and simmer over medium-high heat. Reduce the heat to medium-low and simmer for 10 minutes. Add the chard and corn, return to a simmer, and cook about 10 minutes longer, until the soup has been reduced to a nice thick consistency.

Serve hot, garnished with cilantro, if desired.

NOTE: If using frozen corn kernels, place them in a colander and rinse briefly under warm water to melt off any ice crystals before adding them to the dish. If using fresh corn, you will need about four medium ears to yield 2 cups of kernels.

Summer Squash and Apricot Soup with Fresh Basil and Pine Nuts

YIELD: 4 first-course servings

1½ pounds summer squash

½ cup chopped dried apricots

1 medium yellow onion, diced

½ medium bell pepper, diced

¼ teaspoon salt

½ teaspoon paprika

1 cup loosely packed basil leaves

A few grinds black pepper

2 tablespoons pine nuts, toasted (see page 10) and chopped

Trim off and discard the ends of the squash, dice them, and set aside. In a stockpot, combine the apricots, onion, bell pepper, and the salt with 5 cups of water. Bring to a boil over high heat, then reduce the heat to medium and simmer 10 minutes. Add the squash and paprika. Bring back to a simmer over medium heat and cook 20 minutes. Purée with an immersion blender, or transfer the soup in small batches to a blender and purée.

Return the soup to the stockpot over medium heat and stir in the basil, reserving 4 nice leaves for garnish. When the basil has wilted, stir in the pepper. Serve immediately in warmed bowls, or chill for an hour or two before serving in chilled bowls.

Garnish each bowl with a sprinkling of pine nuts and a reserved basil leaf before serving.

This dish sings of summer and is good either hot or chilled. You may make it using only zucchini, if you wish, but we prefer the golden yellow of crookneck with the basil, so use a combination, if possible. If you are using squash picked from the garden, all the better.

EACH SERVING PROVIDES

125 calories, 4 g protein, 3 g fat,

5 g dietary fiber, 24 g carbohydrates,

156 mg sodium, 0 mg cholesterol

Grilled Butternut Squash Soup with Fresh Shiitake Mushrooms

YIELD: 4 main-dish servings

This exotic-tasting soup combines the sweetness of winter squash with the woody richness of shiitake mushrooms. Wood chips added to the grill accentuate the earthy flavor. Delicious!

EACH SERVING PROVIDES
*204 calories, 6 g protein, 4 g fat,
2 g dietary fiber, 37 g carbohydrates,
230 mg sodium, 0 mg cholesterol*

1 cup hickory or apple wood chips

1 pound butternut squash (about 1 small)

1 teaspoon canola oil

4 ounces fresh shiitake mushrooms

1 teaspoon dark sesame oil

1 tablespoon mirin or dry sherry

2 cloves garlic, minced

2 ½ cups vegetable stock

¼ teaspoon salt

Several grinds black pepper

⅓ cup dried pastina

2 ½ cups plain soy or rice milk

¼ cup minced fresh cilantro

Place the wood chips in a bowl and cover them with water. Set aside to soak for at least 15 minutes. Preheat the grill to medium. Drain the wood chips and place them on the coals just before grilling the squash.

Cut the squash in half lengthwise and scoop out and discard the seeds. Lightly rub the skin of the squash with ½ teaspoon of the canola oil. Place the squash on the grill, skin side down, close the lid, and cook for 20 minutes. Remove from the grill, brush the cut side with the remaining oil, and place back on the grill, cut side down. Close the lid and cook for about 10 minutes longer, until the squash is completely soft. Remove from the grill and set aside to cool.

Meanwhile, wipe off the mushrooms, remove their stems, and cut the caps in half. Chop the halves into bite-sized pieces. Place the sesame oil and mirin in a large skillet over medium heat. Add the garlic and cook for 1 minute, then stir in the mushrooms and sauté for 2 minutes.

When the grilled squash is cool enough to handle, remove the pulp from the skin, discarding the skin. Purée the squash in a food processor, then transfer it to a large saucepan. Add the stock, salt, pepper, and mushrooms and simmer over medium-high heat. Stir in the pastina and simmer rapidly, stirring frequently, for 5 minutes. Add the soy milk and cilantro, return to a simmer, and cook until the pastina is tender and the soup has reduced to a thick soup consistency, about 5 minutes. Serve very hot.

SHIITAKE MUSHROOMS

For centuries, shiitake mushrooms have been recognized in Japan and China as healing foods. Now modern nutritional research is confirming that these delicious fungi help enhance immunity, lower cholesterol, and show promise in cancer prevention and treatment. Fresh shiitakes are showing up more frequently in markets, though sometimes the price tag is steep. Dried shiitakes are readily available at Asian markets and even mainstream supermarkets. Reconstitute the dried variety by covering them with boiling water and soaking for about 30 minutes (alternatively, you may cover them with water and microwave for about 2 minutes). Fresh or reconstituted shiitakes are delicious added to soups and stir-fries. Strain the flavorful mushroom soaking liquid and use it in the dish, as well.

Pumpkin-Rice Soup with Sage and Allspice

YIELD: 4 main-dish servings

Almost Instant

You can prepare this delicious, carotene-rich soup from cooked fresh pumpkin in the autumn, if you wish, but using canned pumpkin makes it an almost instant meal. We use mild Meyer lemon juice for this soup. If you're using another, more sour variety, you may want to reduce the amount. Serve with garlic bread and a leafy salad.

EACH SERVING PROVIDES
*231 calories, 6 g protein, 6 g fat,
8 g dietary fiber, 43 g carbohydrates,
187 mg sodium, 0 mg cholesterol*

5 cups vegetable stock

1 can (29 ounces) pumpkin

3 cloves garlic, minced

⅓ cup uncooked white basmati rice

1 teaspoon dried sage

¼ teaspoon salt

⅛ teaspoon ground allspice

Several grinds black pepper

1 cup plain rice or soy milk

¼ cup minced fresh Italian parsley

3 tablespoons fresh-squeezed lemon juice

¼ cup chopped raw walnuts, toasted (page 10)

4 lemon wedges

In a stockpot combine the stock, pumpkin, and garlic. Cover and bring to a boil over medium-high heat, then stir in the rice, sage, salt, allspice, and pepper. Reduce the heat to medium-low and simmer uncovered for about 20 minutes, until the rice is tender. Stir frequently. Add the rice milk, parsley, and lemon juice, and heat until steaming. Serve hot with a sprinkling of toasted nuts on top. Pass the lemon wedges.

LEMON
The lemon's flavor, like its color, is light and bright, refreshing the palate and stimulating the digestive juices. Its taste is so potent and pleasing that when used as a table condiment—with steamed vegetables, for instance—a squeeze of fresh lemon juice can eliminate our craving for salt. An added bonus is that lemons are quite high in vitamin C and potassium.

Caramelized Red Onion Soup

YIELD: 4 main-dish servings

3 pounds red onions

3 tablespoons olive oil

½ cup brandy

1 tablespoon minced fresh rosemary
leaves

1 tablespoon minced fresh sage

2 tablespoons organic granulated
sugar

6 cups vegetable stock

2 tablespoons vegan Worcestershire
sauce

¼ teaspoon salt

A few grinds pepper

Slow-cooked red onions develop a delicious depth of flavor when cooked with rosemary, sage, and sugar. Serve with hot garlic bread and a spinach salad for a delicious meal.

Trim off the ends of the onions, cut them in half lengthwise, and peel them. Cut each half into thin slices. Heat the oil in a very large skillet over medium-high heat. (If you do not have a skillet large enough to hold the onions in a shallow layer, use two smaller ones.) Add the onions and cook uncovered for 10 minutes. Reduce the heat to medium, and cook for another 10 minutes, stirring frequently, until the onions are very tender and lightly browned. Stir in the brandy, rosemary, sage, and sugar, and increase the heat to medium-high. Cook 5 minutes, or until the liquid evaporates.

Meanwhile, put the stock in a stockpot and bring it to a boil over high heat. Add the Worcestershire sauce and the cooked onions. Return to a boil, reduce the heat to medium, and simmer for 20 minutes. Stir in the salt and pepper and serve hot.

EACH SERVING PROVIDES
*344 calories, 5 g protein, 11 g fat,
6 g dietary fiber, 44 g carbohydrates,
329 mg sodium, 0 mg cholesterol*

Spinach Soup with Oregano and Calamata Olives

YIELD: 4 first-course servings

Serve this soup as a delightful early spring starter course or a light summer meal, accompanied by good bread and a bean salad.

EACH SERVING PROVIDES

170 calories, 6 g protein, 13 g fat,
5 g dietary fiber, 12 g carbohydrates,
459 mg sodium, 0 mg cholesterol

1 ½ pounds fresh spinach (about 2 bunches)

2 tablespoons olive oil

½ cup diced yellow onion

3 cloves garlic, minced

1 teaspoon dried oregano

4 cups vegetable stock

¼ teaspoon salt

A few grinds black pepper

¼ cup fresh-squeezed lemon juice

¼ cup pitted and diced calamata olives

1 tablespoon fresh oregano leaves, minced

Carefully wash the spinach, discarding the stems. You don't need to dry the spinach. Coarsely chop the spinach leaves and set them aside in a colander.

Place the oil in a stockpot over medium heat. Add the onion, garlic, and dried oregano. Sauté for about 2 minutes, stirring frequently, then add the stock. Bring to a boil over high heat and add the spinach. Return to a boil, reduce the heat to medium, cover, and cook 5 minutes. Stir in the salt, pepper, lemon juice, olives, and oregano, then simmer about 3 minutes longer. Serve immediately.

Beet Borscht with Lemon and Dill

YIELD: 4 main-dish servings

6 cups vegetable stock

3 medium fresh beets, peeled and grated

2 medium carrots, peeled and grated

1 medium russet potato, finely diced

1 medium yellow onion, finely diced

1 cup finely diced green cabbage

¼ cup fresh-squeezed lemon juice

1 teaspoon dried dill

¼ teaspoon salt

Several grinds black pepper

In a large stockpot, combine the stock, beets, carrots, potato, and onion. Bring to a simmer over high heat, reduce the heat to medium, and cook 10 minutes. Add the cabbage, lemon juice, dill, salt, and pepper, and cook an additional 10 minutes. Serve hot or chill for a few hours before serving.

We have eaten many versions of beet borscht over the years, and we especially like this light, fresh-flavored one. It is easy to prepare and as nutritious as it is delicious. Rye crackers spread with avocado are the perfect accompaniment. You may want to wear latex gloves when handling the beets, since they will dye your hands red for several hours.

EACH SERVING PROVIDES

118 calories, 4 g protein, 1 g fat, 4 g dietary fiber, 27 g carbohydrates, 218 mg sodium, 0 mg cholesterol

---

BEETS

Beets have a satisfying natural sweetness, but are low in calories. They contain a moderate amount of folic acid and some vitamin C and manganese. But beets' best claim to nutritional fame is their excellent fiber profile, shown to improve bowel function and cholesterol levels. Beet tops are similar in nutrient value to other leafy greens, delivering calcium, iron, and vitamins A and C.

Tofu, Rice, and Seaweed Soup with Garlic and Peas

YIELD: 4 main-dish servings

Almost Instant

This quick and delicious Chinese–inspired soup is guaranteed to cure what ails you.

EACH SERVING PROVIDES
*311 calories, 17 g protein, 11 g fat,
6 g dietary fiber, 40 g carbohydrates,
363 mg sodium, 0 mg cholesterol*

6 cups vegetable stock

12 ounces firm silken tofu, diced

3 cloves garlic, minced

1 tablespoon plus 1 teaspoon soy
  sauce

1 tablespoon dark sesame oil

Several grinds black pepper

2 cups cooked brown rice

2 cups fresh or frozen shelled peas
  (see NOTE)

4 sheets nori seaweed, snipped into
  small pieces

In a stockpot, combine the vegetable stock with the tofu, garlic, soy sauce, dark sesame oil, and pepper. Bring to a simmer and cook over medium-high heat for 5 minutes, uncovered. Add the rice, peas, and nori and bring back to a simmer. Cook 3 minutes longer, until the peas are tender. Serve hot.

NOTE: If using frozen peas, place them in a colander and rinse briefly under warm water to melt off any ice crystals before adding them to the dish.

Chinese Hot-and-Sour Soup

YIELD: 6 first-course servings

2 tablespoons cornstarch

5 tablespoons brown rice vinegar

2 tablespoons soy sauce

¼ teaspoon cayenne pepper

1 tablespoon dark sesame oil

1 small yellow onion, diced

6 fresh or reconstituted shiitake
    mushrooms, destemmed and
    thinly sliced

2 cloves garlic, minced

7 cups vegetable stock

1 medium carrot, very thinly sliced

½ red bell pepper, finely diced

1 cup diced zucchini

1 tablespoon grated fresh ginger

4 ounces firm tofu, cut into
    matchsticks

Almost Instant

Here is our rendition of a classic healing soup from China. If you can't find fresh shiitake mushrooms, reconstitute 6 dried ones (see page 8) and use the strained soaking liquid as part of the 7 cups of soup stock called for below. Try serving the soup with Fried Brown Rice with Veggies (page 175) or your favorite stir-fry. You can also ladle it over cooked brown rice for a delicious meal-in-a-bowl, yielding 4 main-dish servings.

EACH SERVING PROVIDES
*150 calories, 6 g protein, 6 g fat,
3 g dietary fiber, 21 g carbohydrates,
4908 mg sodium, 0 mg cholesterol*

In a small bowl, whisk the cornstarch with the vinegar, soy sauce, and cayenne until the cornstarch is dissolved. Set aside.

In a large saucepan, heat the oil over medium heat. Add the onion and stir and sauté for 3 minutes. Add the sliced mushrooms and garlic and sauté 2 minutes longer. Add the stock, carrot, bell pepper, zucchini, and ginger, and bring to a boil over medium-high heat. Reduce the heat to medium and simmer 5 minutes.

Stir the cornstarch mixture briefly to recombine, then whisk it gently into the soup. Stir in the tofu, return the soup to a strong simmer, and cook 5 minutes.

Taste and add more cayenne if you want a hotter dish. Serve very hot.

Fresh Bean Stew with Corn and Acorn Squash

YIELD: 4 main-dish servings

This Cuban-inspired harvest season stew is hearty and warming. A crusty bread and leafy salad are all that are needed to complete the meal. Purchase 1 medium acorn squash for this dish and you'll have some left over to enjoy later.

EACH SERVING PROVIDES
*473 calories, 24 g protein, 6 g fat,
16 g dietary fiber, 84 g carbohydrates,
313 mg sodium, 0 mg cholesterol*

2 cups shelled fresh cranberry beans or black-eyed peas

2 cups peeled and diced acorn squash

4 cups vegetable stock

1 tablespoon chili powder

1 ½ teaspoons dried oregano

½ teaspoon dried thyme

1 tablespoon olive oil

1 large white onion, diced

½ cup dry red wine

3 cloves garlic, minced

½ teaspoon salt

¼ teaspoon cayenne pepper

1 ½ cups fresh or frozen corn kernels (see NOTE)

½ cup chopped fresh cilantro

In a stockpot, combine the beans with the acorn squash, stock, chili powder, oregano, and thyme. Bring to a boil, cover, reduce the heat to low, and simmer for 20 minutes.

Meanwhile, heat the oil in a small skillet and sauté the onion over medium heat until nicely browned, about 10 minutes, then stir it into the beans. At the end of the 20-minutes simmering time, add the wine, garlic, salt, cayenne, and ¾ cup of the corn kernels. Return to a simmer and cook 20 minutes.

Place the remaining ¾ cup corn kernels in the blender with the cilantro and ⅓ cup of water. Purée the mixture, then add to the beans and cook an additional 15 minutes, until the beans are tender and the liquid has reduced to a thick consistency. Serve hot.

NOTE: If using frozen corn kernels, place them in a colander and rinse briefly under warm water to melt off any ice crystals before adding them to the dish. If using fresh corn, you will need about 3 medium ears to yield 1 ½ cups of kernels.

Cranberry Bean Minestrone with Sage and Marjoram

YIELD: 4 main-dish servings

1 cup dried cranberry beans

4 cups vegetable stock

2 tablespoons olive oil

1 medium yellow onion, chopped

2 ribs celery, finely diced

3 cloves garlic, minced

1 can (14½ ounces) whole pear
　tomatoes

2 tablespoons minced fresh sage

1 tablespoon minced fresh
　marjoram leaves

¼ teaspoon freshly grated nutmeg

½ teaspoon salt

A few grinds pepper

Cranberry beans, also known as borlotti beans, are popular in Italian cooking. The bean is pink with red speckles, similar to a pinto bean, which may be substituted if you cannot find the Italian variety. This minestrone is reminiscent of the country soups in the hillside villages of Tuscany.

EACH SERVING PROVIDES
*287 calories, 13 g protein, 8 g fat,
14 g dietary fiber, 44 g carbohydrates,
462 mg sodium, 0 mg cholesterol*

Sort the beans, discarding any pebbles or other foreign objects you may find. Rinse the beans and place them in a large pan. Cover the beans with plenty of water, cover the pan, and soak for several hours or overnight. Drain in a colander and set aside.

Place the stock over medium-high heat in a large stockpot and add the beans. Bring to a boil, reduce the heat to medium-low, and simmer with the lid ajar for about 45 minutes, until the beans are almost tender.

Meanwhile, place the olive oil in a skillet over medium heat. Add the onion, celery, and garlic, and sauté for about 5 minutes, until the onion is translucent. Chop the tomatoes in a bowl or use your hands to break them up, then add them with their juice to the cooked beans. Stir in the onion mixture, sage, marjoram, nutmeg, salt, and pepper. Cook over medium-low heat, uncovered, for 30 minutes, stirring occasionally. Serve immediately.

Mung Bean and Zucchini Soup with Ginger

YIELD: 6 main-dish servings

In the spirit of East Indian "kichadi," this soup is warming, nourishing, and soothing—everything you want on a cold winter's night. It has a lot of ingredients, but is really quite simple to prepare. Make it one of your new comfort foods.

EACH SERVING PROVIDES
183 calories, 8 g protein, 3 g fat, 8 g dietary fiber, 32 g carbohydrates, 366 mg sodium, 0 mg cholesterol

1 cup whole dried mung beans
1 tablespoon olive oil
1 teaspoon ground coriander
1 teaspoon ground cumin
½ teaspoon mustard seeds
½ teaspoon ground turmeric
1 medium white onion, diced
1 large carrot, diced
½ teaspoon dried thyme
1 5-inch strip dried kombu (optional)

⅓ cup uncooked white basmati rice, rinsed and drained
2 cups diced zucchini
2 tablespoons grated fresh ginger
1 teaspoon salt
⅛ teaspoon cayenne pepper
¼ cup minced fresh cilantro
1 tablespoon fresh-squeezed lime juice

Sort the mung beans, discarding any pebbles or other foreign objects you may find. Rinse the beans well, then cover them with cold water and set aside to soak for 3 or 4 hours.

When the beans have finished soaking, heat the oil in a large pot over medium heat. Add the coriander, cumin, mustard seeds, and turmeric, and sauté until the seeds begin to pop. Add the onion, carrot, and thyme and sauté, stirring frequently, for 3 minutes. Add 7 cups of water, the drained mung beans, and the kombu. Bring to a boil over high heat, reduce the heat to medium-low, and simmer for 30 minutes, stirring occasionally.

Add the rice and simmer for 15 minutes longer, stirring occasionally. Add the zucchini, ginger, salt, and cayenne, and cook until the beans and zucchini are tender, about 15 minutes. Add a tablespoon or two of water at a time, if necessary, to keep the soup from getting too thick and sticking to the bottom of the pan.

When the soup is done, stir the pot to see if the kombu strip is still in one large piece. If so, fish it out of the pot and chop it finely, then return it to the soup. Stir in the cilantro and lime juice and serve hot.

KOMBU

Sea kelp—best known by its Japanese name, kombu—is traditionally used to season and mineralize broths. Kombu may be added to any soup or stock, and is reputed to calm the digestive storm some people experience when eating cooked beans. Simply include a thick strip of this sea vegetable in the pot. By the time the beans are cooked, the kombu will have completely tenderized and will disappear into the broth with a vigorous stir. (Since iodine stimulates the thyroid gland, people with hyperthyroidism should minimize iodine-rich foods in their diets, including sea veggies.)

Provençal Bean and Vegetable Stew

YIELD: 8 main-dish servings

This delicious and nourishing dish is similar in character to a classic "cassoulet," but much simpler to prepare. If you use precooked beans, you will find it comes together quickly. Serve it over polenta or rice, if you wish, with a good crusty bread and raw veggies on the side.

½ pound button mushrooms

2 tablespoons olive oil

1 large white onion, diced

1 cup dry white wine

2 tablespoons tomato paste

2 cloves garlic, minced

2 teaspoons Herbes de Provence (page 310)

2 tablespoons unbleached white flour

1 medium turnip, peeled and diced

1 large carrot, thinly sliced

2 cups chopped cauliflower

½ teaspoon salt

Several grinds black pepper

2 cups cooked flageolet beans or small white beans, drained

¼ cup minced fresh parsley

1 cup fresh or frozen shelled peas

Wipe any loose dirt from the mushrooms and quarter them. Set aside.

Heat the oil in a stockpot or large saucepan over medium heat and sauté the onion, stirring frequently, until it is nicely browned, about 10 minutes. Stir in the wine, tomato paste, garlic, and Herbes de Provence, and cook 5 minutes over medium heat, stirring frequently. Sprinkle the flour into the pan and stir, then add 2 cups of water and the turnip, and bring the mixture to a boil over medium-high heat. Add the carrot, mushrooms, cauliflower, salt, and pepper, and stir to combine well. Simmer, then cover the pan, reduce the heat to medium-low, and cook for 5 minutes. Remove the lid and stir the vegetables, then cover and cook 3 more minutes.

Stir in the cooked beans and parsley. If using fresh peas, also add them at this point. Cover and cook 5 minutes, until everything is heated through. If using frozen peas, add them to the pot for only the last minute or two of cooking time. Serve very hot.

Split Pea Soup with Sweet Potato and Mexican Seasonings

YIELD: 4 main-dish servings

1 tablespoon olive oil

1 medium white onion, diced

1 teaspoon dried rosemary, crushed

2 tablespoons chili powder

7 ½ cups vegetable stock

1 cup dried green split peas

½ teaspoon salt

¾ pound red-skinned sweet potato (about 1 large)

4 cloves garlic, minced

⅓ cup minced fresh cilantro leaves

2 tablespoons fresh-squeezed lime juice

Heat the oil in a stockpot over medium heat and add the onion and rosemary. Sauté, stirring almost constantly, for 3 minutes, then add the chili powder. Stir and cook for another minute to toast the chili powder a bit, then add the stock, split peas, and salt. Bring to a simmer over high heat, then reduce the heat to medium and simmer 15 minutes.

Meanwhile, peel the sweet potato and dice it into ¼-inch pieces. After the soup has simmered for 15 minutes, add the sweet potato and garlic. Bring back to a simmer over medium heat and cook, stirring frequently, 25 to 30 minutes, until the split peas and sweet potato are tender. If needed, you may add more stock a little at a time to keep the soup from getting too thick and sticking to the bottom of the pan. Stir in the cilantro and lime juice and serve very hot.

This nourishing soup makes a marvelous winter meal. The sweet potato and the tart lime give it a delicate quality not usually associated with split pea soups. A small dollop of guacamole would make a nice topping, but the soup is quite delicious without it.

EACH SERVING PROVIDES
*349 calories, 16 g protein, 5 g fat,
16 g dietary fiber, 63 g carbohydrates,
334 mg sodium, 0 mg cholesterol*

Classic Lentil, Tomato, and Potato Stew

YIELD: 6 main-dish servings

This stew makes a satisfying meal on a cold evening. Serve it with a mixed green salad and crusty bread.

EACH SERVING PROVIDES

290 calories, 12 g protein, 8 g fat,
15 g dietary fiber, 44 g carbohydrates,
315 mg sodium, 0 mg cholesterol

3 tablespoons olive oil

2 tablespoons dry sherry

1 yellow onion, diced

3 cloves garlic, minced

6 cups vegetable stock

1 cup dried brown lentils

2 bay leaves

1 tablespoon dried basil

1 can (16 ounces) whole tomatoes, chopped, with juice

1 pound russet potatoes, scrubbed and diced

½ cup minced fresh Italian parsley

½ teaspoon salt

Several grinds black pepper

1 tablespoon fresh-squeezed lemon juice

6 lemon wedges

In a large stockpot, heat the oil and sherry over medium heat. Add the onion and garlic, stir to coat, and cook for several minutes, until the onion is translucent. Add the stock, lentils, bay leaves, and basil. Increase the heat to high, bring to a boil, then reduce the heat to medium-high and cook for 30 minutes. Stir in the tomatoes, along with their liquid, and the potatoes. Continue to cook for about 15 minutes, until the potatoes and lentils are tender. Stir in the parsley, salt, pepper, and lemon juice. Serve piping hot, with lemon wedges on the side.

Curried Barley, Shiitake, and Broccoli Stew

YIELD: 6 main-dish servings

¾ cup pearl barley

2 cups diced red potato (about 2 medium)

1 large carrot, diced

1 medium onion, diced

3 medium cloves garlic, minced

1 tablespoon curry powder

1 teaspoon dried thyme

8 cups vegetable stock

6 cups trimmed and chopped broccoli (about 1½ pounds)

10 fresh shiitake mushrooms, destemmed and sliced

1 tablespoon soy sauce

½ teaspoon salt

Several grinds black pepper

This thick and hearty stew is a meal in a bowl, requiring only a crusty bread and tart leafy salad to accompany it.

EACH SERVING PROVIDES

250 calories, 11 g protein, 1 g fat, 12 g dietary fiber, 50 g carbohydrates, 412 mg sodium, 0 mg cholesterol

Wash the barley by covering it with water in a bowl, then swirling it around with your hands. Add fresh water several times, until the rinse water is fairly clear. Set the barley aside in a strainer to drain thoroughly.

Place the barley, potato, carrot, onion, garlic, curry powder, and thyme in a stockpot and pour in the stock. Bring to a simmer over medium-high heat, then reduce the heat to medium-low and simmer for 10 minutes. Add the broccoli and shiitake mushrooms, bring to a strong simmer over medium-high heat, then reduce the heat to medium and simmer 20 to 25 minutes, stirring frequently, until the barley is tender. The broccoli will fall apart to produce a thick stew consistency. Add a little more stock if the mixture seems too thick. Stir in the soy sauce, salt, and pepper and serve hot.

7

Vegetable Side Dishes

Wasabi Mashed Potatoes

Zucchini with Garlic and Chili Flakes

Baby Bok Choy with Lemon Miso Sauce

Braised Cabbage with Red Onion and Paprika

Brussels Sprouts with Fresh Dill and Pimientos

Fava Beans Sautéed with Ginger and Garlic

Braised Carrots with Lime Juice and Shallots

Fresh Peas and Shallots with Provençal Herbs

Braised Broccoli with Fresh Herbs and Toasted
  Walnuts

Steamed Corn with Pimiento and Horseradish

Roasted Pumpkin and Brussels Sprouts with Garlic
  and Herbs

Green Beans with Orange Allspice Glaze

Snow Peas with Sesame Miso Sauce

Cauliflower in Coriander Cashew Sauce

Asparagus with Watercress and Green Onion Sauce

Beets with Potato Garlic Sauce

Lynn's Southern-Fried Okra with Tomatoes

Breaded Eggplant Slices with Sweet Chili Sauce

Steamed Artichokes with Silken Tofu Dill Sauce

Vegetables help us synchronize our bodies with the seasons. In spring, asparagus, tender peas, and fava beans make frequent appearances on our tables. When the heat of summer is upon us, juicy tomatoes, the many varieties of eggplant, and sweet corn are favorites. The transition into fall is marked by an abundance of peppers, as well as soft- and hard-skinned squashes. Even winter has its stars—many lettuces and greens are at their best in cold weather, and the root and cruciferous vegetables are also plentiful.

Vegetables make delicious snacks when simply washed and eaten, no cooking required. But vegetables are also versatile—they lend themselves to many different cooking techniques and combine well with a wide variety of seasonings. Super-fresh vegetables from a home garden or the farmer's market can inspire an endless parade of great meals.

Vegetables abound in health benefits. They supply a wealth of vitamins and minerals, pigments such as carotenes, and fiber—and they're extremely low in fat and calories. Nutritional scientists are continually discovering new components in the vegetable kingdom that impact favorably on human health. It simply makes sense to eat liberally from this wondrous cornucopia of foods.

Many of the main dishes in this book take their inspiration from vegetables. But when the meal centers around a substantial grain or bean entrée, the vegetable becomes a welcome side dish. Simply steaming leafy greens, broccoli florets, or diced carrots will often do the trick. At other times, though, you'll want a more elaborate side dish.

We begin this chapter with some basic dishes and progress to those that provide more complex flavors. We hope these recipes will make it a pleasure for you to follow mom's advice: "Eat your vegetables!"

Wasabi Mashed Potatoes

YIELD: 6 side-dish servings

Creamy and smooth mashed potatoes are universally appealing. This version is seasoned with the Japanese horseradish called "wasabi," which adds a spicy touch to this steaming dish. Feel free to add more or less wasabi, according to your taste.

EACH SERVING PROVIDES
*191 calories, 4 g protein, 5 g fat,
3 g dietary fiber, 34 g carbohydrates,
320 mg sodium, 0 mg cholesterol*

6 medium red potatoes (about 2 pounds), peeled and diced
¾ teaspoon powdered wasabi
¾ teaspoon unseasoned rice vinegar

1¼ cups plain soy or rice milk
2 tablespoons canola oil
½ teaspoon salt

Place the potatoes in a large pot with enough water to cover them. Bring to a boil over high heat and cook until very tender, about 15 minutes. Drain.

Meanwhile, in a bowl, mix together the wasabi and vinegar, then whisk in the milk.

Whip the potatoes with a whisk or purée in a food processor, along with the wasabi-milk mixture, oil, and salt. Add additional milk, if necessary, to achieve the desired consistency. Serve very hot.

WASABI

The green horseradish condiment familiar to fans of Japanese food can lend its pungency to non-Asian dishes as well. It is not only delicious, but may prevent dental cavities. Researchers in Japan have found that certain chemical compounds in wasabi inhibit the growth of bacteria that cause tooth decay.

Zucchini with Garlic and Chili Flakes

YIELD: 8 side-dish servings

3 pounds zucchini (about 9 medium)

2 tablespoons olive oil

4 cloves garlic, minced

⅛ teaspoon dried red chili flakes

⅛ teaspoon salt

A few grinds black pepper

Wash the zucchini, trim off the stem ends, and cut crosswise into ½-inch slices. Place on a steamer rack in a large saucepan that has a tight-fitting lid. Add about 2 inches of water, cover, and cook over high heat for about 6 minutes; zucchini should still be somewhat crisp. Drain the zucchini well.

Heat the olive oil in a skillet over medium heat and sauté the garlic, chili flakes, salt, and pepper for about 1 minute. Add the zucchini, reduce the heat to low, and cook about 5 minutes, tossing frequently to keep the zucchini coated with the oil and seasonings. When the zucchini is tender and lightly browned, it is ready.

Almost Instant

The humble zucchini squash—prolific in backyard gardens—lends itself to many different preparations. This one is a wonderful side dish for any entrée. The recipe can easily be cut in half; however, leftovers are good served cold the next day with a squeeze of lemon.

EACH SERVING PROVIDES
*57 calories, 2 g protein, 4 g fat,
2 g dietary fiber, 5 g carbohydrates,
39 mg sodium, 0 mg cholesterol*

Baby Bok Choy with Lemon Miso Sauce

YIELD: 6 side-dish servings

Almost Instant

This member of the cabbage family is frequently showing up in supermarkets and at local farmer's markets. It has a milder flavor than other members of the cabbage family. If baby bok choy isn't available, you may substitute a pound of regular bok choy, chopped.

EACH SERVING PROVIDES
*28 calories, 2 g protein, 0 g fat,
1 g dietary fiber, 5 g carbohydrates,
310 mg sodium, 0 mg cholesterol*

1 pound baby bok choy
¼ cup fresh-squeezed lemon juice
2 tablespoons light miso

2 cloves garlic, minced
1 tablespoon arrowroot powder

Slice each bok choy in half lengthwise and place on a steamer rack in a large saucepan that has a tight-fitting lid. Add about 2 inches of water, cover, and bring to a boil over high heat. Reduce the heat to medium-high and cook until fork-tender, about 8 minutes.

Meanwhile, in a small pan, whisk together the lemon juice, miso, garlic, and ¼ cup water. Heat over low heat until steaming. Place 2 tablespoons of water in a small jar and add the arrowroot powder. Cover and shake to dissolve. Whisk the arrowroot mixture into the lemon juice mixture, and cook until thickened, about 1 minute. Do not overcook, as it will get gummy. Drain the bok choy and fan it out on a large serving platter, leaf end out. Drizzle with the sauce and serve immediately.

Braised Cabbage with Red Onion and Paprika

YIELD: 6 side-dish servings

1 small green cabbage (about 1 ½ pounds)

1 medium red onion

1 tablespoon canola oil

2 tablespoons dry sherry

½ teaspoon dried tarragon

¼ teaspoon salt

A few grinds black pepper

1 teaspoon mild paprika

Cut the cabbage in half and remove the center core. Dice the core, except for the thickest stem end, and thinly slice the remaining cabbage. Peel the onion, cut it in half, then cut each half into thin slices. Place the oil and sherry in a skillet over medium-high heat, along with ⅓ cup of water. Add the cabbage, onion, tarragon, salt, and pepper. Cover, reduce the heat to medium, and cook for 10 minutes, until the cabbage wilts and is just fork-tender. Add the paprika, toss, and serve.

Almost Instant

This dish is very easy to prepare and quite delicious, without a hint of the bitterness sometimes associated with cooked cabbage.

EACH SERVING PROVIDES

70 calories, 2 g protein, 3 g fat, 3 g dietary fiber, 10 g carbohydrates, 110 mg sodium, 0 mg cholesterol

---

CRUCIFEROUS VEGETABLES

All members of cabbage family (cruciferae in Latin, so-named for their cross-shaped flowers) appear to act as potent antioxidants. They contain nitrogen compounds called indoles. Indoles work in the stomach and large intestine to protect against certain forms of cancer, and act to dramatically lower LDL cholesterol, the type linked to hardening of the arteries. Many of the crucifers are also moderately high in vitamin C, vitamin A, riboflavin, iron, potassium, and fiber. Choose foods from this impressive family— including broccoli, brussels sprouts, cauliflower, collard greens, kale, mustard greens, rutabagas, and turnips—for frequent consumption.

Brussels Sprouts with Fresh Dill and Pimientos

YIELD: 6 side-dish servings

This has become a traditional Thanksgiving side dish at our tables. It combines perfectly with all of the savory flavors enjoyed on that special day. Fresh brussels sprouts are a must, but dried dill may be substituted for fresh; use only one tablespoon and add it to the stock when you add the brussels sprouts.

EACH SERVING PROVIDES

*54 calories, 2 g protein, 3 g fat,
2 g dietary fiber, 8 g carbohydrates,
63 mg sodium, 0 mg cholesterol*

1 pound fresh brussels sprouts

¾ cup vegetable stock

1 tablespoon olive oil

½ teaspoon organic granulated sugar

⅛ teaspoon dried red chili flakes

2 teaspoons fresh-squeezed lemon juice

2 tablespoons minced fresh dill

1 jar (2 ounces) sliced pimientos, undrained

⅛ teaspoon salt

A few grinds pepper

Trim off the stem ends of the brussels sprouts and remove any wilted or discolored outer leaves. If they are large, cut each one in half; if they are small, leave them whole and make an X incision on the bottom to ensure even cooking. Place the stock, oil, sugar, chili flakes, and lemon juice in a large skillet over medium-high heat, and bring to a simmer. Add the brussels sprouts, reduce the heat to medium, cover, and simmer for 12 to 15 minutes, until just fork-tender. Remove the lid after 12 minutes to make sure there is still a little liquid in the pan; you want the brussels sprouts to brown slightly, but not to scorch. Add a tablespoon or so of water, as needed, and replace the lid. If the brussels sprouts are tender and there is still liquid in the pan, stir and cook, uncovered, for a minute or two, until it has evaporated. Stir in the dill, pimientos, salt, and pepper. Serve immediately.

The Goodness of Greens

Dark green leafy vegetables, such as spinach and beet greens, are wonder foods. They are low in calories and fat, yet deliver impressive quantities of fiber, vitamins, and minerals. In fact, leafy greens prove a useful rule of thumb: The darker the natural color of a food, the higher its mineral content.

We recommend you include a wide variety of greens in your diet. Mustard, collards, chard, broccoli rabe, arugula, watercress, kale, and escarole all offer nutritional benefits you don't want to miss. These foods can be enjoyed raw, simply torn into bite-sized pieces and tossed into a green salad. They are also delicious when cooked. A flash in the pan is all it takes to tenderize greens and infuse them with flavor.

You don't really need a recipe for great sautéed greens. Just begin with a little water, wine, or oil in a hot pan, pile in the cleaned greens (there's no need to dry them), and add herbs and other savory seasonings. Put a lid on the pot, and within minutes you'll have a tasty batch of wilted greens to serve with any grain or bean entrée.

One winning flavor combination that works with any leafy green is minced garlic and a scant splash of soy sauce. Lemon juice or vinegar can be added just before serving, for those who like their greens on the tart side, and black or cayenne pepper adds a pungent note.

Here are some other recommended combinations.

- Chard with garlic, golden raisins, and pine nuts

- Kale with chopped tomatoes and cumin

- Collards with sage and red bell pepper

- Spinach with fresh ginger and miso

- Beet greens with lemon and fresh thyme

Fava Beans Sautéed with Ginger and Garlic

YIELD: 4 side-dish servings

Any number of vegetables lend themselves to this simple and delicious Japanese preparation. Try it with green beans or sliced carrots when fava beans aren't in season.

EACH SERVING PROVIDES

127 calories, 7 g protein, 4 g fat,
4 g dietary fiber, 17 g carbohydrates,
90 mg sodium, 0 mg cholesterol

3 pounds fresh fava beans, in pods (about 2 cups, shelled)

1 tablespoon dark sesame oil

2 tablespoons vegetable stock or water

1 medium clove garlic, minced

2 teaspoons grated fresh ginger

1 teaspoon soy sauce

Bring several cups of water to a boil. Shell the beans, discarding the pods, and add them to the boiling water. Return the water to a boil and blanch the beans for 30 seconds to 2 minutes, depending on their size, until their skins have visibly loosened. Transfer to a colander and rinse well with cold water to stop the cooking. When the beans are cool enough to handle, pop them out of their skins. Discard the skins and set the beans aside.

Heat the oil and stock in a wok or skillet over medium-high heat, add the garlic and ginger, and simmer. Add the fava beans and soy sauce and cook for 2 to 3 minutes, stirring frequently, until the liquid has thickened enough to cling to the beans. Serve hot.

FAVA BEANS

Fava beans, also known as broad beans, are popular in Mediterranean cuisine but little known in the United States, except as a cover crop. They resemble lima beans in shape, but have a more delicate flavor. Favas are high in folacin and vitamin C, and supply moderate amounts of iron and potassium. The tender fresh beans are delicious parboiled and lightly sautéed with fresh herbs. Dried favas are best when cooked slowly with earthy dried herbs like oregano and rosemary.

NOTE: Some people of Mediterranean and African descent have a rare genetic condition called favism—which causes nausea, dizziness, and severe anemia—and should avoid eating fava beans.

Braised Carrots with Lime Juice and Shallots

YIELD: 4 side-dish servings

1 pound carrots

⅛ teaspoon salt

Several grinds black pepper

4 medium shallots, peeled and thinly sliced

2 tablespoons fresh-squeezed lime juice

2 tablespoons minced fresh cilantro

Almost Instant

Nutritious, delicious, and simple to prepare, this is likely to become an old standby for you, as it has for us.

EACH SERVING PROVIDES
65 calories, 2 g protein, 0 g fat,
4 g dietary fiber, 16 g carbohydrates,
109 mg sodium, 0 mg cholesterol

Scrub the carrots and slice them crosswise at a slant into ¼-inch pieces. Set aside.

Place the carrots, salt, and pepper in a heavy-bottomed pan, along with ¼ cup water, and bring to a simmer over medium-high heat. Cover the pan tightly, reduce the heat to medium-low, and cook 8 minutes. Remove the lid and stir in the shallots and lime juice. Cover and cook an additional 4 minutes. Remove the lid and cook, stirring almost constantly, until all the water is absorbed and the carrots are fork-tender. It is fine for the shallots and carrots to brown a bit, but don't let them scorch.

Transfer the carrots to a serving bowl, scraping the pan lightly with a rubber spatula to remove all the juices and bits of browned shallot. Toss with the cilantro and serve hot or at room temperature.

Fresh Peas and Shallots with Provençal Herbs

YIELD: 4 side-dish servings

Almost Instant

Freshly harvested garden peas are a springtime treat, especially when cooked with seasonings that evoke the south of France. When selecting fresh peas at the market, choose plump, bright green pods.

EACH SERVING PROVIDES
*134 calories, 6 g protein, 4 g fat,
6 g dietary fiber, 19 g carbohydrates,
138 mg sodium, 0 mg cholesterol*

1 tablespoon olive oil

3 medium shallots, peeled and
  thinly sliced

2 pounds fresh peas in pods (about
  2 ½ cups shelled)

1 teaspoon Herbes de Provence
  (page 310)

¼ teaspoon salt

Several grinds black pepper

½ cup vegetable stock

2 tablespoons dry white wine

¼ teaspoon freshly grated nutmeg

Heat the olive oil in a heavy-bottomed skillet or sauté pan with a tight-fitting lid. Sauté the shallots for 3 minutes, until they begin to get limp. Stir in the peas, Herbes de Provence, salt, and pepper.

Stir in the stock and wine and immediately cover the pan. Reduce the heat to low and cook for 6 minutes. Remove the lid and continue to stir and cook until the liquid has reduced to a thick sauce and the peas are tender, about 8 minutes. You may add a bit more stock or wine, if needed to prevent the pan from going dry.

Transfer the peas to a warmed serving dish, top with the nutmeg, and serve very hot.

Braised Broccoli with Fresh Herbs and Toasted Walnuts

YIELD: 4 side-dish servings

1 pound broccoli

2 tablespoons dry sherry

1 tablespoon olive oil

1 clove garlic, minced

⅛ teaspoon salt

2 teaspoons minced fresh
   marjoram, oregano, or thyme

A few grinds black pepper

3 tablespoons chopped walnuts,
   toasted (see page 10)

4 lemon wedges

Almost Instant

Quick and simple to prepare, this delectable side dish makes a fine accompaniment to almost any entrée. You may use a combination of fresh herbs rather than a single one if you wish.

EACH SERVING PROVIDES
*95 calories, 3 g protein, 7 g fat,
2 g dietary fiber, 5 g carbohydrates,
54 mg sodium, 0 mg cholesterol*

Cut off and discard the tough stem ends of the broccoli and peel the remaining stalks if they are thick-skinned. Chop the broccoli into uniform bite-sized pieces and set them aside. Combine the sherry in a small bowl with 2 tablespoons of water and set aside.

Heat the olive oil over medium heat in a skillet that has a tight-fitting lid, and sauté the garlic for about a minute. Add the broccoli and salt and stir for a moment. While holding the pan lid in one hand, pour in the sherry mixture and immediately cover the pan. Cook for 4 to 6 minutes, until the broccoli is lightly browned and fork-tender. Remove the lid after 4 minutes to see if there is still a little liquid in the pan. If the pan is dry but the broccoli is not yet tender, add one or two tablespoons of water and replace the lid. If the broccoli is tender but there is still liquid in the pan, cook uncovered for another minute or so, until it has reduced to a thick sauce that is coating the broccoli.

Toss the broccoli in a warmed serving bowl with the herbs, pepper, and toasted walnuts. Serve immediately, garnishing each serving with a lemon wedge.

Steamed Corn with Pimiento and Horseradish

YIELD: 6 side-dish servings

Fresh sweet corn is essential for this dish, so wait to make it until corn is at its peak in late summer. The horseradish adds a mild, not hot, flavor. Increase the amount if you want more fire.

EACH SERVING PROVIDES

*72 calories, 3 g protein, 0 g fat,
2 g dietary fiber, 17 g carbohydrates,
54 mg sodium, 0 mg cholesterol*

3 cups fresh corn kernels (about 6 ears)

1 jar (4 ounces) minced pimientos, undrained

1 teaspoon prepared horseradish

⅛ teaspoon salt

Several grinds black pepper

¼ cup minced fresh Italian parsley

Place the corn kernels on a steamer rack in a saucepan that has a tight-fitting lid. Add about 2 inches of water, cover, and cook over medium-high heat for 8 to 10 minutes, until the corn is tender-crisp.

Meanwhile, place the pimientos in a serving bowl and stir in the horseradish, salt, and pepper. When the corn is done, drain it briefly and add it to the bowl, along with the parsley. Toss to combine and serve immediately.

Roasted Pumpkin and Brussels Sprouts with Garlic and Herbs

YIELD: 6 servings

1 pound brussels sprouts

3 cups peeled, seeded, and diced
  pumpkin (½-inch dice)

2 tablespoons olive oil

3 cloves garlic, minced

1 teaspoon dried sage

1 teaspoon dried thyme

1 teaspoon dried rosemary

A large pinch ground cloves

½ teaspoon salt

Several grinds black pepper

Preheat the oven to 350 degrees F.

Trim off just a sliver of the stem end of each brussels sprout and remove the few outermost leaves. Halve or quarter the brussels sprouts, depending on their size, to create bite-sized pieces. Combine with the pumpkin in a large shallow baking dish.

Drizzle the olive oil over the vegetables and toss to coat. Add the garlic, sage, thyme, rosemary, and cloves and toss again until everything is well distributed. Spread the mixture out to create an even, shallow layer in the dish.

Bake until the vegetables are tender and nicely browned, about 1 to 1¼ hours. Serve hot.

This delectable autumn side dish can accompany any casserole or pilaf. You can use another variety of winter squash, such as Hubbard or acorn, in place of the pumpkin. Any medium-size winter squash will provide plenty for this recipe, plus some to enjoy later.

EACH SERVING PROVIDES
*116 calories, 3 g protein, 5 g fat,
3 g dietary fiber, 18 g carbohydrates,
198 mg sodium, 0 mg cholesterol*

Green Beans with Orange Allspice Glaze

YIELD: 6 side-dish servings

This is a wonderful and unusual way to prepare green beans. Serve with a substantial pilaf, as a side dish at Thanksgiving, or any time you get a craving for it.

EACH SERVING PROVIDES
*47 calories, 2 g protein, 0 g fat,
2 g dietary fiber, 9 g carbohydrates,
92 mg sodium, 0 mg cholesterol*

1 pound fresh green beans

½ cup fresh-squeezed orange juice

2 tablespoons dry sherry

1 teaspoon maple syrup

⅛ teaspoon ground allspice

¼ teaspoon salt

Several grinds black pepper

1 teaspoon arrowroot powder

Rinse the green beans and pat them dry. Remove the stems and any strings, leaving the beans whole. Steam the beans for about 7 minutes, until just fork-tender.

Meanwhile, combine the orange juice, sherry, maple syrup, allspice, salt, and pepper in a small saucepan over high heat. Dissolve the arrowroot powder in a tablespoon of water. When the orange juice is simmering, whisk in the arrowroot mixture. Cook for only a moment longer, until the sauce is smooth and slightly thickened.

Place the steamed green beans in a serving bowl and toss them with the sauce. Serve hot.

Snow Peas with Sesame Miso Sauce

YIELD: 4 side-dish servings

¾ pound fresh snow peas

2 tablespoons plus ½ teaspoon
　　black or brown sesame seeds,
　　toasted (see page 10)

2 tablespoons light miso

¼ cup vegetable stock or water

1 teaspoon brown rice vinegar

¼ teaspoon organic granulated
　　sugar

A pinch of salt

Discard the strings and stems of the peas, leaving the pods whole. Steam them over boiling water until barely fork-tender, about 3 to 4 minutes.

Meanwhile, use a mortar and pestle or spice grinder to coarsely grind 2 tablespoons of the toasted seeds, reserving ½ teaspoon of whole seeds for garnish.

Mash the ground seeds into the miso, then whisk in the vegetable stock, vinegar, sugar, and salt. Heat the miso mixture in a small pan over low heat until it just begins to bubble, then turn off the heat.

Transfer the steamed peas to a serving dish and add the sauce, tossing until it is well distributed. Garnish with the whole sesame seeds and serve hot or at room temperature.

Almost Instant

Cathy Tokubo introduced us to this classic Japanese preparation that uses black sesame seeds ground into miso. Asian markets carry the black seeds, but if you can't find them feel free to substitute the standard brown variety. We recommend you also try this sauce with other favorite vegetables, such as asparagus, green beans, or carrots. It makes a great accompaniment to Fried Brown Rice with Veggies (page 175).

EACH SERVING PROVIDES
*83 calories, 4 g protein, 3 g fat,
3 g dietary fiber, 11 g carbohydrates,
273 mg sodium, 0 mg cholesterol*

Cauliflower in Coriander Cashew Sauce

YIELD: 6 side-dish servings

This scrumptious curry makes a great side dish for any simple pilaf, such as the Brown Rice and Lentil Pilaf on page 168.

EACH SERVING PROVIDES

126 calories, 6 g protein, 6 g fat, 6 g dietary fiber, 16 g carbohydrates, 315 mg sodium, 0 mg cholesterol

⅓ cup raw cashews

2 tablespoons raw sesame seeds

1 cup fresh or canned tomato, seeded and diced

¼ cup chopped fresh cilantro

2 tablespoons fresh-squeezed lime juice

2 teaspoons ground coriander

2 cloves garlic, minced

1 teaspoon turmeric

1 teaspoon organic granulated sugar

¾ teaspoon salt

¼ teaspoon cayenne pepper

1 cup vegetable stock

6 cups chopped cauliflower (1 medium head)

1 cup fresh or frozen shelled peas (see NOTE)

In a blender, combine the cashews and sesame seeds. Grind them into a powder, then add the tomato, cilantro, lime juice, coriander, garlic, turmeric, salt, sugar, and cayenne. Blend until fairly smooth, then add the vegetable stock and puree.

Place the purée and the cauliflower in a large sauté pan over medium-high heat and bring to a simmer. Reduce the heat to medium-low, cover, and simmer for 10 minutes. Lift the lid and stir the contents of the pan. If the sauce is sticking to the bottom, stir in another 2 tablespoons of stock or water, then replace the lid and cook 5 minutes. Add the peas, cover, and cook until the peas are tender, about 2 minutes for frozen peas, 4 minutes for fresh. Serve hot.

NOTE: If using frozen peas, place them in a colander and rinse briefly under warm water to melt off any ice crystals before adding them to the dish.

Asparagus with Watercress and Green Onion Sauce

YIELD: 8 side-dish servings

2 pounds fresh asparagus

3 tablespoons extra-virgin olive oil

2 tablespoons fresh-squeezed
    lemon juice

1/8 teaspoon salt

Several grinds black pepper

1/2 cup watercress leaves, firmly
    packed

2 green onions, coarsely chopped

Almost Instant

Asparagus and watercress both appear in early spring, making this dish a seasonal delight.

EACH SERVING PROVIDES
*69 calories, 2 g protein, 6 g fat,
1 g dietary fiber, 4 g carbohydrates,
45 mg sodium, 0 mg cholesterol*

Rinse the asparagus well to remove any traces of soil. Snap or slice off the tough ends. Place on a steamer rack in a pan with a tight-fitting lid. Add about 2 inches of water and cook over medium-high heat until just fork-tender, about 6 minutes, depending on the thickness of the stems. Be careful not to overcook, as limp asparagus is not very appetizing.

Combine the oil, lemon juice, salt, and pepper in a small bowl. Place the watercress and onions in a blender. Switch on the low setting and add the oil and lemon juice mixture in a slow, steady stream. The resulting sauce will be a bright springtime green. Arrange the cooked asparagus on a serving platter and top with the sauce. Serve hot or at room temperature.

Beets with Potato Garlic Sauce

YIELD: 6 side-dish servings

This succulent sauce, a version of Greek "skordalia," is delicious on bread, potatoes, or steamed vegetables. We find the sweetness of fresh cooked beets to be a wonderful counterpoint to the pungent flavors of the sauce. If you are especially fond of beets, you could make a main dish out of this—it is that delicious and satisfying. A pilaf would be the perfect accompaniment.

EACH SERVING PROVIDES
*162 calories, 2 g protein, 10 g fat,
4 g dietary fiber, 18 g carbohydrates,
164 mg sodium, 0 mg cholesterol*

1 ½ pounds fresh beets (6 medium)

½ pound russet potato (1 large)

2 cloves garlic, minced

¼ teaspoon salt

⅛ teaspoon dried red chili flakes

¼ cup extra-virgin olive oil

1 tablespoon red wine vinegar

1 tablespoon fresh-squeezed lemon juice

¼ cup minced fresh Italian parsley

Place the unpeeled beets in a saucepan and cover them with water. Bring to a boil over high heat, then reduce the heat to medium and cook 20 to 25 minutes, depending on their size, until you can easily pierce each beet all the way through the middle with a sharp skewer or knife. Transfer the cooked beets to a plate and and set aside. When they are cool enough to handle, rub off the skins. Cut into 8 wedges each and arrange in a single layer on a platter.

Meanwhile, bring a few cups of water to a boil and cook the whole potato until it is very tender but not falling apart, about 15 minutes. Remove it from the water and allow it to cool a bit, then peel it and cut it into a few pieces. Place the potato in a food processor along with the garlic, salt, and chili flakes. Process for a few seconds then, with the machine running, slowly add the oil, vinegar, lemon juice, and ½ cup of cold water. Process for only about 30 seconds after each addition. Over-processing will develop the starch in the potato and turn the sauce gooey. If this happens, blend in more water a tablespoon at a time until a smooth, moderately thick consistency is achieved. Drizzle the sauce evenly over the beets, garnish with the parsley, and serve immediately.

Lynn's Southern-Fried Okra with Tomatoes

YIELD: 6 side-dish servings

¾ pound fresh okra pods

½ teaspoon salt

¼ cup fine cornmeal

1 tablespoon unbleached white
    flour

Several grinds black pepper

3 tablespoons canola oil

1 cup diced fresh tomato (1 large)

Rinse the okra pods and pat them dry. Trim off and discard the stem ends, then slice the okra crosswise into ½-inch slices. In a bowl, toss the cut okra with ¼ teaspoon of the salt. Cover the bowl with a clean tea towel and allow it to stand at room temperature for 30 minutes to an hour. The okra will exude some of its "slimy" juice, which will help the cornmeal stick to it.

In a small bowl, combine the cornmeal, flour, remaining ¼ teaspoon salt, and pepper. Just before cooking the dish, sprinkle this mixture over the okra in the bowl and toss to distribute it evenly.

Heat the oil over medium heat in a heavy-bottomed skillet large enough to hold the okra in a single layer. After a couple of minutes, drop a piece of breaded okra into the oil—if it begins to sizzle immediately, the oil is ready. Add the okra and all the cornmeal to the skillet, including the loose meal on the bottom of the bowl, and toss to distribute the oil evenly.

Cook for 10 to 12 minutes, turning the okra frequently with a metal spatula, until it is browned and tender but not mushy. Add the tomato, stir, and cook for about 2 minutes longer, until the tomato is barely warm. Serve immediately.

Inspired by the season's best okra, Lynn Hager cooked this scrumptious dish for us one September evening. If you imagine you don't like okra (perhaps because it's "slimy"), this recipe will probably make a convert of you. Select okra pods that are firm, bright green, and no more than about three inches in length. Large, brownish pods will be stringy and tough. Serve this with a side of seasoned beans like the Whole Pinto Beans with Minced Vegetables on page 183.

EACH SERVING PROVIDES
*111 calories, 2 g protein, 7 g fat,
1 g dietary fiber, 11 g carbohydrates,
183 mg sodium, 0 mg cholesterol*

Breaded Eggplant Slices with Sweet Chili Sauce

YIELD: 6 side-dish servings

This delicious eggplant dish would go well with any substantial rice and bean dish, like the Brown Rice and Lentil Pilaf on page 168. It also makes a great appetizer, with the sauce served in a small bowl in the middle of a platter and the eggplant slices fanned out around it.

EACH SERVING PROVIDES

341 calories, 5 g protein, 20 g fat, 4 g dietary fiber, 38 g carbohydrates, 468 mg sodium, 0 mg cholesterol

¾ cup fresh-squeezed orange juice

¼ cup tomato paste

2 tablespoons grated onion

2 tablespoons apple cider vinegar

1½ tablespoons maple syrup

½ jalapeño chili, seeded and minced

1 pound Chinese or Japanese eggplants (about 3 medium)

1 cup plain soy or rice milk

1 cup fine cornmeal

¼ cup unbleached white flour

1 teaspoon chili powder

1 teaspoon salt

Several grinds black pepper

Peanut or canola oil for frying (about 1 cup)

In a small saucepan, combine the orange juice, tomato paste, onion, vinegar, maple syrup, and jalapeño chili. Bring to a strong simmer over medium heat and cook until reduced to a thin sauce consistency, about 5 minutes, stirring frequently. Set aside.

Wash the eggplants and slice them crosswise into ½-inch slices. Place the eggplant slices in a large shallow baking dish and pour the milk over them. Set aside at room temperature for 15 minutes. Meanwhile, stir together the cornmeal, flour, chili powder, salt, and pepper, and transfer the mixture to a paper or plastic bag. Remove the eggplant slices from the milk, shaking each one a bit to remove most of the milk. Add the eggplant slices to the bag that contains the cornmeal and shake gently to distribute it evenly.

Place ¼ inch of oil in a skillet large enough to hold the eggplant slices in a single layer, and heat it over medium heat until a few grains of the cornmeal sizzles immediately when added to the oil. Place the coated eggplant slices in the hot oil and cook until well browned on one side, about 3 minutes. Turn and cook another 2 or 3 minutes, until well browned and crisp on the other side. As they finish cooking, place the eggplant slices on a folded paper or cloth towel to soak up the residual oil. If you need to fry the eggplant in 2 batches, clean out the pan in between to remove browned bits, then add fresh oil and start over for the second batch. If you have 2 large skillets, you can cook both batches at once.

Serve by overlapping a few slices of eggplant on individual serving plates and drizzling the sauce evenly over them. Serve hot or at room temperature.

Steamed Artichokes with Silken Tofu Dill Sauce

YIELD: 4 side-dish servings

These herb and vinegar infused artichokes are delicious. The dill dipping sauce is a wonderful way to enhance this succulent vegetable.

EACH SERVING PROVIDES

120 calories, 10 g protein, 3 g fat,
7 g dietary fiber, 18 g carbohydrates,
352 mg sodium, 0 mg cholesterol

8 ounces firm silken tofu

1 tablespoon Dijon mustard

3 tablespoons fresh-squeezed
   lemon juice

2 tablespoons minced fresh dill

½ teaspoon granulated garlic

2 bay leaves

3 cloves garlic

¼ teaspoon dried red chili flakes

¼ teaspoon salt

2 tablespoons apple cider vinegar

1 teaspoon dried dill

1 teaspoon dried oregano

4 large artichokes

Cut the tofu into cubes and combine it in a blender with the mustard, lemon juice, dill, and granulated garlic. Purée, then place in a serving bowl and set aside.

Meanwhile, bring about 4 inches of water to a boil in a stockpot over high heat and add the bay leaves, garlic, chili flakes, salt, vinegar, dill, and oregano.

Use a sharp knife to trim off most of the stem of the artichokes and about ½-inch of the pointy ends of their leaves. Put a steaming tray in the stockpot and place the artichokes on the tray, leaf end down. Cover the pan tightly, reduce the heat to medium, and steam 25 to 45 minutes, depending on the size of the artichokes. When the leaves pull off easily and the base (heart) is barely tender when pierced with a fork, the artichoke is done.

Remove the artichokes from the pan with tongs, squeezing gently to remove some of the water. Serve hot, chilled, or at room temperature, with the dipping sauce on the side.

8

Pasta
Dishes

Spaghetti with Artichoke-Pistachio Pesto

Orzo with Peas and Lemon-Herb Sauce

Linguine with Asparagus, Walnuts, and Fresh Herbs

Pasta with Adzuki Beans, Tomatoes, Spinach, and
    Olives

Pasta with Sweet Potato and Roasted Red Bell Pepper

Lasagna Rolls with Tofu Filling and Tomato Coulis

Orrechiette with Tomato Sauce, Basil, and Toasted
    Pine Nuts

Pasta Puttanesca with Artichokes

Rice Noodles with Curried Tofu and Veggies

Soba with Fresh Soybeans and Spicy Tahini Sauce

Sweet-and-Hot Cauliflower with Couscous

Fusilli with Grilled Eggplant and Garbanzos

Pumpkin-Stuffed Shells with Jalapeño-
    Rosemary Sauce

Pasta is universally appealing—almost every region of the globe enjoys some kind of noodle as an accompaniment to sauces, soups, and stews. Fettuccine dressed simply in olive oil and garlic, buckwheat soba smothered in ginger tahini sauce; or couscous with a curried lentil stew—whenever it appears, pasta has an international flair.

No great cooking skill is needed for pasta dishes. The main trick is learning to remove it from the heat and drain it when it reaches the perfect "al dente" stage. This Italian phrase means "to the tooth" and suggests that when we bite into a strand we should meet just a hint of resistance. Overcooked pasta falls apart easily when stirred and feels mushy in the mouth. Don't worry: Just a few tries will teach you to get it right; then a world of pasta pleasures will be yours for the making.

There are a few other simple tips to keep in mind. Use a large pot and plenty of water, bring it to a strong rolling boil before adding the pasta, separate the strands as you put them in the pot, and give the pasta a good stir once or twice as it cooks. Drain the pasta well before adding it to the sauce (unless otherwise directed), and don't rinse it, unless you want to cool it quickly for a pasta salad.

It's true that pasta is a refined carbohydrate, and therefore not advisable as everyday fare. Served with fresh veggies and beans; however, and interspersed among plenty of whole grain meals, pasta can play a delicious role in the healthy vegan diet.

Spaghetti with Artichoke–Pistachio Pesto

YIELD: 4 main-dish servings

Almost Instant

In this simple recipe, the pesto coats the pasta to perfection, making every bite a pleasure.

EACH SERVING PROVIDES
*628 calories, 19 g protein, 17 g fat,
8 g dietary fiber, 101 g carbohydrates,
272 mg sodium, 0 mg cholesterol*

1 can (14 ounces) water-packed
    artichoke bottoms, drained

3 cloves garlic, minced

3 tablespoons extra-virgin olive oil

2 tablespoons fresh-squeezed
    lemon juice

1 cup chopped Italian parsley

¼ cup chopped pistachios

1 pound spaghetti

Put several quarts of water on to boil in a large stockpot.

Place the artichoke bottoms and garlic in a food processor. With the machine running, add the olive oil and lemon juice in a slow steady stream and process until smooth. Add the parsley and process until incorporated. Add the pistachios and pulse to combine. Thin with a tablespoon or two of water, if needed, to achieve a thick but soft consistency.

Cook the pasta in the rapidly boiling water until al dente, drain it briefly, then toss it in a large bowl with the pesto. Serve immediately.

GARLIC

Garlic has been known for its healing powers since ancient times. Modern research has shown it to lower blood levels of cholesterol and triglycerides, promote detoxification, and enhance the immune system. These effects are most pronounced when garlic is eaten uncooked. Garlic bread, salad dressing, pesto, and salsa are good ways to get your daily dose. You can also stir minced raw garlic into hot beans or soup just before serving, for both a flavor and a health boost. Buy garlic bulbs that feel firm and have visibly large cloves. Stored in the open at room temperature, garlic will stay fresh for a few weeks. If the garlic starts sprouting, we recommend that you remove the bitter green sprouts at the center of each clove as you prepare it to use in a recipe.

Orzo with Peas and Lemon–Herb Sauce

YIELD: 4 main-dish servings

2 cups chopped fresh Italian parsley

¼ cup chopped fresh mint

2 cloves garlic, coarsely chopped

¼ cup vegetable stock

¼ cup extra-virgin olive oil

2 tablespoons fresh-squeezed
  lemon juice

1 ½ teaspoons fennel seeds,
  crushed

¾ teaspoon salt

¼ teaspoon dried red chili flakes

1 ⅛ cups fresh or frozen shelled
  peas (see NOTE)

2 cups dried orzo (about 1 pound)

Here is a simple and light, yet quite satisfying, main dish. We like to serve it with braised or steamed carrots for a wonderful combination of colors and flavors.

EACH SERVING PROVIDES

619 calories, 19 g protein, 17 g fat, 7 g dietary fiber, 96 g carbohydrates, 478 mg sodium, 0 mg cholesterol

Bring several quarts of water to a rapid boil in a large stockpot.

Meanwhile, in a food processor or blender, combine the parsley with the mint, garlic, stock, oil, lemon juice, fennel seeds, salt, and chili flakes. Blend until fairly smooth and set aside in a large serving bowl.

When the water comes to a rolling boil, add the peas. Bring the water back to a boil, then remove the peas immediately if using the frozen variety, or cook for 1 minute if using fresh peas. Remove the peas from the water with a wire strainer or slotted spoon and bring the water back to a boil. Drain the peas well, then add them to the sauce in the bowl.

Add the orzo to the boiling water and stir. Bring the pot back to a boil and cook until the orzo is al dente, about 10 minutes, stirring occasionally.

When the pasta is ready, transfer it to a large fine-mesh strainer and drain it well. Add it to the peas and sauce and toss until everything is well combined. Serve immediately.

NOTE: If using frozen peas, place them in a colander and rinse briefly under warm water to melt off any ice crystals before adding them to the dish.

Linguine with Asparagus, Walnuts, and Fresh Herbs

YIELD: 4 main-dish servings

In the tradition of primavera-style pasta, this dish makes the most of spring asparagus and delivers a hefty dose of garlic. It is a satisfying main dish for four hearty appetites. You may use almost any fresh herbs—our favorite blend includes oregano, tarragon, and thyme. Serve with soy Parmesan cheese, if desired.

EACH SERVING PROVIDES
*492 calories, 16 g protein, 11 g fat,
6 g dietary fiber, 81 g carbohydrates,
164 mg sodium, 0 mg cholesterol*

1 pound fresh asparagus
1 medium yellow bell pepper
1 tablespoon olive oil
1 medium yellow onion, diced
6 cloves garlic, minced
1 large carrot, thinly sliced

¼ teaspoon salt
A few grinds black pepper
3 tablespoons dry sherry
3 tablespoons minced fresh herbs
12 ounces dried linguine
⅓ cup walnut pieces, toasted
   (see page 10) and chopped

Put several quarts of water on to boil in a large stockpot.

Rinse the asparagus and break off the tough stem ends. Cut the spears at a slant into 1-inch pieces. Cut the bell pepper in half lengthwise, discard the stem and seeds, and slice the halves into long, thin strips. Set the asparagus and bell pepper aside.

Heat the oil in a heavy-bottomed skillet over medium heat and sauté the onion and garlic for 2 minutes. Add the carrots, salt, and pepper, and stir and sauté for about 3 minutes. Stir in the asparagus and bell pepper, then pour in the sherry and immediately cover the pan tightly. Cook for 6 minutes, then remove the lid and stir in the fresh herbs.

Meanwhile, cook the linguine in the rapidly boiling water until al dente. Drain it well and toss it with the asparagus mixture in a serving bowl, then top with the walnuts. Serve very hot, passing grated soy Parmesan cheese, if desired.

Pasta with Adzuki Beans, Tomatoes, Spinach, and Olives

YIELD: 4 main-dish servings

10 ounces dried corn pasta spirals

2 cups chopped fresh or canned tomatoes, with juice

1 cup vegetable stock

2 cloves garlic, minced

1 teaspoon dried oregano

1/4 teaspoon dried red chili flakes

1/4 teaspoon salt

4 cups chopped spinach or baby spinach leaves, firmly packed

1 cup cooked and drained adzuki beans

1/4 cup chopped calamata olives

1 tablespoon extra-virgin olive oil

Bring several quarts of water to a rapid boil in a large stockpot. Add the pasta and cook, stirring occasionally, until al dente, about 8 to 10 minutes, depending on its size and shape.

Meanwhile, combine the tomatoes, stock, garlic, oregano, chili flakes, and salt in a saucepan over medium heat. Simmer for 7 minutes, stirring occasionally, then add the spinach and adzuki beans, cover, and cook for 3 more minutes.

Drain the pasta well and add it to the tomato mixture, along with the olives and olive oil. Toss until well combined. Serve hot.

Almost Instant

This satisfying dish is great made with vine-ripened tomatoes in the summertime and almost as good made with canned tomatoes in the dead of winter. We recommend corn pasta, as it brings a spectacular color contrast to the dish. A leafy salad and a glass of Merlot make excellent accompaniments.

EACH SERVING PROVIDES
422 calories, 12 g protein, 8 g fat, 8 g dietary fiber, 78 g carbohydrates, 456 mg sodium, 0 mg cholesterol

Pasta with Sweet Potato and Roasted Red Bell Pepper

YIELD: 6 main-dish servings

1 ½ pounds red-skinned sweet potatoes (3 medium)

2 medium red bell peppers

1 cup plain rice or soy milk

¼ teaspoon salt

A few grinds black pepper

¼ teaspoon freshly grated nutmeg

⅛ teaspoon ground mace

2 tablespoons dry sherry

1 pound dried fusilli

½ cup minced Italian parsley

2 tablespoons extra-virgin olive oil

6 lemon wedges

Preheat the grill to medium-high. Scrub the sweet potatoes and pierce them in several places with a fork. Place the whole sweet potatoes on the grill, cover the grill, and cook about 45 minutes, until they are soft, turning occasionally. Remove from the grill and set aside to cool slightly, then peel off the skin and chop the potato.

While you are cooking the sweet potatoes, also place the whole peppers on the grill. Turn them every 10 minutes to blacken and blister the skin, cooking for about 30 minutes. Transfer the blackened peppers to a paper or plastic bag, close the bag, and set aside until the peppers are cool enough to handle. Peel off the blackened skin and discard the stem, seeds, and white membranes. Slice the peppers into long ½-inch strips and set aside. Place the sweet potatoes in a food processor with the milk, salt, pepper, nutmeg, mace, and dry sherry; purée. The sauce should be fairly thick.

Meanwhile, bring several quarts of water to a boil in a large stockpot. Add the pasta and cook until al dente. Before draining the pasta, add about ½ cup of the pasta cooking water to the food processor to heat the sauce and thin it a bit, then add the parsley and pulse to combine.

Drain the pasta well and place it in a large, warmed serving bowl. Drizzle with the olive oil and toss, then add the sweet potato purée and parsley and toss again. Arrange the grilled red pepper strips over the top. Serve immediately, passing the lemon wedges.

SWEET POTATOES

Most vegetables sold as "yams" in the United States are technically sweet potatoes. Sweet potatoes come in many varieties, ranging from orange-tan in color to reddish brown or burgundy red. The true yam is an extremely large tuber that is native to Africa and grows only in very hot regions. Whatever their name, the red-fleshed tubers are an antioxidant powerhouse. Just a few bites, as little as ⅛ of a cup, delivers the recommended daily allowance of vitamin A.

Lasagna Rolls with Tofu Filling and Tomato Coulis

YIELD: 6 main-dish serving

In this dish, lasagna noodles are filled and rolled up jellyroll fashion, then baked with a sauce. Use a semolina lasagna noodle, as it will roll more easily than the whole wheat variety, which tends to break apart.

EACH SERVING PROVIDES
*532 calories, 25 g protein, 17 g fat,
6 g dietary fiber, 73 g carbohydrates,
647 mg sodium, 0 mg cholesterol*

The sauce

1 tablespoon olive oil

3 cloves garlic, minced

2 cans (28 ounces each) pear tomatoes

3 bay leaves

1 teaspoon dried oregano

2 thin slices fresh lemon

1 pound lasagna noodles

The filling

18 ounces firm tofu

¼ cup plain soy or rice milk

¾ cup chopped fresh basil leaves

2 cloves garlic, minced

1 tablespoon olive oil

8 ounces soy mozzarella cheese, grated

To prepare the sauce, heat the olive oil in a large high-walled skillet over medium heat and sauté the garlic for a few seconds. Add the tomatoes, along with their juice, the bay leaves, oregano, and lemon slices. Cook over medium heat for about 45 minutes, stirring frequently to break up the tomatoes and prevent the sauce from scorching. Remove the bay leaves and lemon slices and set the sauce aside.

Meanwhile, preheat the oven to 350 degrees F. Bring several quarts of water to a rapid boil in a large stockpot, as the noodles need a lot of room to move around as they cook. Add the noodles, return the pot to a boil, then reduce the heat slightly. Cook until almost al dente; the noodles will finish cooking in the oven. Remove gently from the water, and place on a tea towel to dry.

Slice the tofu and blot it dry with a clean tea towel or paper towels. Place it in a food processor with the milk, basil, garlic, and olive oil. Alternatively, you may use a fork to mash these ingredients together in a mixing bowl.

Spoon ⅓ of the sauce over the bottom of a 9 × 13-inch baking dish. Place one noodle at a time on the work surface and spread about 1 tablespoon of the tofu mixture over the entire surface of the noodle. Sprinkle about 1/16 of the cheese over the filling and roll up jellyroll style. Place the roll seam side down in the baking dish. Continue until all of the ingredients are used; you will have about 16 rolls. Top with the remaining sauce. Bake, covered, for 25 minutes and serve immediately.

Orrechiette with Tomato Sauce, Basil, and Toasted Pine Nuts

YIELD: 4 main-dish servings

The indentation in the orre-chiette ("little ears") pasta creates the perfect cradle to hold the sauce. Make this in late summer, when the basil's slight peppery flavor will be at its best.

EACH SERVING PROVIDES
555 calories, 18 g protein, 12 g fat, 5 g dietary fiber, 96 g carbohydrates, 480 mg sodium, 0 mg cholesterol

1 can (28 ounces) whole pear tomatoes

2 tablespoons extra-virgin olive oil

3 cloves garlic

¼ teaspoon salt

Several grinds black pepper

2 cups fresh basil chiffonade, loosely packed (see page 4)

16 ounces dried orrechiette

2 tablespoons pine nuts, toasted (see page 10)

Put several quarts of water on to boil in a large stockpot.

Lift the tomatoes out of their juice, and place in a strainer set over a bowl. Coarsely chop the tomatoes, retaining any juice that has collected in the bowl. (Reserve the juice left in the can for another use, such as soup stock or a juice drink.) Heat the oil in a sauté pan over medium heat. Add the garlic and sauté for a minute or so, then add the tomatoes, salt, and pepper. Cook over medium-high heat for about 15 minutes to reduce the liquid. Stir in the basil, then turn off the heat and cover the pan.

Meanwhile, cook the pasta in the boiling water until al dente, then drain well and transfer to a serving bowl. Toss with the sauce, then top with the toasted pine nuts. Serve immediately.

Pasta Puttanesca with Artichokes

YIELD: 4 main-dish servings

2 tablespoons olive oil

4 cloves garlic, finely chopped

½ teaspoon dried red chili flakes

1 can (28 ounces) whole pear tomatoes

2 tablespoons tomato paste

½ cup calamata olives, pitted and halved

¼ cup dry red wine

¼ cup finely chopped fresh basil

2 tablespoons capers, drained

1 teaspoon dried rosemary, crushed

¼ teaspoon salt

1 package (8 ounces) frozen artichoke hearts, thawed and cut into bite-sized wedges

12 ounces spinach spaghetti

Bring several quarts of water to boil in a large stockpot.

In a large, heavy-bottomed pan, heat the olive oil and add the garlic and chili flakes. Stir and cook 30 seconds, then add the canned tomatoes, with their juice. Use a fork or wooden spoon to chop and crush the tomatoes somewhat. Stir in the tomato paste, then add the olives, wine, basil, capers, rosemary, and salt, and bring to a simmer over medium-high heat. Reduce the heat to medium and cook 10 minutes, stirring occasionally. Add the artichokes and cook 5 minutes longer.

Meanwhile, cook the pasta in rapidly boiling water until al dente, about 10 to 12 minutes. Drain well, then add to the sauce. Toss until the sauce ingredients are well distributed, then transfer to a platter and serve piping hot.

This classic robust and spicy tomato sauce is named for the so-called "ladies of the evening." There is certainly nothing bashful about it! It is especially tasty on spinach pasta, but feel free to use another variety instead. If fresh basil isn't available, substitute 1 tablespoon dried basil. Also, you may use cauliflower florets or chopped green beans in place of the artichokes. Simply steam the vegetables until barely fork-tender before adding them to the sauce.

EACH SERVING PROVIDES
529 calories, 16 g protein, 14 g fat, 15 g dietary fiber, 85 g carbohydrates, 1385 mg sodium, 0 mg cholesterol

Rice Noodles with Curried Tofu and Veggies

YIELD: 6 main-dish servings

This makes an excellent rainy night dinner, accompanied by a shredded cabbage salad that has a tart dressing. The degree of spicy heat in the finished dish will depend on the brand of curry powder you have on hand, so adjust the amount according to your taste. Rice vermicelli is available at Asian markets and some natural food stores.

EACH SERVING PROVIDES
*400 calories, 11 g protein, 10 g fat,
8 g dietary fiber, 70 g carbohydrates,
316 mg sodium, 0 mg cholesterol*

½ pound button mushrooms

12 ounces rice vermicelli

2 cups vegetable stock

1 cup coconut milk

1 tablespoon curry powder

1 ½ tablespoons soy sauce

1 large carrot, diced

½ pound firm tofu, diced

1 medium yellow onion, diced

2 ½ cups bite-sized broccoli florets

1 cup fresh or frozen shelled peas
  (see NOTE)

2 tablespoons arrowroot powder

⅓ cup minced fresh mint

6 lime wedges

Bring a large pot of water to a rapid boil and add the rice vermicelli. Return the pot to a rolling boil and cook until the noodles are tender but not mushy, about 7 to 9 minutes, stirring occasionally. (If the pasta is done before the sauce is ready, drain it, toss it with a teaspoon of canola oil, and set aside.)

Meanwhile, brush or wipe any loose dirt from the mushrooms and quarter them. In a large skillet or sauté pan, combine the vegetable stock, coconut milk, curry powder, and soy sauce. Add the tofu, carrot, mushrooms, and onion, and bring to a simmer over medium-high heat. Reduce the heat to medium, cover, and cook 7 minutes. Add the broccoli, cover, and cook 3 minutes. Add the peas and bring back to a simmer. Cook an additional 30 seconds if using frozen peas, about 3 minutes if using fresh peas.

Dissolve the arrowroot powder in 3 tablespoons of water. When the peas are done, stir the arrowroot mixture into the bubbling sauce and cook for about 30 seconds, until the sauce thickens slightly. Do not overcook, as the arrowroot can turn the sauce gummy.

Divide the well-drained rice noodles among 6 shallow serving bowls and pour the sauce evenly over them. Sprinkle on the mint and serve hot, with a lime wedge nestled in each bowl.

NOTE: If using frozen peas, place them in a colander and rinse briefly under warm water to melt off any ice crystals before adding them to the dish.

EDAMAME

The Japanese have found countless ways over the centuries to enjoy the soybean. The most simple of all is to boil fresh soybeans—edamame in Japanese—in their pods, then pop out the beans for a tasty snack. This high-protein, high-fiber vegetable has always been sold at Asian markets in the United States, and now it's stocked in the frozen vegetable case at some mainstream supermarkets. A one-pound bag of soybeans in their pods will yield about 1½ cups of shelled soybeans. If you are following a recipe that calls for shelled beans, buy them already shelled or parboil the pods for a few minutes, cool, then squeeze gently to pop out the beans. Adults and children alike may find them addictive.

Soba with Fresh Soybeans and Spicy Tahini Sauce

YIELD: 4 main-dish servings

Here's a wonderful way to enjoy the earthy Japanese buckwheat noodles called soba. It is simple to prepare and always satisfying—one of those good stand-by recipes. If you don't care much for spicy food, cut the amount of chili flakes in half or omit them altogether. If you can't locate fresh soybeans, you may use broccoli florets for equally good results.

EACH SERVING PROVIDES
*377 calories, 19 g protein, 10 g fat,
4 g dietary fiber, 59 g carbohydrates,
1041 mg sodium, 0 mg cholesterol*

1 cup vegetable stock

3 tablespoons sesame tahini, raw or toasted

2 tablespoons soy sauce

1 tablespoon brown rice vinegar

1 tablespoon grated fresh ginger

2 teaspoons organic granulated sugar

¼ teaspoon red chili flakes, crushed

8 ounces buckwheat soba

1 ½ cups fresh or frozen shelled soybeans (*edamame*)

1 small carrot, sliced very thin

6 green onions, minced

2 tablespoons minced fresh cilantro leaves

1 tablespoon sesame seeds, toasted

Put several quarts of water on to boil in a large stockpot.

In a saucepan, whisk together the stock, tahini, soy sauce, vinegar, ginger, sugar, and chili flakes, and bring to a strong simmer over medium-high heat. Reduce the heat to medium-low and simmer 5 minutes.

Meanwhile, add the soba to the rapidly boiling water and stir gently, then bring back to a boil and cook 5 minutes, stirring occasionally. Add the shelled soybeans and carrot slices, bring back to a boil, and cook 2 to 4 minutes longer, until the soba is tender but not mushy.

Drain well and toss with the sauce and onions in a serving bowl. Serve hot, garnished with the cilantro and sesame seeds.

Sweet-and-Hot Cauliflower with Couscous

YIELD: 6 main-dish servings

1 can (28 ounces) whole pear
    tomatoes

1 tablespoon plus 2 teaspoons
    olive oil

2 medium white onions, chopped

6 cups chopped cauliflower

2 large carrots, diced

½ cup golden raisins

2 cloves garlic, minced

1 teaspoon mild paprika

1 teaspoon ground cumin

½ teaspoon ground cinnamon

½ teaspoon ground cardamom

½ teaspoon salt

⅛ teaspoon cayenne pepper

2 tablespoons fresh-squeezed
    lemon juice

1 ⅓ cups dried couscous

¼ cup minced fresh Italian parsley

¼ cup minced fresh mint

A deliciously aromatic combination of spices makes this dish a mouth-watering favorite. It comes together quickly and makes a satisfying meal, perhaps followed by a flavorful leafy salad.

EACH SERVING PROVIDES

323 calories, 10 g protein, 6 g fat,
9 g dietary fiber, 62 g carbohydrates,
433 mg sodium, 0 mg cholesterol

Chop the tomatoes and set them aside in a bowl. Heat 1 tablespoon of the oil over medium heat in a high-walled skillet that has a tight-fitting lid. Sauté the onions, cauliflower, and carrots for 5 minutes, stirring frequently, then add the tomatoes, raisins, garlic, paprika, cumin, cinnamon, cardamom, ¼ teaspoon of the salt, the cayenne, and 1 cup of water. Cover and reduce the heat to medium-low. Cook for 15 minutes, stirring once about midway through the cooking time. Stir in the lemon juice, cover, and set aside.

Meanwhile, bring 2 cups of water to a boil in a covered saucepan, along with the remaining ¼ teaspoon salt and the remaining 2 teaspoons oil. Stir in the couscous, immediately cover the pan, and remove it from the heat. Let stand at least 5 minutes without disturbing the lid. Just before serving, turn the couscous out onto a warmed serving platter, fluffing with a fork. Arrange the couscous in a ring around the edge of the platter, spooning the hot cauliflower mixture into the center. Sprinkle the parsley and mint evenly over the dish and serve immediately.

Fusilli with Grilled Eggplant and Garbanzos

YIELD: 6 main-dish servings

Enjoy this quick and delicious dish in the late summer, when eggplants are plentiful and the oregano in your garden is in full production. Use whole wheat fusilli for added fiber and nutrients.

EACH SERVING PROVIDES

443 calories, 15 g protein, 9 g fat, 8 g dietary fiber, 76 g carbohydrates, 188 mg sodium, 0 mg cholesterol

1 pound eggplant (about 1 medium)

1 ½ teaspoons canola oil

1 pound dried fusilli

2 tablespoons extra-virgin olive oil

2 cups cooked and drained garbanzo beans, heated

2 tablespoons minced fresh oregano leaves

½ teaspoon salt

A few grinds black pepper

Preheat the grill to medium. Remove the stem of the eggplant, but do not peel it. Cut the eggplant lengthwise into ½-inch slices. Brush or spray one side of each slice with some of the canola oil and place on the grill, oiled side down. Close the lid and cook about 6 minutes. Brush or spray the other side of the eggplant slices with the remaining canola oil, turn them over, and cook an additional 5 minutes. Remove from the grill and set aside. When cool enough to handle, slice into thin strips.

Meanwhile, bring several quarts of water to a rapid boil in a large stockpot. Cook the pasta until al dente, then drain it well and transfer it to a large, warmed bowl. Drizzle the extra-virgin olive oil over the pasta, then add the garbanzo beans, oregano, salt, and pepper. Toss well. Arrange the eggplant strips on top and serve immediately.

Pesto Possibilities

What's so great about pesto? Let's start with the taste. Rich with olive oil, garlic, nuts, and fresh herbs, pesto delivers flavor in abundance.

And it delivers good nutrition. Olive oil has the right kind of fat, raw garlic offers a long list of health benefits, and fresh green herbs are bursting with antioxidant vitamins.

Pesto's other claim to greatness is its simplicity. You can make up a batch in 10 minutes and keep it in the refrigerator for a week—ready when you need a little flavor inspiration. And don't stop at using pesto with pasta. Try stirring pesto into a bowl of beans, eating a dollop on a baked potato, or spreading the delicious stuff on whole wheat bread.

The classic basil concoction that originated in Genoa, Italy, is only one of the fantastic pesto possibilities. All can be created quickly and easily if you have a sturdy blender or food processor.

Each of the following pesto recipes has the same directions. Place the ingredients in the blender and purée until the mixture forms a thick and homogeneous sauce. You may add a bit more stock or other liquid, if necessary, to achieve the desired consistency. Use immediately or keep refrigerated, doling it out a few delicious tablespoons at a time.

CILANTRO AND PUMPKIN SEED PESTO

1 cup chopped fresh cilantro

1 cup chopped fresh parsley

¼ cup extra-virgin olive oil

¼ cup raw unsalted pumpkin seeds

2 tablespoons fresh-squeezed lime juice

1 tablespoon dried oregano

2 cloves garlic, minced

½ teaspoon ground cumin

½ teaspoon salt

¼ teaspoon dried red chili flakes

DRIED TOMATO AND MINT PESTO

¾ cup oil-packed dried tomatoes

½ cup fresh mint leaves, firmly packed

½ cup chopped walnuts

¼ cup vegetable stock

2 tablespoons tomato paste

1 tablespoon fresh-squeezed lemon juice

2 cloves garlic, minced

¼ teaspoon salt

ARUGULA AND ALMOND PESTO

2 cups chopped fresh arugula, firmly
   packed

½ cup fresh basil leaves, firmly packed

⅓ cup whole blanched almonds

¼ cup extra-virgin olive oil

¼ cup vegetable stock

1 tablespoon fresh rosemary leaves

2 cloves garlic, minced

¼ teaspoon salt

Pumpkin-Stuffed Shells with Jalapeño-Rosemary Sauce

YIELD: 6 main-dish servings

Several steps are required to prepare this dish, but none of them are difficult. Serve with warm tortillas and a leafy green salad. This dish is a wonderful autumn treat!

EACH SERVING PROVIDES
415 calories, 11 g protein, 14 g fat, 7 g dietary fiber, 63 g carbohydrates, 277 mg sodium, 0 mg cholesterol

The filling

2 tablespoons dry sherry

2 tablespoons olive oil

3 cloves garlic, minced

2 tablespoons minced fresh rosemary leaves

1 bunch fresh spinach, stems removed, washed, and chopped

1 can (16 ounces) pumpkin

½ teaspoon salt

A few grinds black pepper

12 ounces dried jumbo pasta shells

½ teaspoon olive oil

6 lemon wedges

The sauce

3 tablespoons olive oil

2 cloves garlic, minced

1 tablespoon minced fresh rosemary leaves

3 tablespoons unbleached white flour

1½ cups plain rice or soy milk

1 tablespoon minced pickled jalapeño chilies

First, make the filling: In a large sauté pan, heat the sherry, oil, garlic, and rosemary over low heat and sauté for about 30 seconds. Add the spinach, along with any water clinging to the leaves, and cover the pan. Cook for about 3 minutes, until the spinach wilts, stirring occasionally. Stir in the pumpkin, salt, and pepper. Remove from the heat and set aside.

To make the sauce: Heat the oil in a heavy-bottomed skillet over medium heat. Stir in the garlic and rosemary and cook for about 1 minute. Sprinkle in the flour and continue to cook for about 1 minute, stirring constantly. Whisk in the milk ½ cup at a time, then bring to a simmer, and cook for about 6 minutes, until slightly thickened. Stir in the pickled jalapeños and set aside.

Meanwhile, bring several quarts of water to a rapid boil in a large stockpot. Add the pasta shells and cook until almost al dente, about 6 minutes; the noodles will finish cooking in the oven. Gently remove them from the pan and place them in a colander. Rinse with cold water, then transfer them to a folded tea towel to drain.

Preheat the oven to 350 degrees F, and use the remaining ½ teaspoon olive oil to lightly coat an 8 x 12-inch baking dish.

Place a drained pasta shell in the palm of your hand and gently press the pointed ends toward one another to open the shell's pocket. Stuff with a mounded teaspoon of the spinach-pumpkin filling and place in the baking dish. Pour the sauce evenly over the shells, cover the dish, and bake for 20 minutes to heat through. Serve immediately, passing the lemon wedges.

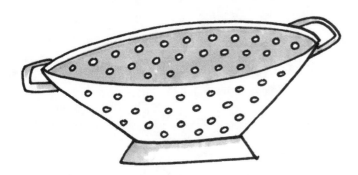

9

Grain and Bean Dishes

Bulgur Pilaf with Garbanzo Beans, Caraway, and
    Mint
Bulgur and Red Lentil Pilaf with Kale and Olives
Brown Rice and Lentil Pilaf
Wild Rice Pilaf
Toasted Orzo and Rice Pilaf
Quinoa Pilaf with Sunflower and Sesame Seeds
Oat and Rutabaga Pilaf with Toasted Walnuts
Barley and Mushroom Pilaf with Toasted Pecans
Serrano Chili Rice
Fried Brown Rice with Veggies
Risotto with Saffron, Peas, and Pine Nuts
Corn, Sweet Pepper, and Cumin Risotto
Risotto with Portobello Mushrooms and Radicchio
Asparagus Risotto with Oyster Mushrooms and
    Ginger
Cannellini Beans with Peppers and Fennel Seeds over
    Soft Polenta
Creamy French Lentils with Celery Root and Garlic
Whole Pinto Beans with Minced Vegetables
White Beans with Tomatoes and Chipotle Chilies
Black Bean Patties with Tomatillo Sauce

At the center of vegan cooking are hearty and healthful grains and beans. Both are ancient sources of nourishment. Long before early humans settled the land and planted crops, they harvested the seeds of wild grasses and other plants, which are the ancestors of today's grains and beans.

Despite the bad reputation of carbohydrates in some circles, to sustain good health, you need a substantial quantity of carbohydrates in your daily diet. It is refined carbohydrates you should try to avoid. Sugar- and flour-based foods like cakes, cookies, and breads are generally empty-calorie foods that can do your body more harm than good when you eat them in excess. Of course, the occasional sweet treat is nothing to worry about!

Complex carbohydrates like whole grains, on the other hand, deliver important fiber, minerals, and vitamins, and provide for a slow release of sugars into the bloodstream. This ensures a steady supply of calm energy—nothing like the "sugar rush" you can experience with refined carbohydrates, which makes you crazy, pushes insulin production into overdrive, and eventually pads your body with fat.

Another grain caveat: Wheat is a common allergen, and some people will need to avoid foods made from it (like pasta and bread). A simple allergy elimination diet can help you discover if wheat is your friend or your foe. Fortunately, the variety of whole grains available at natural food stores and many supermarkets gives you lots of options. Rice, for instance, is a delicious and versatile grain well tolerated by almost everyone (see page 176).

As for beans, some people avoid them because they find them "windy." Cooking beans until they are quite done, chewing them well, and eating them in small portions minimizes this effect for most people. There are also a few kitchen tricks reputed to prevent gassy beans, including skimming any foam off the beans as they cook and adding kombu or other sea vegetables to the pot (see pages 6–7).

We hope the recipes in this chapter convince you that there is nothing monotonous about a diet based on grains and beans. Combined with a wide variety of vegetables and seasonings, these humble staples can provide a world of exciting dishes and a lifetime of good health.

Bulgur Pilaf with Garbanzo Beans, Caraway, and Mint

YIELD: 6 side-dish servings

This distinctive dish goes well with a simple stir-fry or stew, or can become the center of the meal when served with plain steamed vegetables.

EACH SERVING PROVIDES
*183 calories, 7 g protein, 4 g fat,
8 g dietary fiber, 32 g carbohydrates,
186 mg sodium, 0 mg cholesterol*

1½ teaspoons caraway seeds
1 teaspoon coriander seeds
1 teaspoon ground turmeric
½ teaspoon salt
A few grinds black pepper
1 tablespoon olive oil
½ medium white onion, diced

2 cloves garlic, minced
1 large bay leaf
1 cup uncooked bulgur wheat
1½ cups cooked and drained
    garbanzo beans
⅓ cup chopped fresh mint

Combine the caraway seeds and coriander seeds in a mortar and pestle and crush to a coarse powder. Set aside in a small bowl with the turmeric, salt, and pepper.

Heat the oil in a large saucepan over medium heat and sauté the onion for 3 minutes, stirring occasionally. Stir in the garlic and spice mixture, then add 2 cups of water and the bay leaf. Bring to a boil over high heat. Add the bulgur and garbanzo beans and return to a simmer. Reduce the heat to very low, cover, and cook 20 minutes. Turn off the heat, remove the lid, and distribute the mint over the top of the pilaf. Replace the lid and set the pilaf aside for at least 5 minutes before serving.

Transfer the pilaf to a warmed serving bowl or platter. Discard the bay leaf and toss the pilaf with two forks to break up any clumps and distribute all the ingredients evenly. Serve hot.

Bulgur and Red Lentil Pilaf with Kale and Olives

YIELD: 4 main-dish servings

½ cup dried red lentils

2 tablespoons olive oil

1 medium onion, finely diced

2 cloves garlic, minced

1 teaspoon whole cumin seeds

1 teaspoon yellow mustard seeds

1 teaspoon ground coriander

1 cup uncooked bulgur wheat

3 cups chopped fresh kale, lightly packed

2 cups vegetable stock

½ teaspoon salt

¼ cup pitted and chopped green or black olives

The salmon-colored split legume used in this recipe is usually sold as red lentils at natural food stores or "masoor dal" at Indian markets. It lends a nutty flavor to this earthy dish, which is satisfying enough to make a complete meal.

EACH SERVING PROVIDES
334 calories, 14 g protein, 10 g fat, 17 g dietary fiber, 53 g carbohydrates, 484 mg sodium, 0 mg cholesterol

Pick over the lentils, rinse them well, and drain thoroughly.

Heat the oil in a heavy-bottomed saucepan over medium heat. Add the onion and sauté until lightly browned, about 5 minutes. Add the garlic, cumin seeds, mustard seeds, and coriander, and sauté for another minute. Add the bulgur and drained lentils and stir and sauté for 3 minutes. Add the kale, stock, and salt and bring to a simmer.

Cover tightly, reduce the heat to very low, and cook for 25 minutes. Without disturbing the lid, turn off the heat and allow to stand for 15 minutes.

Transfer the pilaf to a serving dish, toss gently with two forks, and scatter the olives over the top. Serve hot.

Brown Rice and Lentil Pilaf

YIELD: 6 side-dish servings

Simple and nutritious, this delicious side-dish goes well with any Mediterranean-inspired vegetable stew or stir-fry. Leftovers will keep well in the refrigerator, to be enjoyed over the course of two or three days.

EACH SERVING PROVIDES
*264 calories, 7 g protein, 6 g fat,
6 g dietary fiber, 45 g carbohydrates,
183 mg sodium, 0 mg cholesterol*

2 tablespoons olive oil

1 medium yellow onion, diced

¼ teaspoon dried red chili flakes

1 ½ cups uncooked long-grain
   brown rice

⅓ cup dried brown lentils

½ teaspoon salt

1 large bay leaf

Heat the oil over medium heat in a heavy-bottomed saucepan that has a tight-fitting lid, and sauté the onion and chili flakes, stirring frequently, for 5 minutes. Add the rice and lentils, stir, and cook 5 minutes more to toast them slightly. (This toasted flavor adds a lot to the finished dish, so don't skimp on this step.)

Add 3 ¼ cups water, the salt, and the bay leaf and bring to a boil over medium-high heat. Reduce the heat to very low, cover, and cook 50 minutes. Remove the pan from the heat and set aside, without disturbing the lid, for at least 5 minutes.

Transfer the pilaf to a warmed serving dish, tossing with two forks to break up any clumps. Serve hot.

Wild Rice Pilaf

YIELD: 4 side-dish servings

½ cup uncooked wild rice

¼ teaspoon salt

1 tablespoon olive oil

1 tablespoon dry sherry

4 green onions, minced

1 small carrot, finely diced

1 teaspoon dried thyme

2 cups vegetable stock, warmed

1 cup uncooked long-grain brown rice

Wild rice has a very strong and nutty flavor that needs to be tamed a bit. Pairing it with brown rice and vegetables results in a delicious side dish.

EACH SERVING PROVIDES
*292 calories, 7 g protein, 5 g fat,
3 g dietary fiber, 54 g carbohydrates,
146 mg sodium, 0 mg cholesterol*

Rinse the wild rice. Bring 3 cups of water to a boil in a medium saucepan over high heat. Add the salt and wild rice, return to a boil, then reduce the heat to low and cook uncovered for about 45 minutes. Most, if not all, of the water will be absorbed, but if any remains drain the rice.

Meanwhile, heat the olive oil and dry sherry in a medium saucepan over medium heat. Add the green onions, carrots, and thyme. Sauté for about 2 minutes, then add the stock and brown rice. Bring to a boil, cover the pan, reduce the heat to very low, and simmer for 45 minutes. Turn off the heat and allow the pan to stand for at least 5 minutes without disturbing the lid. Transfer to a warmed serving bowl, stir in the cooked wild rice, and serve.

WILD RICE

A traditional Native American food, wild rice is not technically rice, but the seed of a different American wild grass species. It has a nutty taste and chewy texture and provides about twice the protein of other rice, as well as more B vitamins. Although wild rice is expensive, it expands a great deal when cooked. One cup of dry wild rice will yield 3 to 4 cups cooked, enough to serve six people. Added to other rices, it increases their nutritional value and adds interesting texture and flavor.

Toasted Orzo and Rice Pilaf

YIELD: 6 side-dish servings

½ cup dried orzo (4 ounces)

1 tablespoon olive oil

1½ cups uncooked white
   basmati rice

1 clove garlic, minced

½ teaspoon salt

Several grinds black pepper

½ cup minced fresh Italian parsley

3 cups vegetable stock

EACH SERVING PROVIDES
*269 calories, 6 g protein 3 g fat,
1 g dietary fiber, 52 g carbohydrates,
186 mg sodium, 0 mg cholesterol*

Preheat a toaster oven or conventional oven to 400 degrees F. Place the orzo on a baking sheet and toast for about 6 minutes, stirring or shaking the pan occasionally, until the orzo is lightly and evenly browned. Immediately remove it from the baking sheet and set it aside.

Heat the oil in a heavy-bottomed saucepan over medium heat and sauté the rice and garlic for 3 minutes, stirring frequently. Add the toasted orzo, salt, pepper, parsley, and stock and bring to a simmer. Cover, reduce the heat to very low, and cook 25 minutes. Without disturbing the lid, remove from the heat, and allow the pot to stand for 10 minutes.

Transfer the pilaf to a serving dish and toss gently with two forks to break up any clumps and to distribute the ingredients evenly. Serve hot.

Quinoa Pilaf with Sunflower and Sesame Seeds

YIELD: 4 side-dish servings

1 ⅓ cups uncooked quinoa

1 tablespoon olive oil

½ medium white onion, finely diced

1 medium carrot, finely diced

1 rib celery, finely diced

1 clove garlic, minced

½ teaspoon dried thyme

2 cups vegetable stock

2 tablespoon tomato paste

¾ teaspoon salt

Several grinds black pepper

2 tablespoons sunflower seeds, toasted

1 tablespoon sesame seeds, toasted

This yummy pilaf is a simple way to enjoy quinoa, the "heirloom" high-protein grain that hails from the Andes Mountains of Peru. It pairs particularly well with vegetable dishes that have a Mediterranean or Mexican flair.

EACH SERVING PROVIDES

317 calories, 10 g protein, 10 g fat, 5 g dietary fiber, 48 g carbohydrates, 435 mg sodium, 0 mg cholesterol

Fill a large bowl with cold water and add the quinoa. Stir around with your fingers for a moment, then transfer to a fine-mesh strainer. Hold the strainer under the tap and rinse the quinoa with cold water for a few seconds, then set it aside to drain.

Heat the oil in a large saucepan over medium heat and add the onion, carrot, and celery. Stir and sauté for 3 minutes. Add the quinoa, garlic, and thyme, then stir and sauté 3 minutes longer.

Add the stock, tomato paste, salt, and pepper and bring to a boil. Reduce the heat to very low, cover, and simmer 15 minutes. Turn off the heat and let the pot stand, covered, for 10 minutes.

Transfer the pilaf to a serving dish, toss with the sunflower and sesame seeds, and serve.

QUINOA

Quinoa (pronounced "keen-wah"), a native of South America, has been cultivated as a food for hundreds of years. It delivers all eight "essential" amino acids (those our bodies can't produce on their own), making it one of the best protein foods in the plant kingdom. Quinoa also provides a healthy dose of fiber and is a good source of potassium, iron, zinc, and B vitamins.

Oat and Rutabaga Pilaf with Toasted Walnuts

YIELD: 6 side-dish servings

Whole oat groats are a minimally processed form of this popular grain that offers superior fiber and mineral content. The oats give this pilaf a delicious nutty taste, accentuated by the walnuts, and satisfying chewy texture.

EACH SERVING PROVIDES

145 calories, 4 g protein, 7 g fat, 3 g dietary fiber, 17 g carbohydrates, 190 mg sodium, 0 mg cholesterol

1 tablespoon olive oil

½ medium yellow onion, diced

1½ cups peeled and finely diced rutabaga

1 cup uncooked oat groats

1 clove garlic, minced

1 teaspoon dried thyme

1 teaspoon celery seeds

2 cups vegetable stock

½ teaspoon salt

Several grinds black pepper

2 tablespoons minced fresh Italian parsley

⅓ cup raw walnut pieces, toasted (see page 10)

Heat the oil over medium heat in a heavy-bottomed saucepan. Add the onion and rutabaga, and stir and sauté for 3 minutes. Add the oat groats, garlic, thyme, and celery seeds and sauté 3 minutes longer. Add the stock, salt, and pepper and bring to a boil. Cover, reduce the heat to very low, and cook 45 minutes. Without disturbing the lid, turn off the heat and allow the pot to stand for 10 minutes.

Transfer the pilaf to a serving dish, add the parsley and walnuts, and toss gently with two forks to distribute everything evenly. Serve hot.

Barley and Mushroom Pilaf with Toasted Pecans

YIELD: 8 side-dish servings

1 cup whole pearl barley	3 cups sliced button mushrooms
1½ tablespoons olive oil	½ teaspoon salt
½ cup uncooked brown basmati rice	3 cups vegetable stock
1 medium onion, diced	⅛ teaspoon cayenne pepper
2 cloves garlic, minced	¼ cup minced fresh Italian parsley
2 teaspoons rubbed sage	¼ cup chopped pecans, toasted (see page 10)
1 teaspoon dried oregano	

A chewy grain that is hearty and satisfying, barley makes a classic combination with mushrooms and sage. This is a great offering for a holiday or harvest celebration. Natural pearl barley retains some of the bran and is darker in color, nuttier in flavor, and higher in vitamins, minerals, and fiber than the typical white supermarket "pearls."

EACH SERVING PROVIDES
205 calories, 5 g protein, 6 g fat,
6 g dietary fiber, 34 g carbohydrates,
141 mg sodium, 0 mg cholesterol

Wash the barley by covering it with cold water in a bowl and swirling it around with your fingers. Drain and add fresh water a few times, until the rinse water is fairly clear. Set the barley aside in a strainer to drain thoroughly.

Heat the oil in a large, heavy-bottomed saucepan over medium heat. Add the barley, rice, onion, garlic, sage, and oregano, and sauté for about 3 minutes, until the onions begin to brown. Add the mushrooms and salt and sauté 3 more minutes.

Add the stock and cayenne and bring to a simmer. Cover, reduce the heat to very low, and cook for 40 minutes. Without disturbing the lid, turn off the heat and allow to stand for 15 minutes.

Transfer the pilaf to a serving dish. Add the parsley and toss gently with two forks to break up any clumps and distribute the ingredients evenly. Scatter the pecans over the dish and serve hot.

Serrano Chili Rice

YIELD: 6 side-dish servings

This is one of our best-ever rice side dishes. The chili strips make it as pretty as it is delicious. They also add a bit of heat, of course, but not too much.

EACH SERVING PROVIDES
204 calories, 4 g protein, 4 g fat, 2 g dietary fiber, 38 g carbohydrates, 261 mg sodium, 0 mg cholesterol

4 medium fresh serrano chilies

1 tablespoon olive oil

1 teaspoon chili powder

1 ½ cups uncooked long-grain
 brown rice

2 cloves garlic, minced

2 ½ cups vegetable stock

½ cup tomato juice

1 teaspoon dried oregano

½ teaspoon salt

Remove and discard the stems of the chilies and use the edge of a spoon to scrape out the seeds for a milder dish. Sliver the chilies lengthwise and set aside.

Heat the oil in a heavy-bottomed saucepan over medium heat. Add the chili powder and stir it around in the pan for about 30 seconds, then add the rice and stir to coat it with the oil and chili powder. Cook, stirring frequently, for about 2 minutes, to toast the rice a bit. Stir in the garlic, then add the stock, tomato juice, oregano, and salt. Stir to combine and bring to a strong simmer over high heat.

Cover the pan, reduce the heat to very low, and cook 30 minutes. Remove the lid, distribute the chili slivers over the rice, and quickly replace the lid. Cook an additional 5 minutes, then turn off the heat and allow the pot to stand without disturbing the lid for at least 10 minutes before serving.

Transfer the rice to a serving bowl and toss with two forks to distribute the chili strips evenly in the rice. Serve hot.

Fried Brown Rice with Veggies

YIELD: 4 main-dish servings

1 cup vegetable stock

1 tablespoon soy sauce

1 tablespoon canola oil

2 teaspoons dark sesame oil

2 teaspoons grated fresh ginger

¼ teaspoon salt

½ pound button mushrooms

5 green onions

1 medium carrot, finely diced

2 cups diced green cabbage

2 cloves garlic, minced

4 cups cooked brown rice, chilled

1 tablespoon sesame seeds, toasted
(see page 10)

2 tablespoons sunflower seeds,
toasted (see page 10)

In a bowl, combine the stock, soy sauce, canola oil, sesame oil, ginger, and salt. Set aside. Brush or wipe any loose dirt from the mushrooms and slice them thinly. Discard all but 2 inches of the green portion of the onions, trim off the root end, and cut the onions into 1-inch pieces. Set aside.

Preheat a wok or large sauté pan over medium-high heat until very hot and pour in ¼ cup of the stock mixture, along with the carrot and mushrooms. This should begin to sizzle and bubble immediately. Stir-fry 3 minutes. Add the green onions, cabbage, and garlic, plus an additional ¼ cup of the stock mixture. Stir-fry 3 minutes. Add the rice and the remainder of the stock mixture. Use two metal spatulas or spoons to keep the rice moving in the pan as it cooks for 5 minutes.

Transfer the rice to a serving dish and garnish with the sesame and sunflower seeds. Serve hot.

Almost Instant

Fried rice makes a simple and delicious breakfast, lunch, or dinner entrée. The key to preventing the rice from sticking to the pan is to use rice that has been chilled and to keep it moving around. This is not a dish you can walk away from, but once you have the vegetables ready to go, the rest of the process takes only a few minutes.

EACH SERVING PROVIDES
*349 calories, 9 g protein, 11 g fat,
6 g dietary fiber, 55 g carbohydrates,
418 mg sodium, 0 mg cholesterol*

Rice: A Healthy Habit

Rice—be it short-grain or long; brown or white; Indian basmati or Italian arborio—offers versatility and nutrient-rich bulk to the daily diet. It is one of the world's most important agricultural crops. In some countries, rice is such an important staple that the word for "to eat" literally means "to eat rice."

Brown rice contains substantially more nutrients than polished white rice, so make it your first choice. Only the husk has been removed during milling. With the bran intact, it provides more fiber and nutrients than more heavily processed rices. Brown rice is a good source of B vitamins and vitamin E, as well as iron, phosphorus, and magnesium. It provides valuable amino acids—notably lysine—that form a complete protein when combined with the amino acids that are plentiful in cooked legumes or soy products.

Brown rice has a rich, nutty flavor that we enjoy as a regular part of our diets. For variety, we also enjoy basmati and arborio rices, even plain white rice on occasion, especially to accompany an entrée inspired by the cooking of the American South. Wild rice, which is technically a fruit rather than a grain, is another delicious variation on the rice theme.

We often cook extra rice as it is a wonderful leftover to have on hand. For breakfast, simmer it with a bit of water, then top with raisins, walnuts, and soy milk. Add a trickle of maple or rice syrup and you have a delicious, high-energy breakfast. For an almost-instant lunch, reheat the rice with a tablespoon or so of water, then wrap it in a tortilla along with cooked beans and salsa. At dinnertime, stir-fry whatever vegetables you have on hand and serve them over reheated rice.

A BASIC BOWL OF BROWN

A big scoop of hot brown rice becomes a healthful snack or meal-in-a-bowl when combined with other nourishing foods or just your favorite seasonings. Cooking instructions for brown rice are on page 298. Get it simmering on the stove, then consult the list below for some interesting ways to dress it up.

- Steamed vegetables and miso
- Soy sauce, flax oil, sesame seeds, and minced green onion
- Dried Tomato Pesto (page 159) and soy cheese
- Baked Tofu (page 308) and sautéed leafy greens
- Hot miso broth and sautéed shiitake mushrooms

Risotto with Saffron, Peas, and Pine Nuts

YIELD: 6 side-dish servings

6 cups vegetable stock

2 tablespoons olive oil

1 medium white onion, diced

1½ cups uncooked arborio rice

½ cup dry white wine

2 cups fresh or frozen shelled peas
(see NOTE)

½ teaspoon crushed saffron
threads

¼ teaspoon salt

¼ cup pine nuts, toasted (see page
10)

This risotto has a delicate yet distinctive flavor and brilliant yellow color. The peas add a bright color accent and the pine nuts a tasty crunch.

EACH SERVING PROVIDES
*329 calories, 9 g protein, 7 g fat,
5 g dietary fiber, 54 g carbohydrates,
142 mg sodium, 0 mg cholesterol*

Heat the stock in a saucepan until just steaming and keep it handy near the stove. Place the oil in a large saucepan over medium heat and sauté the onion for about 5 minutes, until translucent. Add the rice and stir to coat. Add the wine and cook, stirring, until it is almost completely absorbed. Add the hot stock ½ cup at a time, stirring almost constantly and waiting until the liquid is almost completely absorbed before each addition.

Add the peas, saffron, and salt with the last addition of stock. When almost all of the liquid has been absorbed and the rice is tender, transfer it to a warmed serving bowl and top with the pine nuts.

NOTE: If using frozen peas, place them in a colander and rinse briefly under warm water to melt off any ice crystals before adding them to the dish.

Corn, Sweet Pepper, and Cumin Risotto

YIELD: 6 side-dish servings

Depending on the weather and your level of hunger, this recipe makes a wonderful starter, main dish, or side dish for summer. For the perfect accompaniment, serve a leafy green salad with black beans and a cumin vinaigrette.

EACH SERVING PROVIDES
232 calories, 4 g protein, 5 g fat, 3 g dietary fiber, 41 g carbohydrates, 99 mg sodium, 0 mg cholesterol

2 tablespoons olive oil

¼ cup dry sherry

2 cloves garlic, minced

⅛ teaspoon ground cumin

½ teaspoon chili powder

1 medium red bell pepper, seeded and diced

1 medium green bell pepper, seeded and diced

2 cups fresh or frozen corn kernels (see NOTE)

3 ½ cups vegetable stock

¼ teaspoon salt

1 cup uncooked arborio rice

¼ cup chopped fresh basil leaves

A few grinds black pepper

Heat 1 tablespoon of the oil and 2 tablespoons of the sherry in a skillet over medium-high heat. Add the garlic, cumin, and chili powder, and cook for about a minute. Stir in the bell peppers and corn, cover, and cook 10 minutes, stirring occasionally. Remove from the heat and set aside.

Meanwhile, heat the stock until steaming, stir in the salt, and keep this broth handy near the stove. Place the remaining 1 tablespoon oil and 2 tablespoons sherry in a heavy-bottomed saucepan over medium-low heat. Add the rice and stir to coat. Add the broth, about ½ cup at a time, stirring almost constantly and waiting until the liquid is absorbed before each new addition. Add the sautéed corn mixture with the last ½ cup of broth. When the last addition of broth has been absorbed and the rice is tender, add the basil and pepper. Stir to incorporate and serve immediately.

NOTE: If using fresh corn, you will need about 4 ears to yield 2 cups of kernels. If using frozen corn kernels, place them in a colander and rinse briefly under warm water to melt off any ice crystals before adding them to the dish.

Risotto with Portobello Mushrooms and Radicchio

YIELD: 4 main-dish servings

¾ pound portobello mushrooms (about 4 medium)

3 tablespoons olive oil

3 cloves garlic, minced

2 tablespoons balsamic vinegar

2 tablespoons fresh-squeezed lemon juice

1 teaspoon dried thyme

3 ½ cups vegetable stock

¼ teaspoon salt

1 tablespoon dry sherry

1 cup uncooked arborio rice

½ cup minced fresh Italian parsley

1 cup finely diced radicchio

Portobello mushrooms, which can be found in well-stocked grocery stores, develop a delightful flavor when sautéed with olive oil and balsamic vinegar. The enjoyment of this dish begins with its visual appeal: The risotto is topped with the mushrooms, scarlet radicchio, and bright green parsley.

EACH SERVING PROVIDES
*326 calories, 7 g protein, 11 g fat,
3 g dietary fiber, 49 g carbohydrates,
150 mg sodium, 0 mg cholesterol*

Clean the mushrooms with a brush or soft cloth. Trim and discard the bottoms of the stems, and remove the stems from the caps. Slice the mushroom caps into ¼-inch strips. Cut the stems in half lengthwise, then into quarters or eighths, depending on their size. Heat 2 tablespoons of the oil in a large skillet and add the garlic. Sauté for 1 minute, then add the mushrooms, balsamic vinegar, lemon juice, and thyme. Sauté for about 20 minutes, until the mushrooms are tender and their liquid has reduced. Set aside.

Meanwhile, heat the stock in a saucepan until just steaming, stir in the salt, and keep this broth handy near the stove. Place the remaining 1 tablespoon oil and the sherry in a saucepan over medium heat, then add the rice. Stir for about 1 minute to coat the rice, then add the broth, ½ cup at a time, stirring almost constantly and waiting until the liquid is almost completely absorbed before each new addition.

Add the parsley, reserving 1 tablespoon, with the last ½ cup of broth. When the last addition of broth has been absorbed and the rice is tender, transfer the risotto to a warmed serving bowl. Garnish with the sautéed mushroom strips, diced raw radicchio, and remaining parsley. Serve immediately.

Asparagus Risotto with Oyster Mushrooms and Ginger

YIELD: 6 main-dish servings

A true comfort food, risotto is a good choice for evenings when appetites are strong. This stunning Asian-flavored asparagus and mushroom version would be the perfect meal after a day of working in the spring garden.

EACH SERVING PROVIDES
247 calories, 6 g protein, 3 g fat, 3 g dietary fiber, 46 g carbohydrates, 236 mg sodium, 0 mg cholesterol

5 ½ cups vegetable stock

1 tablespoon soy sauce

1 tablespoon grated fresh ginger

¾ pound fresh asparagus

6 ounces fresh oyster mushrooms

½ tablespoon dark sesame oil

4 cloves garlic, minced

¼ teaspoon dried red chili flakes

½ medium red bell pepper, diced

⅛ teaspoon salt

¼ cup dry sherry

½ tablespoon olive oil

1 ½ cups uncooked arborio rice

1 green onion, minced

Heat the stock, soy sauce, and ginger in a saucepan until just steaming, and keep this broth handy near the stove. Rinse the asparagus spears, break off their tough stem ends, and cut them at a slant into 1-inch pieces. Set aside.

Rinse the mushrooms, pat dry, and chop coarsely. In a heavy-bottomed saucepan, heat the sesame oil over medium heat. Add 2 cloves of the garlic and the red chili flakes and sauté a minute or two. Add the bell pepper, asparagus, and salt. Sauté 3 minutes, stirring frequently. Stir in the mushrooms, add the sherry, and cover the pan. Cook 2 minutes, remove from heat and set aside.

In a large, heavy-bottomed saucepan, heat the olive oil over medium heat. Sauté the remaining 2 cloves of garlic for a minute, then add the rice and stir to coat it with the oil and garlic. Add 1 cup of broth to the rice, and stir gently until the liquid is absorbed. Add the remaining broth ½ cup at a time, stirring almost constantly and waiting until the liquid is absorbed before each new addition. When the last addition of broth has been absorbed and the rice is tender, stir in the asparagus and mushrooms, along with their pan juices. Heat through for 1 minute, then transfer to a warmed serving bowl and garnish with the green onion. Serve immediately.

Cannellini Beans with Peppers and Fennel Seeds over Soft Polenta

YIELD: 6 main-dish servings

3 tablespoons olive oil

4 cloves garlic, minced

1 teaspoon fennel seeds

½ teaspoon dried chili flakes

2 medium red bell peppers, seeded
  and diced

4 cups cooked and drained
  cannellini beans

⅓ cup minced fresh Italian parsley

1 teaspoon minced fresh rosemary
  leaves

½ teaspoon salt

⅔ cup bean cooking liquid or water

⅓ cup dry white wine

¾ cup minced white onion

6 cups vegetable stock

1½ cups uncooked polenta

¼ cup grated soy Parmesan cheese

*Here is another satisfying
country supper. If you have
precooked beans on hand, the
dish comes together quickly.
Grilled baby vegetables and a
tart, leafy salad would round
out this meal nicely.*

EACH SERVING PROVIDES

*351 calories, 13 g protein, 9 g fat,
9 g dietary fiber, 55 g carbohydrates,
627 mg sodium, 0 mg cholesterol*

Heat the oil in a heavy-bottomed sauté pan over medium heat. Stir in the garlic, fennel seeds, and chili flakes, then add the bell peppers and reduce the heat to medium-low. Cook 5 minutes, stirring frequently. Stir in the beans, parsley, rosemary, and ¼ teaspoon of the salt. Add the bean cooking liquid and the wine. Increase the heat to medium-high, and cook 10 minutes, stirring occasionally, to reduce. Turn off the heat and stir in the onion. Cover and set aside until the polenta is ready.

Bring the stock to a boil with the remaining ¼ teaspoon salt in a large saucepan over high heat. Gradually pour in the polenta in a slow, steady stream, whisking constantly. Reduce the heat to medium-low, and gently simmer about 20 minutes, stirring almost constantly with a wooden spoon. The polenta thickens as it cooks. When it begins to pull away from the sides of the pan, it is done. Turn off the heat, and stir in the soy Parmesan cheese.

Reheat the bean mixture, if necessary. Distribute the polenta among six warmed serving bowls. Ladle equal portions of the beans over the polenta and serve immediately.

Creamy French Lentils with Celery Root and Garlic

YIELD: 4 main-dish servings

French lentils, also sold as green or "du Puy" lentils, are smaller and less starchy than the standard brown variety. Prepared in this way, they make a rich and creamy dish that's simply scrumptious. For a hearty dinner, serve it over any plain cooked grain or a baked potato.

EACH SERVING PROVIDES

251 calories, 18 g protein, 2 g fat, 16 g dietary fiber, 44 g carbohydrates, 415 mg sodium, 0 mg cholesterol

4 cups vegetable stock

2 cups plain soy milk

1 cup dried French lentils

2 cups peeled and diced celery root (about 1 medium)

2 cloves garlic, minced

1 bay leaf

Several grinds black pepper

½ teaspoon salt

3 tablespoons minced fresh Italian parsley

In a large saucepan over medium heat, combine the stock, soy milk, lentils, celery root, garlic, bay leaf, and pepper. Bring to a simmer, reduce the heat to low, and cook 35 to 40 minutes, until the lentils are tender and the mixture is moderately thick. Purée the beans slightly with an immersion blender or transfer half of the mixture to a blender jar and purée, then return it to the pan. Stir in the salt and parsley and serve hot.

LENTILS

Lentils date back to biblical times and are still a staple in parts of the Middle East and India. Like other legumes, they are high in fiber and amino acids, low in fat and calories, and deliver a substantial amount of folic acid. This nutrient is particularly important for pregnant women, because a folic acid deficiency has been linked to serious birth defects, notably spina bifida. Higher folic acid levels also offer protection against cervical cancer.

Whole Pinto Beans with Minced Vegetables

YIELD: 6 side-dish servings

2 medium fresh serrano chilies

1 tablespoon canola oil

1 medium red or yellow bell
  pepper, seeded and minced

1 medium white onion, minced

1 medium carrot, finely diced

1 medium zucchini, finely diced

2 cloves garlic, minced

2 tablespoons dried oregano

4 cups cooked and drained pinto
  beans

4 canned pear tomatoes, chopped

¼ cup bean cooking liquid or
  vegetable stock

½ cup minced fresh cilantro

This dish makes a great accompaniment to tacos or enchiladas. The beans also make a delicious casual lunch, eaten steaming hot from a deep bowl with warmed corn tortillas on the side. Take the time to chop all the vegetables very finely, since this is what makes the dish so pretty and so delicious.

EACH SERVING PROVIDES
*219 calories, 11 g protein, 3 g fat,
13 g dietary fiber, 39 g carbohydrates,
18 mg sodium, 0 mg cholesterol*

Remove and discard the stems of the chilies, and use the edge of a spoon to scrape out the seeds for a milder dish. Finely mince the chilies and set them aside.

Heat the oil in a deep, heavy-bottomed skillet over medium heat. Add the chilies, bell pepper, onion, carrot, zucchini, garlic, and 1 tablespoon of the oregano. Sauté for 10 minutes, stirring frequently. It is fine if the vegetables brown a bit. Add the beans, tomatoes, and bean cooking liquid or vegetable stock and cook, stirring frequently, 10 minutes. Stir in the cilantro and the remaining tablespoon of oregano. Serve hot.

HANDLING HOT CHILIES

Hot chilies deliver a delicious spicy note to many ethnic dishes, but beware their burn. If you have delicate skin, wear latex gloves when cutting fresh chilies. Even thick-skinned people should take care not to touch their eyes or other sensitive areas for a few hours after handling chilies. When selecting chilies at the market, look for glossy color, smooth skin, and a healthy-looking stem. Withered chilies with blackened stems are past their prime. Store fresh chilies in the refrigerator, loosely wrapped in plastic.

White Beans with Tomatoes and Chipotle Chilies

YIELD: 6 side-dish servings

These white beans have a moist texture and distinctive smoky, slightly spicy flavor. Combine them on a menu with your favorite enchiladas or tacos, or eat them as is, with corn tortillas on the side. The chipotle chilies "en adobo" come in a can and are available at Mexican specialty markets.

EACH SERVING PROVIDES
168 calories, 9 g protein, 3 g fat, 7 g dietary fiber, 28 g carbohydrates, 199 mg sodium, 0 mg cholesterol

1 cup dried small white beans

2 medium fresh tomatoes (about 1 pound)

1 tablespoon canola oil

1 medium white onion, diced

4 cloves garlic, minced

1 tablespoon chipotle chilies en adobo, minced

½ teaspoon salt

Rinse and sort the beans and place them in a stockpot. Cover with hot water and soak for about 2 hours. Drain off the soaking water, and add fresh water to cover. Bring to a boil over high heat, reduce the heat to medium, and cook 45 minutes to 1 hour, until the beans are tender. Add more water, if necessary, during the cooking time to keep the beans barely covered.

Meanwhile, bring a few cups of water to a boil in a small saucepan, and fill a large bowl or basin with ice water. Blanch the tomatoes for 2 to 3 minutes (see page 5). Remove and discard the stem ends and cut the tomatoes in half crosswise. Gently squeeze over the sink to remove the juicy seed pockets, then dice the tomatoes and place them in a bowl.

Heat the oil over medium heat in a heavy-bottomed skillet, and add the onion and garlic. Sauté for 2 to 3 minutes, until the onion begins to soften. Stir in the tomatoes, chili, and salt. Increase the heat to medium-high, and continue to cook for about 5 minutes, stirring occasionally, until the sauce has reduced somewhat. If you are still waiting for the beans to cook, turn off the heat, cover the pan, and set aside.

When the beans are tender and their liquid has reduced to a thick sauce consistency, stir in the tomato sauce. Serve hot.

Black Bean Patties
with Tomatillo Sauce

YIELD: 6 appetizer servings

The sauce

¾ pound fresh tomatillos
(9 medium)

¼ teaspoon salt

½ teaspoon chili powder

¼ teaspoon ground cumin

2 tablespoons vegetable stock

2 tablespoons arrowroot powder

The patties

2 cups cooked and drained black
beans

¼ cup raw unsalted pumpkin seeds

3 tablespoons canned diced mild
green chilies

1 clove garlic, minced

¼ teaspoon salt

Try serving this simple and economical do-ahead dish as a summer appetizer or lunch entrée. The cooked beans are combined with seasonings and ground pumpkin seeds to create delicious patties that require no further cooking. If you serve corn chips on the side, any leftover sauce will be devoured as a dip by your guests.

EACH SERVING PROVIDES
*139 calories, 8 g protein, 4 g fat,
4 g dietary fiber, 21 g carbohydrates,
143 mg sodium, 0 mg cholesterol*

To make the sauce: Remove and discard the husks of the tomatillos, rinse, and place in a saucepan with the salt. Cover with water and bring to a boil. Reduce the heat and simmer about 10 minutes, until they are very tender. Drain, then place in a food processor with the chili powder and cumin. Pulse to combine. Add stock and arrowroot then purée until smooth. Transfer to a small pan, and cook over medium heat 2 to 3 minutes, until the mixture thickens. Do not overcook, or the arrowroot will get gummy. Set aside.

Meanwhile, place the beans in a bowl and mash them thoroughly to form a thick paste. Place the pumpkin seeds in a small food processor or blender and finely chop them to a coarse crumb consistency. Add them to the beans along with the chilies, garlic, and salt. Stir until well combined. (If the paste seems too dry, moisten it with 1 to 2 tablespoons of water.)

Form the bean mixture into 3-inch patties and place them on a large platter. (If you are not going to serve the patties right away, cover the platter with plastic wrap so they do not dry out.) Transfer the tomatillo sauce to a serving bowl and allow guests to spoon the sauce over the patties.

10
Sautés and Stir-Fries

Curried Potato and Bell Pepper Sauté

Stir-Fry of Cauliflower, Tomatoes, Orange, and
   Fresh Basil

Okra with Olives, Tomatoes, Herbs, and Lemon

Artichoke, Squash, and Red Bell Pepper Sauté

Winter Squash with Tomatoes, Chard, and Pine Nuts

Sauté of Many Peppers and Garbanzo Beans

Provençal Black-Eyed Peas with Asparagus

Tofu and Vegetables with Ginger and Coconut Milk

Spicy Chinese Eggplant with Tempeh and Baby Corn

Mushroom-Tempeh Sauté with Sage

A hot wok or skillet sets the stage for a host of easy and easygoing entrées from around the world. Food added to a hot pan—with or without a drizzle of oil—cooks quickly and develops a delicious caramelized flavor.

A simple sauté is the first step in many complex dishes, but in this chapter the sauté stands alone. Put on a pot of rice or another favorite grain, then spend a few minutes prepping veggies, and you're almost there. One of the great attractions of these dishes is that they are quick and easy to prepare.

Sautéing is one of the most basic and universal cooking styles. Since fat has the capacity to hold and transport flavor compounds in foods, beginning a soup or sauce with a vegetable sauté adds a satisfying depth to the taste of the finished dish. Strictly speaking, though, oil is not a necessity. Many lowfat cooks prefer to use stock or wine as a sauté medium. If you own high-quality nonstick cookware, you may find you can accomplish a good sauté without any liquid at all.

If you do use oil, as we do in most of the recipes in this chapter, it is important to choose one that is slow to oxidize. Monounsaturated oils such as olive and canola are perfect for the job, as they remain relatively stable even at high temperatures. Polyunsaturated oils, like safflower and corn, are less stable and readily produce free radicals when heated.

The recipes that follow are all simple yet satisfying main dishes. Call on them when you crave a casual, hearty, and healthy meal.

Curried Potato and Bell Pepper Sauté

YIELD: 6 side-dish servings

Golden Yukon potatoes are especially delicious in this dish, but you may use yellow Finn or white boiling potatoes instead. Serve with grilled or baked tofu strips, if desired, and a leafy green salad.

EACH SERVING PROVIDES
144 calories, 3 g protein, 5 g fat, 3 g dietary fiber, 21 g carbohydrates, 181 mg sodium, 0 mg cholesterol

1 pound yellow Finn potatoes, scrubbed and diced

2 tablespoons olive oil

2 tablespoons dry sherry

1 medium yellow onion, diced

3 cloves garlic, minced

1 red bell pepper, seeded and diced

1 green bell pepper, seeded and diced

1 tablespoon grated fresh ginger

1 teaspoon ground cumin

1 teaspoon ground turmeric

½ teaspoon ground coriander

¼ teaspoon cayenne pepper

¼ cup vegetable stock

2 tablespoons fresh-squeezed lemon juice

1 tablespoon soy sauce

6 lemon wedges (optional)

Place the potatoes in a pot and cover with water. Bring to a boil and cook for 5 to 6 minutes, until barely fork-tender. Drain and set aside.

Meanwhile, heat the oil and sherry over medium heat in a wok or sauté pan and add the onion and garlic. Sauté for about 3 minutes, then add the peppers, ginger, cumin, turmeric, coriander, and cayenne. Stir to coat with the spices, then add the potatoes, stock, lemon juice, and soy sauce. Cook for 2 more minutes, stirring frequently, then serve piping hot. Pass lemon wedges, if desired.

Stir-Fry of Cauliflower, Tomatoes, Orange, and Fresh Basil

YIELD: 4 main-dish servings

1 cup uncooked brown basmati rice	4 cups chopped cauliflower
½ teaspoon salt	½ cup fresh-squeezed orange juice
1 can (12 ounces) tomatillos	½ pound fresh pear tomatoes (about 3 medium), diced
1 tablespoon canola oil	
1 tablespoon dark sesame oil	½ cup chopped fresh basil leaves
1 medium yellow onion, diced	1 tablespoon arrowroot powder

This fresh, light dish highlights a vegetable from the cruciferous family that seldom gets star billing. The smoky sesame oil and peppery basil are great with the orange juice. Start the rice cooking before you start the stir-fry, and everything should be done about the same time.

Place the rice in a large, fine-mesh strainer and rinse under running water for about 30 seconds. Set aside to drain thoroughly. Bring 2 cups of water to a boil, add ¼ teaspoon of the salt and the drained rice, then return to a boil over high heat. Cover the pan, reduce the heat to very low, and simmer 45 minutes. Turn off the heat, and allow the pot to stand, without disturbing the lid, for at least 5 minutes before serving.

Meanwhile, drain the tomatillos, and cut each one in half. Set aside in a bowl.

Heat the canola and dark sesame oils in a wok over medium-high heat and add the onion. Sauté 2 to 3 minutes, until it begins to soften, then stir in the cauliflower and orange juice. Cover and cook 5 minutes, lifting the lid to stir once midway through. Stir in the tomatoes, tomatillos, basil, and remaining ¼ teaspoon salt. Reduce heat to medium-low, cover, and cook 3 to 5 minutes, stirring occasionally, until the cauliflower is just fork-tender.

Meanwhile, combine 2 tablespoons of water with the arrowroot powder in a jar, cover, and shake to dissolve. When the cauliflower is tender, add the arrowroot mixture and stir for a moment or two, until the liquid thickens. Spoon over cooked rice and serve hot.

EACH SERVING PROVIDES
*346 calories, 9 g protein, 9 g fat,
9 g dietary fiber, 61 g carbohydrates,
648 mg sodium, 0 mg cholesterol*

Okra with Olives, Tomatoes, Herbs, and Lemon

YIELD: 6 main-dish servings

Almost Instant

We invented this succulent stewed okra dish in the spirit of Greek cooking. As befits a rustic dish, the olives are added whole. To avoid any unpleasant surprises, let your diners know the pits are there. We recommend serving this with Toasted Orzo and Rice Pilaf (page 170) and a tart, leafy salad—but you can substitute plain cooked rice or another pilaf, if you wish.

EACH SERVING PROVIDES

*216 calories, 4 g protein, 17 g fat,
3 g dietary fiber, 18 g carbohydrates,
1571 mg sodium, 0 mg cholesterol*

1 can (28 ounces) whole pear
  tomatoes
1 pound fresh okra
1 tablespoon olive oil
1 medium white onion, diced
1/2 teaspoon dried red chili flakes
4 cloves garlic, minced

1 teaspoon dried oregano
1/2 teaspoon dried thyme
1/2 teaspoon dried rosemary
1/4 teaspoon salt
1 cup calamata olives, unpitted
1/2 teaspoon minced fresh lemon
  peel

Drain the juice from the can of tomatoes, and reserve it for another use, such as soup or a juice drink. Coarsely chop the tomatoes and set them aside in a bowl. Rinse the okra pods and pat them dry with a tea towel. Use a paring knife to slice off most of the stem portion, leaving the base of the pods intact. Cut the okra pods in half crosswise at a slant, and set them aside in a bowl or colander.

Heat the oil in a heavy-bottomed skillet over medium heat and sauté the onion and chili flakes for 5 minutes, stirring frequently. Add the tomatoes, garlic, oregano, thyme, rosemary, and salt, then stir in the okra. Bring to a simmer, reduce the heat to medium-low, cover, and cook 10 minutes. Remove the lid and stir in the whole olives and the lemon peel. Replace the lid, and cook until the okra is very tender but not mushy, about 5 minutes. Serve hot.

Artichoke, Squash, and Red Bell Pepper Sauté

YIELD: 4 main-dish servings

1 cup brown basmati rice

½ teaspoon salt

1 medium red bell pepper

3 tablespoons dry sherry

1 cup diced yellow crookneck squash

2 cloves garlic, minced

1 teaspoon dried rosemary, crushed

½ teaspoon dill seed

A few grinds black pepper

1 can (8.5 ounces drained weight) quartered artichoke hearts

2 tablespoons fresh-squeezed lemon juice

4 lemon wedges

This is one of the simplest and most succulent dishes we know. Dill and rosemary give it an unmistakable Mediterranean flavor.

EACH SERVING PROVIDES
225 calories, 6 g protein, 2 g fat,
3 g dietary fiber, 45 g carbohydrates,
449 mg sodium, 0 mg cholesterol

Place the rice in a large, fine-mesh strainer and rinse under running water for about 30 seconds. Set aside to drain. Bring 2 cups of water to a boil, add ¼ teaspoon of the salt and the drained rice, then return to a boil over high heat. Cover, reduce the heat to very low, and simmer 45 minutes. Turn off the heat, and allow the pot to stand, without disturbing the lid, for at least 5 minutes before serving.

Cut the pepper in half lengthwise and discard the stem, seeds, and white membrane. Chop the pepper into 1-inch cubes. Heat the sherry with 3 tablespoons of water in a heavy-bottomed skillet that has a tight-fitting lid. When it begins to simmer, stir in the pepper, squash, garlic, rosemary, dill seed, remaining ¼ teaspoon salt, and black pepper. Cover, reduce the heat to medium-low, and cook 5 minutes. Remove the lid and cook, stirring frequently, 2 to 3 minutes, until the pepper is tender and there is still a little liquid remaining in the pan.

Meanwhile, drain the artichoke hearts, and remove any choke material you find. When the pepper is cooked, add the artichokes and lemon juice, and stir gently as you cook for about 2 minutes longer. You want the artichokes to just heat through. Serve hot over rice, garnished with lemon wedges.

Winter Squash with Tomatoes, Chard, and Pine Nuts

YIELD: 6 main-dish servings

This succulent dish has great color, texture, and flavor—not to mention antioxidant power. We call for bulgur here, but you may serve it over rice or another favorite grain instead.

EACH SERVING PROVIDES
241 calories, 9 g protein, 5 g fat,
11 g dietary fiber, 46 g carbohydrates,
444 mg sodium, 0 mg cholesterol

1 ½ cups uncooked bulgur wheat

¼ cup minced fresh Italian parsley

¾ teaspoon salt

1 ¼ pounds acorn squash (1 medium)

1 pound fresh chard

1 tablespoon olive oil

3 cloves garlic, minced

2 teaspoons dried oregano

¼ teaspoon dried red chili flakes

1 large red onion, coarsely chopped

1 ¼ cups vegetable stock

½ pound fresh pear tomatoes (about 3 medium), diced

2 tablespoons balsamic vinegar

2 tablespoons pine nuts, toasted (see page 10) and chopped

Bring 3 cups of water to a boil in a saucepan, and add the bulgur, parsley, and ¼ teaspoon of the salt. Bring back to a boil, cover, reduce the heat to very low, and cook 20 minutes. Turn off the heat and allow the pot to stand for at least 5 minutes without disturbing the lid.

Meanwhile, cut the acorn squash in half and discard the seeds. Slice the squash into wedges and peel them, then coarsely chop the squash. Set aside. Carefully wash the chard. Remove and slice the stems and set aside. Don't dry the chard leaves; tear them into large pieces and set aside in a colander.

Heat the olive oil in a large, heavy-bottomed skillet over medium heat. Sauté the garlic, oregano, and chili flakes for 1 minute, then add the squash, onion, chard stems, and remaining ½ teaspoon salt. Sauté, stirring frequently, 5 minutes. Add the stock, cover, and cook 7 minutes. Remove the lid and stir in the tomatoes. Cook, uncovered, for 5 minutes.

Meanwhile, place the chard leaves in a saucepan over medium-low heat, cover, and cook until well wilted, about 5 minutes. Make a bed of the chard on a warmed platter. Add the vinegar to the squash mixture and gently stir. Spoon the squash evenly over the chard and sprinkle with the pine nuts. Serve hot.

WINTER SQUASH

The nutrition picture for winter squash varies from type to type, but most winter squashes are excellent sources of complex carbohydrates, vitamin C, beta carotene, and fiber. Botanically speaking, the pumpkin is a summer squash, but it more closely resembles the winter varieties in flavor, nutrition, and preparation.

If a recipe calls for chopped pumpkin or winter squash, use a heavy knife to cut a deep slit in the skin to hold the knife in place, then use lots of elbow grease or a mallet to force the knife all the way through the squash, cleaving it in two. Scrape out the seeds and cut the squash into wedges or large chunks. These are easily peeled using a sharp knife, then the flesh can be chopped according to recipe directions.

Sauté of Many Peppers and Garbanzo Beans

YIELD: 4 main-dish servings

Make this dish in the late summer, when peppers are at their best. The colors satisfy the senses nearly as much as the aroma and flavors do. Serve in a bowl, with garlic bread and a leafy salad to round out the meal.

1 cup uncooked brown rice

⅛ teaspoon plus ¼ teaspoon salt

1 large yellow bell pepper

1 large red bell pepper

1 large green bell pepper

2 tablespoons olive oil

½ teaspoon dried chili flakes

3 cloves garlic, minced

1 medium yellow onion, diced

1 teaspoon dried oregano

A few grinds black pepper

¼ cup minced fresh Italian parsley

¼ cup dry sherry

2 cups cooked and drained garbanzo beans

EACH SERVING PROVIDES
448 calories, 13 g protein, 11 g fat, 12 g dietary fiber, 73 g carbohydrates, 216 mg sodium, 0 mg cholesterol

Bring 2 cups of water to a boil in a saucepan with a tight-fitting lid. Add the rice and ⅛ teaspoon of the salt and return to a boil. Tightly cover the pan, turn the heat down to very low, and cook the rice for 45 minutes. Turn off the heat and allow the pot to stand, without disturbing the lid, for at least 5 minutes before serving.

Meanwhile, cut the bell peppers lengthwise into quarters. Discard the stems, seeds, and white membrane, and slice across each section to create uniform ¼-inch strips. Heat the oil in a wok or sauté pan over medium heat, add the chili flakes and garlic, and stir for a moment before adding the peppers, onion, oregano, remaining ¼ teaspoon salt, and black pepper.

Sauté for 10 minutes, stirring frequently, then increase the heat to medium-high and add the parsley, sherry, and garbanzo beans. Cook until the beans are hot, about 2 more minutes. Transfer to a warmed bowl and serve immediately over hot rice.

Provençal Black-Eyed Peas with Asparagus

YIELD: 4 main-dish servings

1 pound fresh asparagus

1 ½ tablespoons olive oil

1 medium white onion, diced

1 medium red bell pepper, diced

2 cups cooked and drained
  black-eyed peas

2 cloves garlic, minced

1 tablespoon Herbes de Provence
  (page 310)

1 large bay leaf

½ teaspoon salt plus a pinch

Several grinds black pepper

3 cups vegetable stock

2 teaspoons arrowroot powder

2 tablespoons minced fresh Italian
  parsley

1 ½ cups uncooked couscous

This light and delicious entrée is a great way to celebrate spring. When asparagus is out of season, you can use green beans or diced zucchini instead.

EACH SERVING PROVIDES

*457 calories, 19 g protein, 7 g fat,
12 g dietary fiber, 82 g carbohydrates,
326 mg sodium, 0 mg cholesterol*

Snap off and discard the tough stem ends of the asparagus, and cut the spears crosswise at a slant into 1-inch pieces.

Heat the olive oil over medium heat and sauté the onion and bell pepper until they begin to brown, about 6 minutes, stirring frequently. Add the asparagus, black-eyed peas, garlic, Herbes de Provence, bay leaf, ½ teaspoon of the salt, black pepper, and ¾ cup of the stock. Bring to a strong simmer, then cover and cook until the asparagus is barely tender, about 5 to 8 minutes, depending on its thickness. Stir once or twice during cooking.

Dissolve the arrowroot powder in a tablespoon of water in a small bowl. When the asparagus is tender, stir in the arrowroot mixture, and cook for another 30 seconds or so, until the sauce thickens. Stir in the parsley.

Meanwhile, bring the remaining 2 ¼ cups of stock to a boil. Stir in the couscous and the remaining pinch of salt. Cover the pan and remove from the heat. Let it sit with the lid undisturbed for 5 minutes, then transfer to a serving dish and fluff with a fork. Serve the asparagus hot over mounds of hot couscous.

Tofu and Vegetables with Ginger and Coconut Milk

YIELD: 6 main-dish servings

10 ounces firm tofu

1 ½ cups uncooked brown basmati rice

½ teaspoon salt

1 pound fresh green beans

4 green onions

½ cup coconut milk

½ cup vegetable stock or water

2 tablespoons minced fresh cilantro

1 tablespoon grated fresh ginger

1 tablespoon soy sauce

2 teaspoons arrowroot powder

1 tablespoon dark sesame oil

2 cloves garlic, minced

¾ pound yellow summer squash (about 2 medium), coarsely chopped

Dice the tofu into ½-inch cubes and wrap them in a clean tea towel to absorb excess moisture. Set aside.

Place the rice in a large, fine-mesh strainer and rinse under running water for about 30 seconds. Set aside to drain thoroughly. Bring 3 cups of water to a boil, add ¼ teaspoon of the salt and the drained rice, and return to a boil over high heat. Cover the pan, reduce the heat to very low, and simmer 45 minutes. Turn off the heat, and allow the pot to stand, without disturbing the lid, for at least 5 minutes before serving.

Meanwhile, remove and discard the stems and strings of the green beans, and cut in half at a slant. Discard all but 2 inches of the onions' green portion, then slice them at a slant into 1-inch pieces. In a bowl, combine the coconut milk, stock, cilantro, ginger, soy sauce, and arrowroot powder. Set aside.

In a wok or heavy sauté pan, heat the oil over medium-high heat. Add the garlic and stir a moment, then add the beans, squash, onions, and remaining ¼ teaspoon salt. Cook, stirring almost constantly, about 5 minutes, then add the tofu and sauté 5 minutes longer, stirring frequently. Give the coconut milk mixture a good stir and add it to the pan. Cook just 1 minute, until heated through and slightly thickened. Serve immediately, over scoops of hot basmati rice.

Spicy Chinese Eggplant with Tempeh and Baby Corn

YIELD: 4 main-dish servings

We like to serve this scrumptious eggplant dish over hot brown or basmati rice, with steamed broccoli on the side. This isn't a scorcher, but if you have low tolerance for spicy foods, you may omit the dried red chili flakes and still enjoy a full-flavored dish.

EACH SERVING PROVIDES

421 calories, 16 g protein, 11 g fat, 7 g dietary fiber, 64 g carbohydrates, 485 mg sodium, 0 mg cholesterol

1 ¼ cups uncooked brown rice

¼ teaspoon plus ⅛ teaspoon salt

2 large Chinese or Japanese eggplants (about ¾ pound)

2 tablespoons canola oil

1 medium white onion, halved then sliced

6 ounces soy tempeh, diced

2 cloves garlic, minced

¼ teaspoon dried red chili flakes

1 ½ cups vegetable stock

1 tablespoon grated fresh ginger

1 tablespoon maple syrup

1 tablespoon soy sauce

6 ounces frozen or canned baby corn (see NOTE)

1 tablespoon arrowroot powder

2 tablespoons minced fresh cilantro

Bring 2 ½ cups of water to a boil in a saucepan, then add the rice and ¼ teaspoon of the salt. Bring back to a boil, cover, reduce the heat to very low, and cook 45 minutes. Turn off the heat and allow the pot to stand with its lid undisturbed for at least 5 minutes before serving.

Meanwhile, wash and dry the eggplants, then cut them crosswise at an angle into 1-inch slices. Heat the oil in a wok or other large, high-walled pan over medium-high heat until the oil is sizzling hot. Add the eggplant, onion, and remaining ⅛ teaspoon salt, and use a spatula to toss the vegetables frequently as they cook for 4 minutes. The eggplant and onion should be browning nicely.

Add the tempeh, garlic, and chili flakes and continue to cook and toss for 4 more minutes. Add the stock, ginger, maple syrup, and soy sauce and bring to a simmer. Stir in the baby corn and return to a simmer, then cook 2 minutes.

Meanwhile, in a small bowl, dissolve the arrowroot powder in 2 tablespoons of cold water. When the simmering time is up, re-stir the arrowroot mixture, add it to the pan, and stir and cook for about 30 seconds, until the sauce has thickened. Immediately turn off the heat. Stir in the cilantro and serve hot over scoops of brown rice.

NOTE: If using frozen baby corn, place it in a colander and rinse briefly under warm water to melt off any ice crystals before adding it to the dish. If using canned corn, rinse and drain the corn before adding it.

ARROWROOT

Arrowroot is a fine white powder ground from a tropical tuber. We usually prefer it to cornstarch as a thickening agent because the latter is a highly processed substance. Arrowroot will thicken a hot liquid almost instantly and should not be cooked longer than a minute or so, or it may turn gummy. Cornstarch, on the other hand, needs to cook for a few minutes in order to do the job of thickening.

Mushroom–Tempeh Sauté with Sage

YIELD: 4 main-dish servings

This is an earthy dish that fills the kitchen with wonderful aromas. You may substitute about 1 teaspoon rubbed dried sage if fresh is not available.

EACH SERVING PROVIDES

360 calories, 17 g protein, 11 g fat, 4 g dietary fiber, 44 g carbohydrates, 399 mg sodium, 0 mg cholesterol

1 cup uncooked brown basmati rice

¼ teaspoon salt

½ pound button mushrooms, sliced

2 tablespoons olive oil

1 medium yellow onion, diced

2 cloves garlic, minced

8 ounces soy tempeh, cubed

¼ cup dry sherry

1 tablespoon soy sauce

2 tablespoons minced fresh sage

⅛ teaspoon ground allspice

Place the rice in a large, fine-mesh strainer and rinse under running water for about 30 seconds. Set aside to drain thoroughly. Bring 2 cups of water to a boil, add ¼ teaspoon of the salt and the drained rice, and return to a boil over high heat. Cover the pan, reduce the heat to very low, and simmer 45 minutes. Turn off the heat, and allow the pot to stand, without disturbing the lid, for at least 5 minutes before serving.

Meanwhile, brush or wipe any loose dirt from the mushrooms and slice them. Heat the oil in a wok over medium-high heat and add the mushrooms, onion, and garlic. Sauté until the mushrooms have released their liquid, about 7 to 10 minutes, then add the tempeh, sherry, and soy sauce. Continue to cook for 10 minutes, stirring frequently, then stir in the sage and allspice. Stir to combine and cook for about 3 more minutes. Serve hot with the steamed rice.

11
Baked and Grilled Entrées

Bell Peppers Stuffed with Dill-Seasoned Rice

Zucchini Stuffed with Mushroom-Quinoa in Tomato
Coulis

Baked Rice with Black Beans, Corn, Tomatoes, and
Epazote

Enchiladas with Green Chili Sauce

Eggplants Stuffed with Rice, Tomatoes, Herbs, and
Pine Nuts

Lasagnette with Cinnamon-Cumin Tomato Sauce

Eggplant Enchiladas with Almond Mole

Curried Bulgur Casserole with Garbanzo Beans

Polenta and Onion Casserole with Fennel Seed and
Soy Mozzarella

Summer Squash, Black Beans, and Rice en Papillote

Tofu and Mushrooms Misoyaki en Papillote

Pizza with Baked Garlic and Grilled Eggplant

Pizza with Zucchini, Artichokes, and Soy Mozzarella

Broiled Portobello Mushroom "Pizzas"

Grilled Sweet Pepper, Summer Squash, and Tempeh
Fajitas

Skewers of Baby Squash and Tempeh in Pineapple-
Ginger Marinade

Skewers of Tofu, Cherry Tomatoes, and Sweet
Peppers

The recipes in this chapter span the seasons. In winter we lean toward baking. Slow-cooked food is deeply satisfying, and the warmth of the oven keeps the kitchen cozy. Conversely, in summer we are drawn to our flower-festooned backyards during the long, light evenings, and the patio grill becomes the heart of our outdoor kitchens.

Turning on the oven and setting a timer is a simple task, but successful grilling takes some practice. There is a mystique surrounding grilling, but this very simple cooking method has been around since the discovery of fire. Become familiar with the unique features of your grill, stay close by so food doesn't overcook, and you'll soon have the skill mastered. Then it's likely to become one of your favorite styles of cooking.

Both charcoal and gas grills work well, so when purchasing a grill, simply choose what suits your needs and your budget. Charcoal grills, while inexpensive, are fairly messy and take considerable time to preheat. Gas grills, on the other hand, preheat almost instantly, and some brands provide handy features like cutting boards and multilevel racks. If you live in a climate that allows for a lot of outdoor cooking, a well-designed gas grill on wheels might be a great investment. Countertop and stovetop grills are also widely available, allowing you to enjoy the look and flavor of grilled foods even in inclement weather.

Grilling times are affected by the condition of the coals (if using a coal grill) and the distance of the grill rack from the heat source. Our grilled recipes were tested on a gas grill with the rack 5 inches from the heat. You may have to adjust the cooking times to suit your particular grill.

We present a wide range of recipes in this chapter, including stuffed vegetables, foods cooked in parchment paper, skewers, pizzas, and casseroles. Try one of these dishes soon, whatever the weather.

Bell Peppers Stuffed with Dill-Seasoned Rice

YIELD: 4 main-dish servings

Choose any color peppers to stuff with this deliciously seasoned rice. You may cut them in half and serve them as a side dish for eight, or as an entrée.

EACH SERVING PROVIDES

566 calories, 19 g protein, 14 g fat, 10 g dietary fiber, 95 g carbohydrates, 888 mg sodium, 0 mg cholesterol

2 tablespoons olive oil

2 tablespoons dry sherry

1 medium yellow onion, chopped

1 cup uncooked long-grain white rice

½ pound fresh pear tomatoes (about 3 medium), sliced

¼ cup dried currants

¼ cup minced fresh dill

1 teaspoon salt

½ teaspoon Chinese Five-Spice Powder (page 311)

4 large green bell peppers

1 cup firm silken tofu

2 tablespoons plain soy or rice milk

2 cloves garlic, minced

4 rounds whole wheat pita bread

2 tablespoons pine nuts, toasted (see page 10)

Place the oil and sherry in a large sauté pan or skillet over medium heat. Add the onion and sauté 3 minutes. Add 2 cups of water, the rice, tomatoes, currants, dill, ¾ teaspoon of the salt, and five-spice powder. Cover, increase the heat to high, and bring to a boil. Reduce the heat to very low and cook for 20 minutes. Turn off the heat and set aside without disturbing the lid.

Preheat the oven to 350 degrees F. Cut out the stem ends of the peppers, and discard the seeds and white membranes. Place the peppers upright in a shallow baking dish. Spoon equal portions of rice into the pepper halves, reserving any leftover rice. Pour hot water into the dish to measure about ½ inch up the sides of the peppers. Cover and bake 45 minutes.

Meanwhile, place the tofu, soy milk, garlic, and remaining ¼ teaspoon salt in the blender and purée. Set aside in a serving dish. Wrap the pita bread in foil and place it in the oven for 10 minutes just before serving.

Remove the peppers from the oven and place two halves on each plate, along with a portion of the reserved rice, if any. Garnish with the pine nuts, passing the tofu sauce and pita bread.

Zucchini Stuffed with Mushroom–Quinoa in Tomato Coulis

YIELD: 6 main-dish servings

EACH SERVING PROVIDES

350 calories, 12 g protein, 16 g fat, 10 g dietary fiber, 45 g carbohydrates, 151 mg sodium, 0 mg cholesterol

½ ounce dried shiitake mushrooms

1 tablespoon olive oil

2 tablespoons dry sherry

2 cloves garlic, minced

1 medium yellow onion, diced

1 medium red bell pepper, seeded and diced

½ pound fresh button mushrooms

1 teaspoon dried oregano

⅛ teaspoon salt

1 cup uncooked quinoa

3 pounds zucchini (about 6 large)

1½ cups Tomato Coulis (see page 312)

½ cup slivered raw almonds, toasted (see page 10)

Place the shiitake mushrooms in a bowl and pour 2 cups of hot water over them. Cover and steep for 30 minutes. Lift the mushrooms from their soaking liquid, reserving the liquid. Chop the mushrooms finely and set them aside. Strain the liquid through a very fine-mesh strainer or a paper coffee filter that has been moistened with water (otherwise it will soak up some of the mushroom liquid). Set aside.

Meanwhile, brush or wipe any loose dirt from the mushrooms and slice them thinly. Heat the oil and sherry in a large skillet over medium heat and add the garlic, onion, and bell pepper. Sauté for 2 minutes, stirring occasionally, then add the button mushrooms, oregano, and salt. Stir to combine, then cover the skillet and cook until the mushrooms have released their liquid, about 10 minutes. Add the chopped shiitakes and 2 tablespoons of water, and continue to sauté for 5 minutes, stirring occasionally.

Meanwhile, place the quinoa in a bowl in the sink and thoroughly rinse it by rubbing the grains together with your hands. Drain it thoroughly in a fine-mesh strainer. Measure the reserved mushroom soaking liquid and add water to yield 2 cups. Place this stock in a pan and bring to a boil. Add the quinoa, cover, and reduce the heat to very low. Cook for 15 minutes, then turn off the heat and allow the pan to stand for at least 5 minutes without disturbing the lid. Stir the quinoa into the mushroom mixture and set aside.

Preheat the oven to 350 degrees F. Cut the zucchinis in half lengthwise. Using a melon baller or spoon, scrape out and discard the center seed area, leaving a ¼-inch-thick shell. Spoon half of the tomato coulis over the bottom of a glass baking dish. Fill the zucchini halves with equal amounts of the quinoa mixture, reserving any that is leftover, and arrange the stuffed zucchini in the baking dish. Spoon the remaining coulis over the top. Sprinkle with the toasted almonds. Cover the pan and bake for 30 minutes. To serve, reheat the reserved quinoa and mound a portion on each plate. Place two zucchini halves on top of the mound and drizzle with the sauce from the baking dish.

Baked Rice with Black Beans, Corn, Tomatoes, and Epazote

YIELD: 8 main-dish servings

This hearty dish could serve as a casual main course, with the addition of warm corn tortillas and a green salad, or as a side dish with tacos or enchiladas. The recipe makes enough for a crowd—perfect for a south-of-the-border party. If there are any leftover, they may be stored in a covered container in the refrigerator and enjoyed over the course of a few days.

EACH SERVING PROVIDES

273 calories, 9 g protein, 3 g fat, 6 g dietary fiber, 52 g carbohydrates, 153 mg sodium, 0 mg cholesterol

2 medium fresh serrano chilies

1 teaspoon cumin seeds

1 tablespoon canola oil

1 medium white onion, diced

1 ½ cups uncooked long-grain brown rice

2 cloves garlic, minced

2 teaspoons dried oregano

1 can (28 ounces) whole tomatoes

1 ⅔ cups vegetable stock

2 cups fresh or frozen corn kernels (see NOTE)

2 cups cooked and drained black beans

½ cup chopped fresh epazote leaves (or 1 tablespoon dried)

½ teaspoon salt

If you have a high-walled Dutch oven that can go directly from the stovetop to the oven, use it for this dish. Otherwise, use a stockpot or large saucepan for the first steps, then transfer the mixture to a lightly oiled 3-quart covered casserole dish for baking.

Remove and discard the stems of the chilies and scrape out the seeds for a milder dish. Finely mince the chilies and set them aside. Crush the cumin seeds thoroughly with a mortar and pestle and set them aside.

Preheat the oven to 375 degrees F. Heat the oil in a Dutch oven or stockpot over medium heat. Add the onion and sauté, stirring frequently, for 3 to 4 minutes, until it turns translucent. Stir in the rice, then add the garlic, oregano, and cumin seeds; sauté 3 to 4 minutes. Add the undrained tomatoes and the stock, then stir in the corn, beans, chilies, epazote, and salt.

Bring the mixture to a strong simmer over high heat, then cover the pan (or transfer the mixture to the covered casserole dish) and bake for 45 minutes. Remove from the oven and allow to stand at room temperature for at least 10 minutes without disturbing the lid. Serve hot.

NOTE: If you are using fresh corn, you will need about 4 medium ears to yield 2 cups of kernels. If you are using frozen corn, rinse it under warm water for a moment to melt any ice crystals before adding it to the dish.

EPAZOTE

This odiferous yet delicious roadside weed grows prolifically in Mexico and is an important culinary herb in Meso-American cuisine. It is easy to grow north of the border, as well. The plants are frost sensitive, though, so move them indoors during the winter or collect their seeds and replant in the early spring. Epazote is responsible for the authentic flavor of many traditional dishes. If you can't find or grow fresh epazote, you may be able to locate the dried herb in Mexican groceries or well-stocked supermarkets. Use it sparingly, as its flavor is quite potent.

Enchiladas with Green Chili Sauce

YIELD: 4 main-dish servings

These tasty enchiladas go well with Serrano Chili Rice (page 174) and Salsa Fresca (page 309), but any side dish rice and store-bought salsa could also be served.

EACH SERVING PROVIDES
*592 calories, 34 g protein, 29 g fat,
8 g dietary fiber, 54 g carbohydrates,
1030 mg sodium, 0 mg cholesterol*

The sauce

2 cans (4 ounces each) mild green
  chilies, drained

1 cup chopped fresh cilantro

2 cups vegetable stock

½ cup raw unsalted pumpkin seeds

½ medium yellow onion, diced

3 cloves garlic, minced

1 tablespoon chili powder

1 teaspoon ground coriander

1 teaspoon brown rice syrup

¼ teaspoon salt

Several grinds black pepper

The enchiladas

8 flour tortillas

12 ounces frozen firm tofu,
  defrosted and patted dry

1 tablespoon chili powder

1 tablespoon ground cumin

2 tablespoons canola oil

8 ounces Monterey Jack–style soy
  cheese, grated

Preheat the oven to 350 degrees F.

First, make the sauce: In a blender or food processor, combine the green chilies, cilantro, stock, pumpkin seeds, onion, garlic, chili powder, coriander, rice syrup, salt, and pepper. Purée, then transfer the mixture to a heavy-bottomed skillet and bring it to a simmer over medium-high heat. Reduce the heat to medium-low and simmer gently, stirring frequently, for about 15 minutes.

Meanwhile, warm the tortillas by heating them one at a time over a gas burner or in a hot skillet for about 30 seconds, turning once or twice during this time. Wrap them in a clean tea towel to keep them warm.

Spread ½ cup of the sauce over the bottom of a 9 × 13-inch glass baking dish. Set aside. Leave the remaining sauce in the skillet.

Crumble the tofu into a bowl and toss with the chili powder and cumin. Heat the oil over medium-high in a separate skillet. Add the tofu mixture and stir and cook for about 5 minutes. Remove from the pan and set aside.

Working with one tortilla at a time, briefly immerse it in the sauce remaining in the skillet to coat it lightly. Place the tortilla flat on a plate and, with your hands, place about ⅛ of the tofu and ⅛ of the cheese in a narrow heap across the tortilla, slightly off-center. Loosely roll up the tortilla around the filling, and place it seam side down in the dish.

When all of the tortillas have been filled and placed in the dish, pour the remaining sauce over them, including any that has collected on the plate. Cover and bake for 20 minutes, then allow to stand at room temperature for 5 minutes before serving.

Eggplants Stuffed with Rice, Tomatoes, Herbs, and Pine Nuts

YIELD: 4 main-dish servings

Eggplant is widely used in Mediterranean cooking, and it is frequently stuffed. We enjoy this dish often during late summer and early autumn, when garden eggplants are at their peak.

EACH SERVING PROVIDES

222 calories, 8 g protein, 6 g fat,
9 g dietary fiber, 39 g carbohydrates,
340 mg sodium, 0 mg cholesterol

2 medium eggplants (about 2 pounds)

1 can (14½ ounces) diced tomatoes

1½ cups cooked brown or white rice

¼ cup pine nuts

4 green onions, minced

2 cloves garlic, minced

1 teaspoon dried oregano

1 teaspoon dried marjoram

1 teaspoon dried basil

1 teaspoon dried rosemary

½ teaspoon salt

A few grinds black pepper

Preheat the broiler. Wash and dry the eggplants and cut them in half lengthwise. Place the eggplants cut side up 4 inches under the broiler for 10 minutes. They will char a bit on top. Remove them from the oven, and set aside to cool for a few minutes. Turn off the broiler, and preheat the oven to 375 degrees F.

Drain the tomatoes, reserving their juice for another use, such as soup or a juice drink. In a large bowl, combine the rice with the tomatoes, pine nuts, green onions, garlic, oregano, marjoram, basil, rosemary, salt, and pepper. When the eggplants are cool enough to handle, use a sharp knife to cut out the eggplant flesh, leaving a ½-inch-thick shell. Chop it and add it to the rice mixture, stirring to combine well. Mound the filling into the eggplant shells and place the stuffed eggplants on a baking sheet.

Bake for 35 to 40 minutes, until the eggplant shells are fork-tender in their thickest part. Serve immediately.

Lasagnette with Cinnamon–Cumin Tomato Sauce

YIELD: 6 main-dish servings

8 ounces lasagnette noodles

1 can (28 ounces) peeled and
    crushed pear tomatoes

½ medium yellow onion, chopped

3 cloves garlic, minced

½ teaspoon ground cinnamon

½ teaspoon chili powder

½ teaspoon ground cumin

⅛ teaspoon dry mustard

⅛ teaspoon ground cloves

1 pound firm tofu

½ cup plain soy or rice milk

¼ cup minced fresh basil leaves

¼ teaspoon olive oil

¼ cup soy Parmesan cheese

Lasagnette noodles, or "mafalda," are narrow, long ribbons resembling skinny lasagna noodles. Look for them in well-stocked supermarkets or Italian specialty stores. Bake this casserole in a large glass dish or, for a particularly pretty presentation, in individual oval baking dishes, decreasing the cooking time by five minutes.

EACH SERVING PROVIDES
*269 calories, 14 g protein, 7 g fat,
3 g dietary fiber, 41 g carbohydrates,
355 mg sodium, 0 mg cholesterol*

Bring several quarts of water to a boil for the pasta. Use a large pan so the noodles have room to move around for even cooking. Cook the pasta until almost al dente, then lay flat on tea towels to drain. It will finish cooking in the oven.

Meanwhile, purée the tomatoes, onion, and garlic in a blender or food processor. Pour into a medium saucepan and add the cinnamon, chili powder, cumin, mustard, and cloves. Cook over medium-low heat for about 10 minutes, stirring frequently.

Preheat the oven to 350 degrees F. Rinse the tofu and pat it dry, then crumble it into a bowl and stir in the soy milk and basil. Rub a 9 × 9 × 2-inch pan with the olive oil, and spread half the sauce evenly over the bottom. Layer with half the noodles, then spread them evenly with the tofu mixture. Top with the remaining noodles and sauce. Sprinkle with the Parmesan cheese, cover, and bake 20 minutes. Uncover and bake 5 minutes longer. Allow to cool for about 5 minutes before serving.

Eggplant Enchiladas with Almond Mole

YIELD: 6 main-dish servings (12 enchiladas)

Though the Mexican word "mole" translates loosely to "sauce" or "mixture," most of us think immediately of the traditional mole poblano, a dark and rich sauce made with sweet as well as savory spices, nuts, and cocoa. This out-of-the-ordinary mole is based on almonds seasoned with anise and allspice—really delicious with the eggplant filling. This dish is fit for a very special occasion.

EACH SERVING PROVIDES
412 calories, 12 g protein, 18 g fat, 11 g dietary fiber, 57 g carbohydrates, 261 mg sodium, 0 mg cholesterol

1 medium green bell pepper

2 pounds eggplant (about 2 medium)

1 1/2 tablespoons canola oil

1 1/2 medium white onions, diced

1 medium carrot, diced

6 cloves garlic, minced

1/2 teaspoon salt

1 teaspoon cumin seeds

1 1/4 cups whole blanched almonds, toasted (see page 10)

1/4 cup golden raisins, chopped

12 standard-sized corn tortillas

2 medium dried ancho chilies

2 1/2 cups vegetable stock

4 canned pear tomatoes

4 whole allspice berries, or 1/8 teaspoon ground allspice

1/2 teaspoon anise seeds

1/2 teaspoon coriander seeds

Preheat the oven to 350 degrees F.

Dice the bell pepper, discarding the stems, seeds, and white membranes. Set aside. Slice off and discard the stem ends of the eggplants and, without peeling them, cut the eggplant into 1/4-inch cubes. Heat 1 tablespoon of the oil over medium heat in a large heavy-bottomed skillet. Sauté 1 diced onion, along with the bell pepper and carrot, for 3 minutes, then add the eggplant, 4 cloves of the minced garlic, and 1/4 teaspoon of the salt. Crush the cumin seeds thoroughly with a mortar and pestle, and stir them into the eggplant. Sauté, stirring frequently, 10 to 15 minutes, until the eggplant and carrot are tender. Meanwhile, finely chop 1/4 cup of the toasted almonds. Stir the raisins and chopped almonds into the eggplant mixture and set aside.

Warm the tortillas by heating each one over a gas burner or in a hot skillet for about 30 seconds, turning once or twice during this time. Wrap them in a clean tea towel to keep them warm. Now make the sauce: Heat a dry heavy-bottomed skillet or cast-iron griddle over medium-high heat. Use your hands to tear the chilies into large pieces, discarding the seeds and stems. Place the chili pieces on the hot griddle, and toast for 1 to 2 minutes, occasionally pressing down on them with a spatula. They will blister a bit and begin to lighten in color. Turn them over and toast the other side briefly.

When the chilies are lightly toasted, place them in a blender. Add the remaining 1 cup toasted almonds, along with the stock, tomatoes, and the remaining diced ½ onion, 2 cloves minced garlic, and ¼ teaspoon salt. Coarsely crush the allspice berries and anise seeds with a mortar and pestle and add them to the blender. Blend on high until the mixture is thoroughly puréed. Heat the remaining ½ tablespoon oil in a heavy-bottomed skillet and add the purée. Cook over medium heat, stirring frequently, for 5 minutes. Set aside near your work surface.

Spread ½ cup of the sauce evenly over the bottom of a 9 × 13-inch glass or ceramic baking dish and place it on your work surface, along with a clean dinner plate. If necessary, reheat the remaining sauce until it is steaming hot but not simmering, and place it near your work surface. Set the eggplant filling nearby.

Working with 1 tortilla at a time, briefly immerse it in the sauce remaining in the skillet to coat it lightly. Place it on the plate and place a portion of the eggplant filling in a narrow, even heap across the tortilla, slightly off center. Loosely roll up the tortilla around the filling, and place the enchilada seam side down in the baking dish.

When all of the tortillas have been filled, rolled, and placed snugly in the baking dish, pour the remaining sauce over them, including any that has collected on the plate. Cover and bake 15 to 20 minutes, then allow to stand 5 minutes before serving.

Curried Bulgur Casserole with Garbanzo Beans

YIELD: 6 main-dish servings

The fragrance satisfies long be-fore this dish is taken from the oven. Warm and creamy in texture, it is sure to become a family favorite. For a variation, you may use cilantro in place of the parsley.

1 ½ cups uncooked bulgur

2 tablespoons olive oil

1 medium red bell pepper, seeded and diced

3 green onions, minced

1 cup fresh or frozen shelled peas (see NOTE)

2 cups cooked garbanzo beans, drained

1 tablespoon curry powder

¼ teaspoon salt

¾ cup plain soy or rice milk

½ cup minced fresh parsley

6 fresh lemon wedges (optional)

EACH SERVING PROVIDES
*293 calories, 12 g protein, 7 g fat,
13 g dietary fiber, 49 g carbohydrates,
126 mg sodium, 0 mg cholesterol*

Bring 3 cups water to a boil in a saucepan over high heat. Stir in the bulgur, reduce the heat to low, cover, and simmer for about 20 minutes. Remove from the heat and set aside until needed.

Meanwhile, preheat the oven to 350 degrees F. Heat the olive oil in a skillet over medium heat. Add the bell pepper and onions and sauté for about 2 minutes. Stir in the peas, garbanzo beans, curry powder, and salt and cook 1 minute, then stir in the soy milk and parsley.

Combine the garbanzo mixture with the cooked bulgur in a large bowl. Fold the ingredients together until well blended, then spoon the mixture into a 1 ½-quart casserole dish. Cover and bake for 20 minutes. Serve hot—with lemon wedges, if desired.

NOTE: If using frozen peas, place them in a colander and rinse briefly under warm water to melt off any ice crystals before adding them to the dish.

Polenta and Onion Casserole with Fennel Seed and Soy Mozzarella

YIELD: 8 main-dish servings

2 teaspoons fennel seed

¼ teaspoon dried red chili flakes

1 tablespoon plus ¼ teaspoon olive oil

4 cloves garlic, minced

3 medium red onions

⅛ teaspoon salt

1 can (28 ounces) whole tomatoes

2 tablespoons capers, drained and minced

¼ teaspoon granulated garlic

A few grinds black pepper

1½ cups uncooked polenta

1 cup grated soy mozzarella cheese (about 4 ounces)

The preparation of this dish requires two burners and the oven, but it is not difficult. The resulting casserole is warming, rich, and delicious—a great meal to share with friends in front of a roaring fire.

EACH SERVING PROVIDES
*196 calories, 8 g protein, 4 g fat,
5 g dietary fiber, 31 g carbohydrates,
316 mg sodium, 0 mg cholesterol*

Use a mortar and pestle or small food processor to coarsely grind the fennel seed with the dried chili flakes. In a large heavy-bottomed skillet, heat 1 tablespoon of the olive oil over medium heat. Add the ground spices and the garlic and stir for a minute, then add the onions and salt. Sauté, stirring frequently, about 5 minutes, until the onions are soft. Add the tomatoes, including the juice, and the capers. Bring to a simmer, reduce the heat to medium-low, and cook 15 minutes, stirring occasionally. Break up the large pieces of tomato with a wooden spoon as the mixture cooks.

Meanwhile, preheat the oven to 375 degrees F. Rub a 2-quart casserole dish with the remaining ¼ teaspoon olive oil and set aside.

Bring 4 cups of water to a boil in a saucepan, along with the granulated garlic and pepper. Reduce to medium, and pour the polenta into the water in a slow, steady stream, whisking constantly. Cook, whisking almost constantly to prevent sticking, until the mixture is very thick, then whisk in ½ cup cold water and bring back to a bubble. Stir in half the cheese and pour into the oiled dish. Top with the onion mixture and the remaining cheese. Bake for 25 minutes, then allow to cool for 5 minutes before serving.

Summer Squash, Black Beans, and Rice en Papillote

YIELD: 4 main-dish servings

This satisfying dish is perfect for early autumn, when the thin-skinned squashes, like zucchini and crookneck, are plentiful. Parchment paper dishes make for an interesting presentation, and cleanup is minimal.

EACH SERVING PROVIDES

508 calories, 19 g protein, 7 g fat, 11 g dietary fiber, 96 g carbohydrates, 134 mg sodium, 0 mg cholesterol

2 cups uncooked brown basmati rice

1 teaspoon ground cumin

1 teaspoon chili powder

½ teaspoon granulated garlic

⅛ teaspoon salt

2 cups cooked and drained black beans

1 pound summer squash, diced

½ medium red bell pepper, thinly sliced

½ small red onion, diced

¼ cup minced fresh cilantro

¼ cup raw unsalted pumpkin seeds

4 pieces cooking parchment, about 15 × 18 inches each

Place 2 cups of water in a medium saucepan over high heat and bring to a boil. Add the rice, cover, reduce the heat to very low, and cook for 45 minutes. Remove from the heat and allow to stand for at least 5 minutes without disturbing the lid.

Meanwhile, place the cumin, chili powder, garlic, and salt in a small bowl and stir to combine. Arrange the cooked rice, black beans, squash, bell pepper, onion, cilantro, and pumpkin seeds in separate containers near your work surface.

Preheat the oven to 400 degrees F. Fold each piece of parchment in half and crease it to create a rectangle. Use scissors to cut each rectangle into a large half-heart shape. Open out the hearts and place ¼ of the rice, beans, squash, bell pepper, onion, cilantro, and pumpkin seeds on each piece of parchment, building a mound near the center of the crease. Sprinkle equal portions of the spice mix over the top, then drizzle about a tablespoon of water over each portion.

Close the heart so that the edges of the paper meet. Beginning at the round end, fold over about ½-inch of the paper and crease sharply. Work your way around the shape of the heart, folding in the edges and creasing sharply in overlapping pleats. Gently twist the pointy end to seal everything tightly in the paper packet. Be careful not to tear the paper, or you will have to begin again with a fresh piece. Repeat this process with the remaining packets, then place them in a single layer on a baking sheet, and bake for 15 minutes.

Transfer the packets to warmed serving plates and instruct your guests to pinch and tear the paper to release the aromatic steam. The contents may then be lifted out onto the plate and the paper removed from the table and discarded.

Tofu and Mushrooms Misoyaki en Papillote

YIELD: 4 main-dish servings

Cooking in parchment paper creates an entrée that is marvelously moist and aromatic, with all the juices intact. This special dish can be served with simple steamed rice or with boiled soba noodles that have been tossed with a few drops each of sesame oil, soy sauce, and rice vinegar.

EACH SERVING PROVIDES
*217 calories, 14 g protein, 10 g fat,
4 g dietary fiber, 23 g carbohydrates,
329 mg sodium, 0 mg cholesterol*

1 large carrot

12 button mushrooms

8 fresh or reconstituted shiitake mushrooms

1 pound firm tofu

¼ cup vegetable stock

2 tablespoons dark miso

2 tablespoons mirin or dry sherry

2 clove garlic, minced

2 teaspoons freshly grated ginger

2 teaspoons sesame seeds, toasted (see page 10)

4 pieces cooking parchment, about 15 × 18 inches each

1 medium white onion, cut into 8 wedges

Peel or scrub the carrot and cut it crosswise at a slant into ½-inch pieces. Brush or wipe any loose dirt from the button mushrooms and quarter them. Remove the stems of the shiitakes and cut the caps into ¼-inch slices. Cut the tofu into 12 equal-sized pieces. Set these ingredients aside separately.

In a small bowl, stir together the vegetable stock, miso, mirin, garlic, and ginger, until the miso is dissolved. Grind the sesame seeds in a spice grinder or with a mortar and pestle and add to the mixture. Stir to combine well and set aside.

Preheat the oven to 400 degrees F.

Fold each piece of parchment paper in half and crease to create 9 × 12-inch rectangles. Use scissors to cut each folded rectangle into a half-heart shape. Open out the hearts and distribute the tofu pieces evenly among the hearts, positioning them near the center of each crease. Drizzle each piece of tofu with a little of the miso mixture as you go.

Top the tofu with the button and shiitake mushrooms and nestle a few chunks of carrot and 2 wedges of the onion alongside each portion. Drizzle the remaining miso mixture evenly over the contents of the packets.

Close the hearts so the edges of the paper meet. Beginning at the rounded end, fold over about ½ inch of the paper and crease sharply. Work your way around the shape of the heart, folding in the edges and creasing sharply in overlapping pleats. Gently twist the pointy end to seal everything tightly in the paper packet. Be careful not to tear the paper, or you will have to begin again with a fresh piece. Repeat this process with the remaining packets.

Place the packets in a single layer on a baking sheet, and bake for 15 minutes. Transfer the packets to warmed serving plates and instruct your guests to pinch and tear the paper to release the aromatic steam. The contents may then be lifted out onto the plate and the paper removed from the table and discarded.

MISO

Miso is a flavoring paste made from fermented soybeans. It has been a staple in Japanese cooking for centuries, lending its salty richness to soups and sauces. Miso is rich in B-vitamins, including a form of B_{12}, which is generally lacking in the vegan diet. Like other naturally fermented foods, it contains beneficial microorganisms that help with healthy digestion. In fact, a heaping teaspoon of miso stirred into a cup of hot water and slowly sipped will often relieve an upset stomach.

Pizza with Baked Garlic and Grilled Eggplant

YIELD: 4 main-dish servings

The vegetables for this pizza need to be lightly coated with oil before they are grilled. If you have olive oil in a sprayer, all the better because you can distribute it evenly and will need less. You can vary the vegetables according to the season—try this pizza in the early spring with grilled asparagus and steamed spinach.

EACH SERVING PROVIDES

171 calories, 3 g protein, 8 g fat, 5 g dietary fiber, 24 g carbohydrates, 239 mg sodium, 0 mg cholesterol

1 12-inch pizza crust (page 302)
2 tablespoons yellow cornmeal
1 medium bulb garlic
1 medium eggplant (about 1 pound)
2 tablepoons olive oil

¼ teaspoon salt
A few grinds black pepper
1 medium red bell pepper
1 medium green bell pepper
½ pound fresh red or yellow tomatoes, sliced

Make a pizza crust according to the directions on page 302 or use a commercially prepared one. Place the uncooked crust on a round baking pan or a baker's peel that has been sprinkled with cornmeal. Set aside.

Preheat the oven to 450 degrees F, or heat the grill to high—about 500 degrees F. Rub the loose paper husks off the garlic, then wrap it in foil or place it in a garlic baking dish. Bake in the oven or on the grill until very soft when gently squeezed, about 25 minutes.

Remove and discard the stem end of the eggplant and cut the eggplant lengthwise into ¾-inch thick slices. Using some of the oil, spray or brush one side of the eggplant slices and sprinkle lightly with salt and pepper. Place the slices oiled side down on the grill or oiled side up under a broiler. Cook for about 5 minutes, until nicely browned. Lightly spray or brush the other side of the slices with oil, lightly salt and pepper, turn, and cook for 5 minutes, until the eggplant is nicely browned and soft. Set aside.

Remove and discard the stems, seeds, and white membrane of the bell peppers. Cut them into thick strips, lightly oil the strips, and place them on the grill or under the broiler. Cook for several minutes, until tender and slightly charred. Turn to cook the other side.

Break apart the individual cloves of baked garlic and squeeze out the paste directly onto the pizza crust. Spread around to coat evenly, leaving about a 1-inch border. Arrange the grilled eggplant and bell pepper slices in a decorative pattern on top of the garlic. Top with the tomato slices.

Transfer the pizza to the hot grill and close the lid or place the pizza in the hot oven. Bake until the crust is crisp and golden brown, about 10 to 12 minutes for a freshly made crust or 5 minutes for a precooked one. Serve immediately.

Pizza with Zucchini, Artichokes, and Soy Mozzarella

YIELD: 4 main-dish servings

We prepare this pizza any time of the year, but especially enjoy it during the summer, cooked on the outdoor grill.

EACH SERVING PROVIDES

341 calories, 12 g protein, 11 g fat, 9 g dietary fiber, 53 g carbohydrates, 553 mg sodium, 0 mg cholesterol

1 12-inch pizza crust (page 302)

2 tablespoons yellow cornmeal

1 can (14 ounces) water-packed artichoke hearts

2 tablespoons olive oil

2 cloves garlic, minced

1 tablespoon dried oregano

1 medium zucchini

2 ounces soy mozzarella cheese, grated

¼ red onion, thinly sliced

A few grinds black pepper

Prepare a pizza crust from the recipe on page 302, or use a commercially prepared crust. Place the uncooked crust on a round pizza pan or a baker's peel that has been sprinkled with cornmeal. Preheat a coal or gas grill to high, about 500 degrees F, or preheat the oven to 450 degrees F.

Drain the artichoke hearts, lightly pat them dry, and cut out and discard any "choke" portion. Coarsely chop them and place in a bowl with the oil, garlic, and oregano. Remove the ends of the zucchini and cut it into very thin oblong slices.

Distribute half of the soy mozzarella over the pizza crust, leaving about a 1-inch border. Arrange the onion and zucchini slivers over the top, then spread on the artichoke mixture to evenly cover the other vegetables. Top with the remaining cheese and the pepper.

Transfer the pizza to the hot grill and cover the grill, or place the pizza in the hot oven. Bake until the crust is crisp and golden brown, about 10 to 12 minutes for a freshly made crust or 5 minutes for a precooked one. Serve immediately.

Broiled Portobello Mushroom "Pizzas"

YIELD: 4 main-dish servings

4 medium portobello mushrooms, of uniform large size

½ teaspoon salt

¼ teaspoon ground black pepper

1 cup diced fresh or canned tomatoes, drained

½ cup finely chopped fresh spinach leaves

2 tablespoons minced fresh basil leaves

2 cloves garlic, minced

½ teaspoon dried oregano

½ cup coarse dry bread crumbs

½ cup shredded soy cheese

1½ tablespoons olive oil

Preheat the broiler. Brush or wipe both sides of the mushrooms with a mushroom brush or moistened paper towel to remove any bits of soil. Use half the salt and pepper to lightly season the caps of the mushrooms, and place the mushrooms cap side up on a broiler pan. Place the pan about 6 inches from the heat source and cook until lightly browned and tenderized, about 8 to 10 minutes.

Meanwhile, combine the tomatoes, spinach, basil, garlic, oregano, and remaining salt and pepper in a mixing bowl. Toss to combine well and set aside. In a separate bowl, combine the bread crumbs, soy cheese, and olive oil. Toss to combine well and set aside.

When the mushroom caps are ready, turn them over and spoon the tomato filling evenly into the caps. Top evenly with the bread crumb mixture. Return the pan to the broiler and cook until the cheese has melted and the crumbs are lightly browned, about 4 to 5 minutes. Serve immediately.

This simple and delicious entrée will go well with your favorite grain pilaf and a tart, leafy salad. If weather permits, cook the mushrooms on the grill for stupendous results. You can even make the sauce and crumb mixtures ahead of time, wrap everything tightly, and do the assembly and cooking at a campground.

EACH SERVING PROVIDES
*127 calories, 5 g protein, 7 g fat,
1 g dietary fiber, 13 g carbohydrates,
496 mg sodium, 0 mg cholesterol*

The Thrill of the Grill

Grilling is one of the oldest forms of cooking known to humankind, and it is still enjoyed by many people. In warm weather, the grill can become an outdoor kitchen, bringing you and your family and friends out into the garden to enjoy the long, light evenings.

With a host of convenient gas grills available at reasonable prices, you no longer need to wait for charcoal to heat up or guess at the correct heat setting. Just turn the dial to the desired temperature and become familiar with how the flame looks at the different settings. Some grills come with a built-in temperature gauge.

If you have no interest in investing in a gas grill, you can use the standard charcoal type with good results. Regardless of what type of grill you use, the following tips apply.

- Set up the grill in an open area away from the house, and don't attempt to move the grill once it is hot

- Preheat a charcoal grill for about 20 minutes before cooking; preheat a gas grill for about 10 minutes

- Hardwood chips, which add unique flavors, are available for use with gas or charcoal grills; soak them in water 15 minutes before adding to the fire

- Lightly brush vegetables with oil so they do not stick to the grill

- Avoid wearing a flowing garment when cooking on a grill

- Use long-handled utensils and wear heavy-duty mitts

- Do not cook on a charcoal fire in high winds

- If using charcoal, make sure the ashes are completely cold before discarding them

- The grill is easiest to clean when hot; scrape the rack with a stiff wire brush to remove any charred food particles before storing

Grilled Sweet Pepper, Summer Squash, and Tempeh Fajitas

YIELD: 6 main-dish servings

8 ounces soy tempeh

2 tablespoons dark sesame oil

2 tablespoons unseasoned rice vinegar

2 tablespoons soy sauce

2 cloves garlic

3 medium yellow onions

1½ pounds assorted sweet peppers, such as bells and anaheims

1 pound small to medium golden and green zucchini

2 tablespoons canola oil

12 fajita-sized tortillas, warmed

This is a great recipe for a casual dinner party. Serve salsa and guacamole to accompany the fajitas, with ears of grilled corn and steamed brown rice on the side. We cook this in a cast-iron skillet that can go directly on the grill, but a pan made especially for grill cooking would also work well. Feel free to substitute another summer squash for the zucchini.

EACH SERVING PROVIDES
444 calories, 16 g protein, 17 g fat, 6 g dietary fiber, 61 g carbohydrates, 636 mg sodium, 0 mg cholesterol

Cut the tempeh into strips about ½ inch wide and 3 inches long. Whisk together the sesame oil, vinegar, soy sauce, and garlic in a shallow dish and add the tempeh strips. Gently toss to coat, cover, and marinate in the refrigerator for about an hour.

Heat the grill to medium-high. Peel the onions and cut them crosswise into ¾-inch slices. Cut the peppers in half lengthwise, discarding the stems, seeds, and white membranes. Cut the halves into strips about ¾-inch wide. Trim off the stem ends of the zucchini and quarter them lengthwise.

Place onions, peppers, and zucchini in a bowl with the oil and toss to coat. Place onions on the grill and cook about 20 minutes, until tender and slightly charred. Simultaneously, grill the peppers and squash about 15 minutes, until tender and slightly charred.

Meanwhile, heat each tortilla on the grill or over a gas flame for several seconds, turning with tongs to lightly char. Wrap in a tea towel to keep warm.

Heat a cast iron skillet on the grill or over high heat on the stovetop. Add the tempeh and its marinade and sizzle and cook for 5 minutes. Add the grilled vegetables and serve from the hot skillet, passing the tortillas and condiments of choice.

Skewers of Baby Squash and Tempeh in Pineapple–Ginger Marinade

YIELD: 4 main-dish servings

Baby squashes make a great presentation here, but you can substitute slices of larger squash. The pineapple juice, cilantro, and fresh ginger make a great flavor combination.

EACH SERVING PROVIDES
*376 calories, 13 g protein, 5 g fat,
6 g dietary fiber, 69 g carbohydrates,
540 mg sodium, 0 mg cholesterol*

¼ cup unseasoned rice vinegar

¼ cup mirin

¼ cup unsweetened pineapple juice

¼ cup minced fresh cilantro

2 tablespoons grated fresh ginger

1 ½ tablespoons soy sauce

2 cloves garlic, minced

16 baby summer squashes

8 ounces soy tempeh, cut into 1-inch cubes

1 cup uncooked long-grain brown rice

¼ teaspoon salt

1 large red bell pepper

1 ½ cups peeled and cubed pineapple (see NOTE)

8 wooden skewers, soaked in water for 10 minutes

Combine the vinegar, mirin, pineapple juice, cilantro, ginger, soy sauce, and garlic in a large shallow dish. Add the squash and tempeh, toss gently to coat, cover, and refrigerate. Allow to marinate for about 1 hour.

Preheat the grill to medium-high. Place 2 ¼ cups of water in a medium saucepan over high heat and bring to a boil. Add the rice and salt, cover, reduce the heat to very low, and cook for about 35 minutes. Turn off the heat and allow to stand for at least 5 minutes before serving.

Meanwhile, cut the bell pepper in half lengthwise. Remove and discard the stem, seeds, and white membrane. Cut the pepper into about 1 ½-inch-square pieces. Just before grilling, evenly distribute the squashes, tempeh, red bell pepper, and pineapple among the skewers, arranging in an alternating pattern. Reserve the remaining marinade. Place the skewers on the grill and cook for 4 minutes, then turn and grill about 4 minutes longer. Mound the rice into the center of each serving plate. Place two skewers atop each serving. Strain the reserved marinade and pass it as a sauce.

NOTE: Fresh pineapple is best in this dish, but drained canned pineapple chunks may be substituted. Buy a brand that has no added sugar, if possible.

Skewers of Tofu, Cherry Tomatoes, and Sweet Peppers

YIELD: 4 main-dish servings

Fresh, juicy cherry tomatoes and crisp sweet peppers make this skewered tofu dish as visually pleasing as it is delicious.

EACH SERVING PROVIDES

319 calories, 15 g protein, 10 g fat, 4 g dietary fiber, 48 g carbohydrates, 447 mg sodium, 0 mg cholesterol

1 pound firm tofu

¼ cup apple cider vinegar

2 tablespoons unsulfured molasses

1 tablespoon Dijon mustard

2 tablespoons catsup

1 teaspoon soy sauce

1 teaspoon dried red chili flakes

12 cherry tomatoes

1 large red or yellow bell pepper

1 cup uncooked white basmati rice

¼ teaspoon salt

8 wooden skewers, soaked in water for 10 minutes

Rinse the tofu and cut it into 1-inch cubes. Place on paper towels and pat dry. Whisk together the vinegar, molasses, mustard, catsup, soy sauce, and chili flakes. Place the tofu in a shallow baking dish and pour the sauce over it. Gently turn the tofu over using a rubber spatula, then marinate it at room temperature for an hour or so.

Preheat the oven to 350 degrees F. Transfer the dish of marinated tofu to the oven and bake for about 30 minutes, turning the tofu over midway through the cooking time. Remove from the oven and set aside to cool a bit. Any unabsorbed marinade will be used later when serving the skewers.

Discard the stems of the tomatoes and leave the tomatoes whole. Remove and discard the stem, seeds, and white membranes of the bell pepper and chop it into about 1½-inch-square pieces. Set aside.

Meanwhile, place 2¼ cups of water in a medium saucepan over high heat and bring to a boil. Add the rice and salt, cover, reduce the heat to very low, and cook for 20 minutes. Turn off the heat and allow to stand with the lid in place for at least 5 minutes before serving.

Preheat the grill to medium. Evenly distribute the tofu, tomatoes, and pepper pieces among the skewers, arranging them in an alternating pattern. Grill for 4 minutes, then turn over and grill 4 more minutes.

Mound the rice in the center of each serving plate and place two skewers atop each portion. Strain any remaining marinade and drizzle some over each serving. Serve immediately.

12
Sandwiches and Wraps

Hummus Sandwich with Cucumber and Tomato
    Relish
Avocado and Watercress Sandwich with Dried Tomato
    Mayo
Grilled Veggie Sandwich with Red Bell Pepper Sauce
Cumin-Seared Tofu Wrap
Savory Mushroom, Oat, and Almond Burgers
Tofu Tostadas with Kidney Beans
Mushroom and Soy Cheese Quesadillas
Soft Tacos with Tofu and Pickled Jalapeños
Mushrooms and Corn Tacos with Serrano Chilies
Curried Tempeh in Pita Pockets
Falafel in Pita Bread with Cucumber Sauce
Soft Tacos with Potatoes and Tofu Chorizo "Sausage"

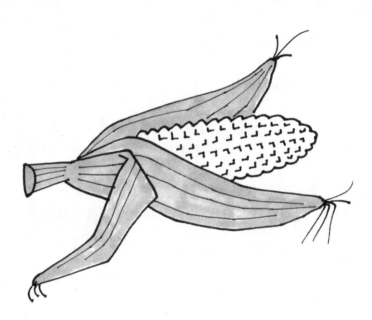

Every region of the world has its version of the sandwich: bread or some other wrapper stuffed with savory or sweet ingredients, and the whole package enlivened with condiments. We have drawn heavily on the foods of Mexico in this chapter, including scrumptious tacos and quesadillas among our chosen recipes. Pita bread from the Middle East turns up with a couple of different fillings, and the unique Japanese "wrap" called sushi is also present here. Of course, we haven't neglected the simple sandwich: slices of bread holding together a mouthwatering combination of ingredients.

Bread is a beloved food, perhaps too much so for many people. As discussed elsewhere, flour products may be filling and delicious, but they don't deliver the fiber, vitamins, and minerals of whole grains. Most breads are high-calorie, low-nutrient foods, so they should have only a minor place in your overall diet. What's more, most bread is made from wheat, a common allergen, making it troublesome for people who are sensitive to this common grain. These caveats aside, however, the occasional sandwich is a wonderful treat.

When it comes to sandwich condiments, there are infinite possibilities. Some of our recipes provide instructions for making just the right sauce or relish. Others can be seasoned to your liking with mustard, soy mayonnaise, catsup, and the like, or you can serve your favorite salsa with the tacos and quesadillas. The sandwich allows for individual tastes.

Sandwiches and wraps are a casual and easy warm weather entrée because most of them don't require turning on the stove. These are fun meals to share with family and friends. Enjoy!

Hummus Sandwich with Cucumber and Tomato Relish

YIELD: 8 sandwiches

You may use any hearty bread for this sandwich, but we especially enjoy a whole wheat walnut variety made by a local bakery. Offer extra napkins, as the filling drips a bit. Any leftover hummus and relish may be stored in the refrigerator for up to a week.

EACH SERVING PROVIDES
*295 calories, 10 g protein, 13 g fat,
8 g dietary fiber, 39 g carbohydrates,
406 mg sodium, 0 mg cholesterol*

2 cups cooked and drained garbanzo beans

1/3 cup fresh-squeezed lemon juice

1/4 cup sesame tahini, raw or toasted

3 green onions, minced

2 cloves garlic, minced

1/2 teaspoon mild paprika

1/2 teaspoon salt

3 tablespoons extra-virgin olive oil

1 pound fresh tomatoes, diced

1 medium cucumber

2 tablespoons minced fresh Italian parsley

2 tablespoons unseasoned rice vinegar

A few grinds black pepper

16 slices walnut wheat bread

In a blender or food processor, combine the garbanzo beans, lemon juice, tahini, 2 tablespoons of water, green onions, garlic, paprika, 1/4 teaspoon of the salt, and 2 tablespoons of the olive oil. Purée until smooth. Set aside or refrigerate for several hours to allow the flavors to develop.

Meanwhile, discard the stem ends of the tomatoes. Finely dice tomatoes and set them aside in a bowl. If the skin of the cucumber is tough or tastes bitter, peel it. Cut the cucumber in half lengthwise and use a teaspoon to remove the seeds. Finely dice the cucumber and add it to the tomatoes in the bowl, along with the parsley, vinegar, remaining tablespoon of olive oil, remaining 1/4 teaspoon of salt, and black pepper.

To assemble the sandwiches, spread a slice of bread generously with the garbanzo spread, then top with some of the relish. Place another slice of bread on top and serve. Serve immediately because the relish tends to make the bread soggy if allowed to sit.

Avocado and Watercress Sandwich with Dried Tomato Mayo

YIELD: 4 sandwiches

4 ounces fresh watercress, including stems

¼ cup soy mayonnaise

¼ cup reconstituted dried tomatoes (see page 8), minced

8 slices whole grain bread

2 ounce soy cheese, thinly sliced

1 perfectly ripe Hass avocado

Rinse the watercress well and pat it dry. In a small bowl, combine the mayonnaise with the dried tomatoes. Spread this mixture evenly over the 8 slices of bread. Layer the cheese slices and watercress on 4 of these slices.

Discard the pit of the avocado and slice or mash the flesh. Divide the avocado among the remaining 4 slices of bread. Put the two sides of the sandwiches together, cut them in half diagonally, and serve immediately.

Almost Instant

This sandwich is a fine choice any time you have a really great avocado on hand. Serve it with carrot sticks or other raw vegetables for a very satisfying lunch.

EACH SERVING PROVIDES
328 calories, 11 g protein, 21 g fat, 6 g dietary fiber, 27 g carbohydrates, 424 mg sodium, 0 mg cholesterol

---

AVOCADO

Avocados are high in fat and calories, which has given them a bad reputation with some health enthusiasts. But an avocado's fatty acids are mostly beneficial monounsaturates that can help lower LDL cholesterol. In addition, avocados are an excellent source of potassium and glutathione, a potent antioxidant. Of course, they are also quite delicious! Eaten in moderation, they are a fine addition to the vegan diet.

Grilled Veggie Sandwich with Red Bell Pepper Sauce

YIELD: 4 sandwiches

We enjoy this warm sandwich for lunch or dinner. You can include other vegetables if you wish, but always use an eggplant. Roast a red bell pepper when you are grilling the vegetables or use a prepared one from a jar for the sauce.

EACH SERVING PROVIDES

469 calories, 9 g protein, 32 g fat, 9 g dietary fiber, 43 g carbohydrates, 720 mg sodium, 0 mg cholesterol

½ cup soy mayonnaise

½ cup chopped roasted red bell pepper

1 clove garlic, minced

1 medium eggplant (about 1 pound)

2 medium yellow onions

2 medium zucchini

3 tablespoons olive oil

½ teaspoon granulated garlic

½ teaspoon salt

A few grinds black pepper

8 slices whole grain or sourdough bread

Prepare the red bell pepper sauce by combining the mayonnaise, red bell pepper, and minced garlic in a blender. Purée until smooth. Set aside in the refrigerator until needed.

Preheat the grill to medium-high. Remove the stem end of the eggplant, and slice it crosswise into ½-inch-thick pieces. Cut the onions crosswise into ¼-inch slices. Remove the stem end of the zucchini and cut it lengthwise into ¼-inch slices. Whisk together the oil, granulated garlic, salt, and black pepper. Lightly brush the oil mixture on one side of the vegetable slices, taking care to keep the onion slices intact. Place the vegetables on the grill and cook for 4 to 6 minutes, then brush the top sides with a little oil and turn to cook on the other side. The onions and zucchini will cook faster than the eggplant, so place them on a cooler part of the grill and check them frequently.

Toast the bread, if you wish, then spread with some of the red bell pepper mayonnaise. Pile on a layer of the vegetables, top with another slice of bread, and serve.

Cumin-Seared Tofu Wrap

YIELD: 6 wraps

2 pounds firm tofu

2 tablespoons canola oil

3 tablespoons vegan Worcestershire
    sauce

1 teaspoon ground cumin

4 cloves garlic, minced

¼ teaspoon cayenne pepper

¼ teaspoon salt

6 chapati or whole wheat tortillas

6 tablespoons soy mayonnaise

3 cups shredded lettuce

*We all need convenient foods
that we can easily eat on the run.
This recipe is great to enjoy at the
table or to package and enjoy as
a lunch on the road.*

EACH SERVING PROVIDES
*430 calories, 20 g protein, 26 g fat,
6 g dietary fiber, 37 g carbohydrates,
478 mg sodium, 0 mg cholesterol*

Rinse the tofu and pat dry with a tea towel. Cut into ½-inch cubes.
Heat the oil in a skillet over medium-high heat and add the
Worcestershire sauce, cumin, garlic, cayenne, and salt. Gently fold
in the tofu, tossing to coat with oil and seasonings. Cook until the
tofu has released its liquid and most of it has cooked away, about 12
minutes, gently stirring it occasionally.

Meanwhile, wrap the chapatis in a tea towel and place in a 250
degree F oven until heated through, about 10 minutes. Lay a chapati on the work surface and mound ⅙ of the tofu in the center.
Top with 1 tablespoon of the mayonnaise and ½ cup of the lettuce.
Fold up the bottom and fold in the sides, then roll up tightly. Fill
the remaining chapatis in the same manner. Serve immediately or
wrap tightly in plastic or waxed paper to be enjoyed as a nourishing
meal-on-the-go.

Savory Mushroom, Oat, and Almond Burgers

YIELD: 8 burgers

Serve this yummy burger with mustard, relish, soy mayo, and/or catsup—as you wish. Uncooked patties can be frozen individually for future use. Simply stack them with squares of waxed paper in between, then wrap the stack in plastic before freezing.

EACH SERVING PROVIDES

416 calories, 14 g protein, 15 g fat, 7 g dietary fiber, 56 g carbohydrates, 555 mg sodium, 0 mg cholesterol

⅔ cup whole blanched almonds

½ pound button mushrooms

1 tablespoon olive oil

1 tablespoon dry sherry

2 shallots, minced

1 teaspoon dried oregano

1½ cups rolled oats

½ cup rice or soy milk

2 teaspoons vegan Worcestershire sauce

1 teaspoon arrowroot powder

½ teaspoon salt

¼ cup fine bread crumbs

2 tablespoons canola oil

8 whole wheat burger buns

8 fresh tomato slices

8 butter lettuce leaves

½ medium red onion, thinly sliced

Place the almonds in a blender or food processor and grind them to a fine meal consistency. Set aside. Brush or wipe any loose dirt from the mushrooms and finely chop them. Heat the olive oil and sherry in a skillet over medium heat, then add the shallots, mushrooms, and oregano. Sauté for about 5 minutes, stirring frequently, until the mushrooms release their liquid and most of it has evaporated, then remove from the heat and set aside.

Place 1 cup of the oats in a blender or food processor and process until ground to a fairly fine consistency. Put them in a bowl and add the remaining ½ cup rolled oats, along with the ground almonds. Toss to combine. Whisk together the milk, Worcestershire sauce, arrowroot powder, and salt. Stir this into the oat mixture, along with the bread crumbs and mushrooms. Mix well. Use your hands to form the mixture into 8 patties, setting them aside on waxed paper. Heat 1 tablespoon of the canola oil in a skillet over medium-high heat and place 4 burgers in the pan. Cook for several minutes on each side until lightly browned. Add a bit more oil as needed. Repeat with the remaining 4 burgers.

Place the cooked burgers and buns on a large platter, along with the tomatoes, lettuce leaves, and sliced onions. Set out your favorite condiments and let diners serve themselves.

OATS

Modern research has finally confirmed what folk wisdom has long proclaimed: Oats increase vitality, especially in men. Make this ancient grain a regular part of your diet, and you'll soon be "feeling your oats." It is also well documented that regular oat consumption significantly reduces serum cholesterol in individuals with high levels. The fatty acids in oats, as well as their fiber, contribute to this result. This means that rolled oats (also called oatmeal) and oat bran are probably equal in cholesterol-lowering effect, because the former contains more fatty acids and the latter more fiber. Whole oats (oat groats) and the steel-cut variety contain both compounds in good measure. Oats are also an excellent source of complex carbohydrates and have a good amino acid (protein) profile. In addition, they provide iron, manganese, copper, folacin, vitamin E, and zinc.

Tofu Tostadas with Kidney Beans

YIELD: 12 tostadas

This is a fun meal to present—set out all the fixings and invite diners to craft their own tostadas. Serve with guacamole and your favorite salsa.

EACH SERVING PROVIDES
135 calories, 6 g protein, 4 g fat, 4 g dietary fiber, 23 g carbohydrates, 32 mg sodium, 0 mg cholesterol

1 small serrano chili

1 tablespoon canola oil

1 cup fresh or frozen corn kernels (see NOTE)

½ cup minced green bell pepper

3 green onions, minced

1 clove garlic, minced

½ teaspoon chili powder

½ teaspoon ground cumin

½ pound firm tofu, mashed and drained in a strainer

1 cup cooked and drained kidney beans, heated

3 cups shredded lettuce

2 large tomatoes, thinly sliced

12 crisp corn tortillas

Remove and discard the stem of the chili and scrape out the seeds for a milder dish. Mince the chili and set aside.

Heat the oil in a large skillet over medium heat. Add the corn, bell pepper, onions, serrano, garlic, chili powder, and cumin. Sauté for about 5 minutes, then add the tofu. Continue to cook for about 10 minutes, until the vegetables are tender. Transfer to a warmed serving bowl.

Meanwhile, place the kidney beans in a bowl and mound the lettuce, tomatoes, and tortillas on a platter. Serve immediately.

NOTE: If using fresh corn, you will need 2 medium ears to yield 1 cup kernels. If using frozen corn kernels, place them in a colander and rinse briefly under warm water to melt off any ice crystals before adding them to the dish.

Mushroom and Soy Cheese Quesadillas

YIELD: 4 quesadillas

1 medium serrano chili

½ pound button mushrooms

1 tablespoon olive oil

1 tablespoon dry sherry

½ medium white onion, thinly sliced

¼ teaspoon ground cumin

¼ teaspoon salt

4 standard-size chapatis or whole wheat tortillas

4 ounces sliced soy mozzarella cheese

Quick cooking quesadillas are perfect for lunch, a light supper, or appetizers. Cut into wedges and serve as an appetizer for 6, or serve whole as an entrée for 4. Offer a selection of table salsas.

EACH SERVING PROVIDES

339 calories, 15 g protein, 12 g fat, 5 g dietary fiber, 43 g carbohydrates, 710 mg sodium, 0 mg cholesterol

Remove and discard the stem of the chili and scrape out the seeds for a milder dish. Mince the chili and set aside. Brush or wipe any loose dirt from the mushrooms and thinly slice them.

Heat the oil and sherry in a skillet over medium heat. Add the chili, mushrooms, onion, cumin, and salt. Cook the mushrooms until they are limp and the liquid has evaporated, about 8 to 10 minutes, then remove from the heat and set aside.

Heat a cast-iron griddle or heavy-bottomed skillet over medium heat for a few minutes. Place 1 tortilla in the pan and cook several seconds. Turn the tortilla over and distribute a quarter of the cheese over half of the tortilla. Top with a quarter of the mushroom mixture. Use a spatula to fold the tortilla in half, enclosing the filling. Cook, turning once or twice, until the cheese melts and the tortilla browns. If the tortilla is browning too quickly, reduce the heat a bit.

Repeat the process with the remaining ingredients. Serve the quesadillas whole or cut into wedges, hot or at room temperature.

Soft Tacos with Tofu and Pickled Jalapeños

YIELD: 12 tacos

Serve these deliciously spicy soft tacos with salsa, steamed rice, and fresh corn. You can also prepare these in advance and tightly wrap them for a wonderful "on-the-go" lunch.

EACH SERVING PROVIDES

141 calories, 6 g protein, 6 g fat, 3 g dietary fiber, 19 g carbohydrates, 140 mg sodium, 0 mg cholesterol

1 pound firm tofu

2 tablespoons canola oil

1 medium yellow onion, diced

2 cloves garlic, minced

2 teaspoons cumin seeds

1 teaspoon chili powder

1 teaspoon dried oregano

½ teaspoon dried thyme

⅛ teaspoon black pepper

½ cup prepared tomato sauce

2 teaspoons minced pickled jalapeño chilies

12 standard-sized corn tortillas

2 medium tomatoes, diced

2 cups shredded lettuce

Cut the tofu into ½-inch slices and blot dry on a tea towel. Crumble it into a bowl and set aside. Heat the oil over medium-high heat in a large, heavy-bottomed skillet and add the onion, garlic, cumin, chili powder, oregano, thyme, and black pepper. Sauté for about 2 minutes, then add the tomato sauce and pickled jalapeño and stir to combine. Stir in the tofu and cook until heated through, about 5 minutes, stirring frequently.

Wrap the tortillas in a clean tea towel and heat in a 250 degree F oven for 10 minutes right before serving time.

Arrange the tomatoes and lettuce on a serving platter. Transfer the tofu mixture to a warmed bowl. Place all the ingredients on the table, along with condiments, and allow diners to fill their own tacos.

Mushroom and Corn Tacos with Serrano Chilies

YIELD: 8 tacos

¾ pound button mushrooms

1 tablespoon canola oil

2 medium serrano chilies, seeded and minced

⅓ cup finely chopped white onion

2 cloves garlic, minced

1 cup fresh or frozen corn kernels (see NOTE)

2 tablespoons minced fresh epazote leaves

¼ teaspoon salt

8 standard-sized corn tortillas

1½ cups finely shredded green cabbage

Brush or wipe any loose dirt from the mushrooms and quarter them. Heat the oil over medium-high heat in a heavy-bottomed skillet that has a tight-fitting lid. Sauté the chilies, onion, and garlic, stirring frequently, until the onion begins to get limp, about 3 minutes. Add the mushrooms, and sauté 2 minutes longer, then stir in the corn, epazote, and salt. Add 2 tablespoons of water and immediately cover the pan.

Reduce the heat to low and cook 10 minutes. Remove the lid and continue to cook 1 to 2 minutes, if necessary, until there is no more than about a tablespoon of liquid remaining in the pan.

Meanwhile, wrap the tortillas in a clean tea towel and heat them in a 250 degree F oven for 10 minutes right before serving time.

Transfer the mushroom mixture to a serving bowl and place on the table. Put the shredded cabbage on a plate and place it on the table, along with the warmed tortillas. Serve immediately, inviting diners to make their own tacos.

NOTE: If using fresh corn, you will need about 2 medium ears to yield 1 cup kernels. If using frozen corn kernels, place them in a colander and rinse briefly under warm water to melt off any ice crystals before adding them to the dish.

Almost Instant

This is a delightful combination of traditional Mexican flavors. If you can't find fresh epazote, you may substitute cilantro. These delicious tacos come together very quickly—you'll want to make them often. Serve your favorite salsa on the side.

EACH SERVING PROVIDES
119 calories, 3 g protein, 3 g fat, 3 g dietary fiber, 22 g carbohydrates, 96 mg sodium, 0 mg cholesterol

Sushi Savvy

Sea veggies are true health foods. They deliver good quantities of important minerals and vitamins in an easy-to-assimilate form, and the fibers they contain are particularly beneficial to the bowel. When it comes to nori, the paper-thin seaweed sheets from Japan, our favorite preparation is the nori roll, better known as sushi. You might think of sushi as you think of the sandwich: The filling possibilities are limitless and should be guided by your personal tastes. We provide several suggestions below.

There is nothing difficult about making sushi. Contrary to popular belief, it doesn't require any special equipment—not even a bamboo roll. Brown rice will work just fine for sushi, when properly prepared. It won't have the same texture as traditional white suchi rice, but it tastes great. After the first few tries, you'll feel quite comfortable with the sushi-making process and will come to depend on this handy and healthy food.

Sushi is best eaten immediately, but it will still be good the next day if you store it in the refrigerator in an airtight container. Make up a batch on Sunday, eat some for dinner, and pack the rest for a nourishing Monday lunch.

Sushi is pretty to serve, which makes it great party food. But be forewarned: Lots of people love sushi and will gobble it up, so make plenty. Mix up some wasabi (Japanese horseradish) powder with a bit of water to form a thick paste, then thin the paste down with a bit more water and soy sauce to taste. This makes a great dipping sauce for sushi, but be careful—too much can lead to a brief, but painful, sinus inflammation. Pickled ginger is also a good accompaniment, clearing the palate and aiding digestion.

(Any unfamiliar ingredients mentioned below are discussed in our glossary and can be found at all Asian markets and many natural food stores.)

THE BASIC TECHNIQUE

1. Cook a pot of short-grain brown rice, using 3 cups of water and 1 ⅓ cups of rice. This will yield a moister, stickier rice than usual, perfect for making sushi. Cook according to the standard directions on page 298, but leave the heat on for a full 50 minutes. Then turn off the heat, and let the pot stand with the lid undisturbed for an additional 10 minutes.

2. Spread the hot rice out in a large baking dish or on a baking sheet with a raised edge. Dissolve 2 teaspoons of organic granulated sugar in 1 ½ tablespoons of unseasoned rice vinegar, and drizzle it over the hot rice. Sprinkle on a tablespoon or 2 of raw sesame seeds.

3. Toss gently with a spatula or wooden spoon to distribute the vinegar and hasten the cooling of the rice. Keep tossing for about 2 minutes. The rice will get stickier as you go, which is desirable. Set the rice aside until it has cooled to room temperature.

4. Meanwhile, toast 4 sheets of nori by passing them very quickly above a low gas flame or electic burner. If you buy nori sheets that say "toasted" on the package, you can skip this step. Lay a sheet of toasted nori on a cutting board. Use your fingers to spread cooled rice in a ¼-inch layer over it, leaving a 2-inch border free of rice on one long edge. Combine a few drops of unseasoned rice vinegar with a few tablespoons of water and keep your fingers moistened with this solution to minimize sticking.

5. Position the nori with the rice-free border away from you. Add the filling ingredients of your choice (see suggestions below), making a small mound horizontally down the center of the rice.

Moisten the rice-free border of nori with water, then roll up the filled nori as you would a rug, using both hands and starting with the rice-filled edge. Squeeze gently as you go to create a nice, tight roll. When you're finished rolling, use the moistened nori edge to "glue" the roll closed.

Use a very sharp knife moistened with water to cut the roll into 1- to 2-inch pieces. Now it's time to eat!

Some sushi filling suggestions:

- Steamed carrot sticks with pickled ginger
- Avocado and cucumber strips with wasabi paste
- Steamed asparagus with baked tofu slices
- Steamed daikon radish sticks smeared with miso
- Sautéed shiitake mushrooms

Curried Tempeh in Pita Pockets

YIELD: 4 main-dish servings

This dish is finger food, so provide lots of napkins. The fresh tomato and cucumber salsa is the perfect complement to the spicy curried tempeh.

EACH SERVING PROVIDES

*438 calories, 18 g protein, 19 g fat,
11 g dietary fiber, 53 g carbohydrates,
671 mg sodium, 0 mg cholesterol*

3 tablespoons tomato juice

2 tablespoons olive oil

2 tablespoons fresh-squeezed lime juice

1 tablespoon grated fresh ginger

1 teaspoon ground cumin

½ teaspoon ground coriander

¼ teaspoon turmeric

⅛ teaspoon cayenne pepper

8 ounces soy tempeh

1 medium cucumber

2 medium tomatoes, diced

¼ cup unseasoned rice vinegar

2 tablespoons dark sesame oil

4 green onions, minced

½ cup minced fresh parsley

½ cup minced fresh cilantro

½ teaspoon salt

4 whole wheat pita rounds

In a medium bowl, whisk together the tomato juice, olive oil, lime juice, ginger, cumin, coriander, turmeric, and cayenne. Cut the tempeh into ½-inch cubes, and place in the marinade. Toss gently to coat, then set aside in the refrigerator to marinate for about 1 hour. Toss several times during this period to make sure all sides of the tempeh cubes get saturated with marinade.

If the cucumber has a tough or bitter skin, peel it. Cut the cucumber in half lengthwise and use a spoon to scrape out the seeds. Dice the cucumber and combine it in a bowl with the tomatoes. Whisk together the vinegar and dark sesame oil and pour it over the tomatoes and cucumbers. Stir in the onions, parsley, cilantro, and salt. Set aside at room temperature.

About 10 minutes before serving time, cut the pita rounds in half, wrap them in a clean tea towel, and place them in a 250 degree F oven to warm.

Place a large skillet over medium-high heat. Add the tempeh and its marinade. Stir and cook for several minutes, until the tempeh is browned and the liquid is almost completely absorbed.

To serve, place the pita bread, tempeh, and tomato-cucumber mixture on the table. Have diners separate the layers of the pita halves to create bread pockets, then fill the pockets with the tempeh and tomato-cucumber mixture.

GINGER

For centuries, ginger has been a revered medicinal food in the Far East, where it is used to combat nausea as well as for its warming and cleansing properties. Ginger also acts as an anti-inflammatory, and its cancer-fighting potential is currently being studied by the National Cancer Institute. Fresh ginger root should be stored in the refrigerator, where it will stay fresh and juicy for about 2 weeks.

Falafel in Pita Bread with Cucumber Sauce

YIELD: 6 main-dish servings

Enjoy this high-protein pocket sandwich for lunch or dinner. The garbanzo patties can be made ahead, individually wrapped in wax paper and frozen, then defrosted and fried for an instant meal.

EACH SERVING PROVIDES

410 calories, 18 g protein, 13 g fat, 9 g dietary fiber, 62 g carbohydrates, 545 mg sodium, 0 mg cholesterol

The falafel patties

1½ cups French bread, cut into ¾-inch cubes

1½ cups cooked and drained garbanzo beans

2 tablespoons fresh-squeezed lemon juice

¼ cup minced red onion

2 cloves garlic, minced

2 tablespoons minced fresh cilantro

¼ teaspoon ground cumin

¼ teaspoon ground coriander

¼ teaspoon salt

½ teaspoon baking powder

A pinch cayenne pepper

2 tablespoons unbleached white flour

3 tablespoons olive oil

The sauce

12 ounces firm silken tofu

3 tablespoons fresh-squeezed lemon juice

2 cloves garlic, minced

1 tablespoon minced fresh dill

½ medium cucumber

6 whole wheat pita rounds

2 medium tomatoes, diced

6 thin red onion slices

Place the bread cubes in a bowl and add cold water to just cover them. Set aside for about 15 minutes. Preheat the oven to 375 degrees F. Place the garbanzo beans in a food processor and pulse until they are finely chopped. Add the lemon juice, onion, garlic, cilantro, cumin, coriander, salt, baking powder, and cayenne, then process until smooth. Drain the bread and squeeze the water out, then add it to the food processor. Process until smooth.

Form the mixture into 12 balls about 1-inch in diameter, flattening them slightly. Place the flour on a plate and place the patties in it to lightly coat both sides. Use ¼ teaspoon of the oil to lightly coat a baking sheet. Place the patties on the sheet and bake for 6 minutes. Turn and continue to bake 6 minutes.

To make the sauce, place the tofu in a blender with the lemon juice, garlic, and dill. Purée, then transfer to a bowl. If the cucumber has a tough or bitter skin, peel it. Use a spoon to scrape out the seeds, then finely dice the cucumber and stir it into the tofu sauce. Refrigerate until ready to serve.

About 10 minutes before serving time, cut the pita rounds in half, wrap them in a clean tea towel, and place them in a 250 degree F oven to warm.

Heat 2 teaspoons of the remaining oil in a skillet over medium-high. When it is hot enough to sizzle a drop of water, add half of the patties to the pan. Cook them for 3 to 4 minutes, until they are golden brown on the bottom. Add a bit of the remaining oil, turn the patties, and continue to cook for 3 to 4 minutes. Remove them from the pan with a slotted spatula and place on a platter lined with paper towels. Cook the remaining patties, using the remaining oil as needed.

To serve, remove the paper towels from the platter. Transfer the falafel patties, tofu sauce, and pita bread to the table. Invite diners to separate the layers of the pita halves to create bread pockets, then place 2 falafel patties in each pocket, along with tomatoes and onion slices. The cucumber sauce is added last.

Soft Tacos with Potatoes and Tofu Chorizo "Sausage"

YIELD: 12 tacos

Here is a vegan version of a traditional combination—potatoes and spicy sausage. Our chorizo sausage is made from tofu, and even die-hard sausage fans agree it's a delicious facsimile. Make a batch of the chorizo up to a day or two ahead of time, and these tacos can come together almost instantly.

EACH SERVING PROVIDES

*167 calories, 5 g protein, 4 g fat,
4 g dietary fiber, 26 g carbohydrates,
217 mg sodium, 0 mg cholesterol*

¾ pound red or white potatoes

1 tablespoon canola oil

1 medium white onion, diced

2 teaspoons chili powder

¼ teaspoon salt

1½ cups Tofu Chorizo Sausage (page 306)

12 standard-sized corn tortillas

2 cups finely shredded green leaf lettuce

2 cups Salsa Fresca (page 309), or a store-bought variety

Scrub the potatoes and finely dice them. Heat the oil over medium heat in a heavy-bottomed skillet that has a tight-fitting lid. Sauté the onion and chili powder for about 3 minutes, then add the potatoes and salt. Sauté, stirring frequently, for 5 minutes. Holding the lid of the skillet in one hand, pour ½ cup of water into the pan and immediately put the lid in place. Reduce the heat to low and cook for 10 minutes.

Remove the lid, stir in the chorizo, and continue to cook for a minute or two, until the potatoes are tender and there is no more than about a tablespoon of liquid remaining. If the liquid has evaporated but the potatoes are not yet tender, add another 1 or 2 tablespoons of water and continue to cook, covered, about 5 minutes, or until the potatoes are tender.

Meanwhile, warm the tortillas by laying them one at a time directly on a medium gas burner and turning every few seconds until each one blisters and browns just a bit. Wrap the warmed tortillas in a clean tea towel as you go.

Transfer the potato and chorizo filling to a serving bowl. Place the filling, tortillas, lettuce, and salsa on the table and serve immediately, allowing diners to create their own tacos.

13
Morning
Meals

Overnight Oat, Apple, and Seed Porridge

Rye Porridge

Polenta Porridge with Hot Fig Compote

Granola with Dried Cranberries and Apricots

Blueberry-Applesauce Muffins

Oat and Buckwheat Pancakes with Blueberry Sauce

Lemon-Poppy Seed Muffins

Tofu and Potato Hash

Tempeh Rancheros

High-Mineral Morning Shake

Tropical Rice Milk Smoothie

Banana-Strawberry Soy Smoothie

Your first meal of the day is an important one. The body and brain need to be well-nourished to get them awake and functioning. However, don't force yourself to eat immediately upon arising. It's fine to start the morning with a healthy hot beverage or fruit juice. But when you do get hungry, be sure to eat something nutritious.

For many of us, the mornings are rushed, and there's only time for a quick piece of toast and seasonal fruit before heading off to work or school. But when time allows, it's fun to give yourself and your family the gift of a special breakfast or brunch.

Complex carbohydrates provide steady energy to fuel the morning's activities, so hot grain porridge is always a good choice. For a protein-rich breakfast, consider a tofu scramble or hash, or tempeh rancheros, a south-of-the-border treat. For an occasional sweet indulgence, try our handy and delicious muffins or pancakes, a sure crowd pleaser. For lighter appetites, a smoothie is a good choice for breakfast.

The morning meal impacts your energy and mood for the entire day. Take the time to prepare a healthy one.

Overnight Oat, Apple, and Seed Porridge

YIELD: 2 servings

We learned about this delicious breakfast from a Hungarian friend who says it is a tradition in his family. Taking a few minutes to prepare this before going to bed gives you the pleasure of waking up to a healthy meal. Simply multiply the ingredients for more servings.

EACH SERVING PROVIDES

387 calories, 14 g protein, 15 g fat,
10 g dietary fiber, 55 g carbohydrates,
39 mg sodium, 0 mg cholesterol

¾ cup rolled oats

2 tablespoons raw unsalted pumpkin seeds

2 tablespoons raw unsalted sunflower seeds

2 tablespoons raisins

¼ teaspoon ground cinnamon

1 medium apple, finely chopped or grated

½ cup soy, rice, or nut milk

1 to 2 tablespoons maple syrup (to taste)

2 tablespoons flaxseed (freshly ground, if desired)

Combine the oats, pumpkin seeds, sunflower seeds, raisins, and cinnamon in a medium-sized bowl. Boil 1¼ cups water and pour it over the mixture, cover the bowl, and allow to stand at room temperature overnight.

In the morning, chop or grate the apple and stir it into the oat mixture. Divide between two bowls and add half the soy milk, maple syrup, and flaxseed to each serving.

JUST THE FLAX

Flaxseed contains lignan, a fiber compound with anticancer, antiviral, and antifungal properties. It is also one of the best plant sources of omega-3 fatty acids, the superheroes of the fat family. You can buy whole organic flaxseed and flax oil in well-stocked natural food stores. Sprinkle the whole or ground seeds on cereal and salads, add them to smoothies, or stir them into juice. Flax oil has a rich taste that is good on salads or drizzled in a bowl of soup. A tablespoon or two of flaxseed and/or flax oil per day is all you need to reap its important health benefits. High heat alters the beneficial fatty acids, so be sure to use both the seed and the oil in their raw state.

Rye Porridge

YIELD: 2 servings

¾ cup rolled rye flakes

½ teaspoon salt

½ cup chopped apple

½ teaspoon ground cinnamon

2 tablespoons maple syrup

Bring 1 ½ cups of water to a boil and add the rye and salt. Return to a boil, cover, reduce the heat to low and simmer for 3 minutes. Stir, then remove from the heat and set aside for about 7 minutes. Stir in the apples and cinnamon, cover again, and set aside for about 3 minutes. Serve with the maple syrup drizzled over the top.

Almost Instant

This grain is a great alternative to rolled oats. It cooks fast and has a mild flavor. You may vary the fruit according to your tastes and the season—pears, apricots, and blueberries are other favorites.

EACH SERVING PROVIDES
*194 calories, 5 g protein, 1 g fat,
7 g dietary fiber, 43 g carbohydrates,
534 mg sodium, 0 mg cholesterol*

Polenta Porridge with Hot Fig Compote

YIELD: 4 servings

This yummy breakfast combo is comfort food at its most wholesome. It will provide enough energy for a good morning's work or play.

EACH SERVING PROVIDES
311 calories, 4 g protein, 3 g fat, 7 g dietary fiber, 73 g carbohydrates, 61 mg sodium, 0 mg cholesterol

8 ounces dried figs, stems snipped off

¼ cup fresh-squeezed orange juice

4 ¼-inch slices fresh ginger

2-inch cinnamon stick

1 ½ cups plus ½ cup rice milk

1 tablespoon maple syrup

½ teaspoon ground cinnamon

¾ cup uncooked polenta

Combine the figs, orange juice, ginger, and cinnamon stick with ⅔ cup of water in a medium saucepan. Place it over medium heat and bring it to a simmer, then reduce the heat to medium-low, cover, and cook for 10 minutes. Remove the ginger and cinnamon, then transfer the figs and their cooking liquid to a blender. Coarsely purée the mixture to create a thick and chunky texture. Add a tablespoon or two of water while processing, if necessary, to achieve the right consistency.

Combine 1 ½ cups of the rice milk with 1 ½ cups of water, the maple syrup, and ground cinnamon in a large saucepan. Bring to a boil over medium-high heat. Pour in the polenta in a slow, steady stream, stirring constantly with a wire whisk or wooden spoon. Reduce the heat to medium-low and cook, whisking almost constantly, until the polenta is tender and the mixture is beginning to pull away from the sides of the pan, about 10 minutes. The more you whisk the polenta as it cooks, the creamier it will be. Whisk in a few more tablespoons of water if the mixture gets too thick before the polenta is fully cooked. It should be very tender, with no hard grains at all.

Place equal portions of the polenta in warmed shallow bowls. Top each portion with a dollop of the fig compote and pour about 2 tablespoons of the remaining rice milk over each serving. Serve immediately.

FIGS

Fresh figs are wonderfully sweet and soft when fully ripe, but they have a very short shelf life. Because of this, most of the commercial fig crop is dried. Whether fresh or dried, figs are high in dietary fiber and are a good source of potassium, iron, and calcium. If you have access to fresh figs, enjoy them raw as a healthy snack. For a delicious dessert, pierce fresh figs with a fork and place them on a baking pan, sprinkle with fruit juice, and bake for about 20 minutes at 300 degrees F. Serve plain or with Sweet Soy Cashew Topping (page 292).

Granola with Dried Cranberries and Apricots

YIELD: About 14 cups (18 ¾-cup servings)

This makes a lot of granola, but it keeps well in a tightly closed jar in the pantry. Enjoy it as a cold cereal or heat some with soy or rice milk for an instant hot breakfast.

EEACH SERVING PROVIDES

408 calories, 10 g protein, 13 g fat, 8 g dietary fiber, 65 g carbohydrates, 68 mg sodium, 0 mg cholesterol

8 cups rolled oats

2 cups rye flakes

1 cup wheat bran

1 cup turbinado sugar

1 cup roasted and salted sunflower seeds

½ cup canola oil

½ cup brown rice syrup

3 teaspoons pure vanilla extract

1 teaspoon ground cinnamon

¼ teaspoon ground nutmeg

1 cup finely chopped dried apricots

1 cup dried cranberries

Preheat the oven to 350 degrees F. Place the oats, rye, bran, sugar, and sunflower seeds in a large bowl and toss well to combine. Set aside. In a saucepan, heat the oil, rice syrup, vanilla, cinnamon, and nutmeg. Heat until bubbly, then pour over the grains, tossing with a wooden spoon to distribute the liquid evenly. Add the apricots and cranberries, then toss again to combine. Place in a thin layer on large baking sheets and bake for 20 to 30 minutes, until the grains are lightly browned, tossing about every 10 minutes. Place the baking sheets on cooling racks and allow the granola to cool completely before storing in a tightly closed jar.

Blueberry–Applesauce Muffins

YIELD: 16 muffins

2 cups unbleached white flour

1 teaspoon baking powder

1 teaspoon baking soda

¼ teaspoon salt

¾ cup organic granulated sugar

¼ cup wheat germ

12 ounces firm silken tofu

⅛ cup plain soy milk

2 tablespoons canola oil

1 tablespoon lemon juice

½ cup unsweetened applesauce

1½ cups fresh or frozen blueberries (see NOTE)

Light and airy, these muffins will become favorite breakfast treats.

EACH SERVING PROVIDES

143 calories, 4 g protein, 3 g fat, 1 g dietary fiber, 25 g carbohydrates, 149 mg sodium, 0 mg cholesterol

Preheat the oven to 325 degrees F. Into a large bowl, sift together the flour, baking powder, baking soda, and salt. Stir in the sugar and wheat germ. In a food processor, purée the tofu, soy milk, oil, and lemon juice. Stir into the dry ingredients, along with the applesauce, until well combined, then gently fold in the blueberries.

Place paper liners into the cups of a muffin tin. Spoon the batter in, filling the liners almost to the top. Bake for 25 minutes, until lightly browned on top. Remove from the muffin tin and allow to cool on a rack for about 15 minutes before eating. The muffins will stay fresh for a few days, stored in a jar or plastic bag at room temperature. (Cool completely before storing.)

NOTE: If using frozen blueberries, place them in a colander and rinse briefly under cold water to melt off any ice crystals before adding them to the recipe.

Oat and Buckwheat Pancakes with Blueberry Sauce

YIELD: About 12 4-inch pancakes

Made-from-scratch pancakes take a little more time than those from a box, but the extra flavor, texture, and nutrition are worth it. This version uses flaxseed as a binder, rather than eggs. The resulting cakes have a wonderful chewy texture, and the blueberry sauce tops them to perfection.

EACH SERVING PROVIDES
194 calories, 4 g protein, 5 g fat, 3 g dietary fiber, 36 g carbohydrates, 196 mg sodium, 0 mg cholesterol

1 ½ pounds fresh or frozen blueberries

¼ cup maple syrup

3 tablespoons orange juice concentrate

¼ teaspoon allspice

½ cup rolled oats

½ cup buckwheat flour

1 ½ cups whole wheat pastry flour

1 tablespoon baking powder

¼ teaspoon salt

2 tablespoons whole flaxseed

2 ½ tablespoons canola oil

1 ¾ cups plain rice or soy milk

1 teaspoon pure vanilla extract

In a saucepan over medium-low heat, combine the blueberries, 2 tablespoons of the maple syrup, the orange juice concentrate, and the allspice. Cover the pan and cook for 10 minutes, then turn off the heat and allow the pan to stand while you cook the pancakes.

Meanwhile, place the rolled oats in a blender and grind to a coarse meal consistency. Transfer to a large bowl, using a rubber spatula to remove the ground oats from the blender. Add the flours, baking powder, and salt to the ground oats, stirring to combine well. Set aside.

Place the flaxseeds in the blender and grind them to a powder, then add ⅓ cup water and blend for 30 seconds. Add 2 table-spoons of the canola oil, the remaining 2 tablespoons maple syrup, the rice milk, and vanilla, and purée. Add this wet mixture to the flour mixture and stir well, so that all the flour is saturated with liquid.

Heat a heavy griddle or cast-iron skillet over medium heat. Rub the griddle with about ¼ teaspoon of oil. Pour the batter onto the griddle in ¼-cup amounts. Cook for about 2 minutes, until the liquidy top of the pancake is stippled with air holes, then use a metal spatula to quickly turn the pancake over. Cook a minute or two longer, until the pancake is cooked through. (If in doubt, you can cut a small slit in the pancake with the edge of the spatula and take a look at the inside; it should look spongy, not liquidy.)

Serve the pancakes as they come off the griddle or transfer them to a plate in a warm oven while you cook the rest. Just before serving, transfer the blueberry mixture to the blender and purée, then pour into a small pitcher or gravy boat. Serve the pancakes hot, passing the blueberry sauce.

BLUEBERRIES

These flavorful small berries are low in calories yet packed with vitamin C, and they provide potassium, iron, vitamin A, and fiber. Studies have shown that blueberries are similar to cranberries in their ability to fight off E. coli bacteria, the cause of some urinary tract infections. What's more, a compound in blueberries called anthocyanosides has been found to retard vision loss. The humble blueberry is so good for us, it should be a fruit of choice throughout the year. Fresh blueberries will stay crisp and delicious for up to 5 days when stored in the refrigerator, longer than most berries. When blueberries aren't in season, keep the freezer stocked with the frozen variety.

Lemon–Poppy Seed Muffins

YIELD: 15 muffins

Make these simple muffins and enjoy them over the course of a few days. The kitchen will be filled with a light lemon fragrance as they bake.

EACH SERVING PROVIDES
*158 calories, 5 g protein, 4 g fat,
1 g dietary fiber, 26 g carbohydrates,
160 mg sodium, 0 mg cholesterol*

2 cups unbleached white flour

1 teaspoon baking powder

1 teaspoon baking soda

¼ teaspoon salt

¾ cup organic granulated sugar

¼ cup wheat germ

¼ cup poppy seeds

12 ounces firm silken tofu

¼ cup plain soy milk

2 tablespoons canola oil

1 tablespoon fresh-squeezed
   lemon juice

1 teaspoon lemon extract

½ cup unsweetened applesauce

Preheat the oven to 325 degrees F. Into a large bowl, sift together the flour, baking powder, baking soda, and salt. Stir in the sugar, wheat germ, and poppy seeds. In a food processor, purée the tofu, soy milk, oil, lemon juice, and lemon extract. Stir into the dry ingredients, along with the applesauce, until everything is well blended.

Place paper liners into the cups of a muffin tin. Spoon the batter in, filling the liners almost to the top. Bake for 25 minutes, until lightly browned on top. Remove from the muffin tin and allow to cool on a rack for about 15 minutes before eating. The muffins will stay fresh for a few days, stored in a jar or plastic bag at room temperature. (Cool completely before storing.)

Tofu and Potato Hash

YIELD: 6 servings

1 pound tofu, frozen then defrosted

2 tablespoons canola oil

1 yellow onion, diced

1 pound russet potatoes (about 2
large), finely diced

1 teaspoon dried oregano

½ teaspoon soy sauce

½ pound pear tomatoes (about 3
medium), chopped

½ teaspoon salt

Several drops Tabasco sauce

Crumble the tofu into a bowl, then blot firmly with a paper towel or clean tea towel to remove any excess moisture. Set aside. Heat the oil in a large deep skillet and add the onion. Sauté until the onion is translucent, about 4 minutes, then add the potatoes and sauté for 5 minutes, stirring frequently. Add ⅓ cup water to the pan, along with the oregano and soy sauce, and continue to cook for about 5 minutes, until the potatoes are tender and the liquid is almost completely absorbed. Add the tomatoes, salt, Tabasco sauce, and tofu. Cook, stirring frequently, until the hash is lightly browned and crusty, about 2 to 3 minutes. Serve immediately.

Place a standard water-packed tofu container in the freezer overnight or for up to 2 months. If you buy bulk tofu, simply place the slabs in a plastic bag before freezing. Before starting the recipe, defrost the tofu on the countertop for several hours. Serve the hash with toast and fresh fruit for a hearty breakfast.

EACH SERVING PROVIDES
215 calories, 9 g protein, 10 g fat,
3 g dietary fiber, 25 g carbohydrates,
217 mg sodium, 0 mg cholesterol

Tempeh Rancheros

YIELD: 4 servings

The satisfying chewy texture of tempeh makes it a good and hearty breakfast food. Here it is topped with a south-of-the-border ranchero sauce, laced with cumin and chili, to create an irresistible brunch entrée.

EACH SERVING PROVIDES

392 calories, 19 g protein, 16 g fat, 7 g dietary fiber, 47 g carbohydrates, 500 mg sodium, 0 mg cholesterol

8 ounces soy tempeh

2 tablespoons canola oil

1 teaspoon soy sauce

½ teaspoon granulated garlic

½ yellow onion, diced

½ green bell pepper, diced

½ red bell pepper, diced

½ jalapeño pepper, seeded and minced

1 can (14 ounces) diced tomatoes

1 teaspoon chili powder

½ teaspoon ground cumin

⅛ teaspoon salt

8 corn tortillas, warmed

2 ounces soy cheese, grated

Preheat a toaster or conventional oven to 400 degrees F. Cut the slab of tempeh crosswise into 4 equal-sized pieces, then slice each piece lengthwise to create 2 thin slices. In a small bowl, combine 1 tablespoon of the oil with the soy sauce and granulated garlic. Use your hands to rub this oil mixture onto the tempeh slices. Place the seasoned tempeh on a baking sheet and cook for 20 minutes, turning once midway through the cooking time.

Meanwhile, heat the remaining 1 tablespoon of oil in a skillet over medium heat and sauté the onion, green and red bell peppers, and jalapeño pepper until they begin to brown, about 3 minutes. Add the diced tomatoes, including the juice, along with 2 tablespoons of water, the chili powder, cumin, and salt. Bring to a simmer and cook over medium heat for 10 minutes, stirring occasionally.

Heat the tortillas one at a time by laying each one directly on a gas burner for about 10 seconds, then turning it over two or three-more times, until it is softened and fragrant. Wrap the tortillas in a clean tea towel as you go to keep them warm. (Alternatively, you may wrap the tortillas in a clean tea towel and heat them in a 250-degree-F oven for about 10 minutes before serving.)

When the tempeh is done, overlap 2 slices on each of four serving plates. Top with equal portions of the sauce, then sprinkle on the cheese. Serve piping hot, passing the tortillas.

Scrambled Logic

If a scrambled egg was your idea of comfort food back in your prevegan days, there's a way to satisfy that old craving. Just like eggs, scrambled tofu is quick and easy to make, tastes great piled on toast or wrapped in a tortilla, and can be seasoned in an abundance of ways. It's probably even good with plain catsup!

BASIC TECHNIQUE

1. Crumble medium to firm tofu into a skillet over medium heat, along with a drizzle of oil and seasonings of your choice (see suggestions below).

2. Stir frequently as the water is released from the tofu, to prevent sticking.

3. When the tofu is as dry as you'd like it, serve it hot, with your favorite condiments.

Tofu's basic blandness means it can be taken in 101 different flavor directions. Below are just a few of the possibilities. Quantities are according to your taste. As a rule of thumb, start with a modest amount of any single ingredient, then add more if you want a stronger flavor.

- Basil pesto and roasted red bell pepper bits (add at the end of cooking)

- Curry powder (add at the beginning of cooking) and mango chutney (add at the end)

- Corn kernels (add in the middle of cooking) with minced cilantro and fresh salsa (add at the end)

- Fresh or canned diced tomato (add in the middle of cooking) and minced fresh herbs, such as mint, chives, and/or tarragon (add at the end)

High-Mineral Morning Shake

YIELD: 2 servings

¼ cup raw unsalted pumpkin seeds

¼ cup chopped dried apricots

1 cup plain soy milk

1 medium ripe banana

1 tablespoon blackstrap molasses

1 tablespoon fresh-squeezed lemon juice

In a bowl, cover the pumpkin seeds and apricots with 1 cup boiling water. Cover the bowl and let it stand overnight at room temperature. In the morning, place the soaked fruit and soaking liquid in a blender and purée briefly, then add the soy milk, banana, molasses, and lemon juice. Purée and serve immediately.

Almost Instant

This tasty breakfast beverage delivers good doses of iron, potassium, and calcium—very replenishing if you've been feeling run-down. If you want a more substantial breakfast, you can serve it over cooked brown rice or another cooked cereal. For this purpose, the recipe will easily serve four.

EACH SERVING PROVIDES
*271 calories, 10 g protein, 9 g fat,
3 g dietary fiber, 43 g carbohydrates,
75 mg sodium, 0 mg cholesterol*

Tropical Rice Milk Smoothie

YIELD: 2 servings

This smoothie makes a light and refreshing breakfast drink or snack. If you use canned pineapple, look for a brand that has little or no added sugar and drain it before measuring.

EACH SERVING PROVIDES

437 calories, 4 g protein, 11 g fat,
7 g dietary fiber, 88 g carbohydrates,
144 mg sodium, 0 mg cholesterol

1 ½ cups plain rice milk

1 cup diced fresh or canned pineapple

1 cup diced fresh or frozen mango, (see NOTE)

2 tablespoons grated coconut

2 teaspoons fresh-squeezed lemon juice

Combine all the ingredients in a blender and purée.

NOTE: If using fresh mango, you will need about 1 large fruit to yield 1 cup diced mango. If using frozen mango, place it in a colander and rinse briefly under warm water to melt off any ice crystals before adding it to the blender.

Banana–Strawberry Soy Smoothie

YIELD: 2 servings

1 large banana

2 cups sliced fresh strawberries

6 ounces plain cultured soy "yogurt"

1 cup plain soy milk

Place all ingredients in a blender and purée for about 1 minute. Add ½ to 1 cup of crushed ice if you prefer a frosty cold smoothie. Pour into glasses and garnish with mint sprigs, if desired.

Use this smoothie recipe as a template from which you can create many variations. Always include the banana, but you may substitute any seasonal fresh fruit for the strawberries. During the winter, you might also enjoy using frozen mango or raspberries. Add a sweetener as your taste dictates.

EACH SERVING PROVIDES
213 calories, 6 g protein, 3 g fat, 7 g dietary fiber, 44 g carbohydrates, 73 mg sodium, 0 mg cholesterol

SMOOTHIE ENHANCEMENTS

There are many ways to add a little extra nutrition to your favorite smoothie. Try any of the following, starting with a small amount to see how the flavor works out:

> *Brewer's yeast*
>
> *Ginseng extract*
>
> *Ground flaxseed*
>
> *Oat or wheat bran*
>
> *Protein powder*
>
> *Spirulina or other concentrated "green foods"*

14
Desserts

Jessica's Chocolate Chip Cookies

Oatmeal-Raisin Cookies with Fresh Nutmeg

Arborio Rice Pudding with Pears

Dried Apricot and Coconut Pudding

Carob-Almond Pudding

Chocolate-Cinnamon-Walnut Cake

Lemon-Poppy Seed Cake

Fabulous Fruit Crisp

Apple-Cranberry Pie with Butter-Free Crust

Banana Date Freeze

Grilled Fruit with Rum Glaze and Sweet Soy
     Cashew Topping

Oasis Orbs

Sweet Soy Cashew Topping

Creamy Vanilla Sauce

Desserts can be a delightful indulgence when eaten all by themselves as an afternoon snack or as the crowning glory of an elaborate feast. Our recipes range from the simplest cookie to an elegant fruit-filled crepe. If there's a fantastic dessert you're eager to try, plan a special occasion menu around it. Grilled Fruit with Rum Glaze and Sweet Soy Cashew Topping, for instance, can inspire an outdoor summer party that might include other grilled delicacies (see our complete menu plan on page 32).

The recipes we created for this chapter satisfy the sweet tooth without overloading our bodies with empty calories and our minds with guilt. Some recipes call for sugar, but we always choose granulated sugar that is minimally refined from organic cane. No bonemeal or bleach is used in its processing. Other sweeteners we frequently use are maple syrup, molasses, and brown rice syrup.

Although we don't include desserts in our daily meal plans, we chose to feature them in this book because many of our readers are fond of sweets and have asked us for healthy inspiration. We invite you to enjoy these treats on occasion—with no regrets.

Jessica's Chocolate Chip Cookies

YIELD: 1 ½ dozen

A 17-year-old friend developed this recipe for a delicious, not-too-naughty sweet treat.

EACH SERVING PROVIDES

105 calories, 1 g protein, 3 g fat,
0 g dietary fiber, 20 g carbohydrates,
37 mg sodium, 0 mg cholesterol

1 ¼ cups unbleached white flour
½ teaspoon baking soda
¼ teaspoon ground cinnamon
⅔ cup organic granulated sugar

⅓ cup unsweetened applesauce
1 teaspoon pure vanilla extract
1 cup vegan chocolate chips

Preheat the oven to 375 degrees F. Stir together the flour, baking soda, and cinnamon in a medium bowl. In a larger bowl, combine sugar, applesauce, and vanilla extract. Mix until the sugar is well incorporated. Add the flour mixture, stirring until all ingredients combine to form a stiff dough. Fold in the chocolate chips.

Mound rounded teaspoons of batter onto an ungreased baking sheet. Bake for 12 to 15 minutes, until golden brown. Remove from the oven and transfer the cookies to a cooling rack. Allow to cool completely before storing in an airtight container.

Oatmeal–Raisin Cookies with Fresh Nutmeg

YIELD: 2 dozen

1 cup unbleached white flour

½ cup rolled oats

½ teaspoon baking soda

Scant ⅛ teaspoon freshly grated nutmeg

⅔ cup organic granulated sugar

⅓ cup unsweetened applesauce

1 teaspoon pure vanilla extract

½ cup raisins

These cookies come together very quickly, and as they bake, the aroma of the nutmeg fills the kitchen.

EACH SERVING PROVIDES

57 calories, 1 g protein, 0 g fat, 0 g dietary fiber, 13 g carbohydrates, 27 mg sodium, 0 mg cholesterol

Preheat the oven to 375 degrees F. Stir together the flour, rolled oats, baking soda, and nutmeg in a medium bowl. In a larger bowl, combine the sugar, applesauce, and vanilla extract. Mix until the sugar is well incorporated. Add the flour mixture, stirring until all ingredients combine to form a stiff dough. Fold in the raisins.

Mound rounded teaspoons of batter onto an ungreased baking sheet. Bake for 12 to 15 minutes, until golden brown. Remove from the oven and transfer the cookies to a cooling rack. Allow to cool completely before storing in an airtight container.

Arborio Rice Pudding with Pears

YIELD: 6 servings

This pudding calls for the starchy medium-grain rice used to make risotto, and has a satisfying creaminess. It's great for breakfast as well as for dessert.

EACH SERVING PROVIDES
287 calories, 3 g protein, 2 g fat, 2 g dietary fiber, 64 g carbohydrates, 166 mg sodium, 0 mg cholesterol

1 cup uncooked arborio rice

5 cups plus 2 tablespoons rice or soy milk

2 cups diced fresh pears

¼ cup organic granulated sugar

½ teaspoon ground cinnamon

¼ teaspoon salt

½ teaspoon pure vanilla extract

Fresh nutmeg for garnish

In a heavy saucepan over medium heat, combine the rice with 4 cups of rice milk, the pears, sugar, cinnamon, and salt. Bring to a simmer and cook uncovered over medium heat, stirring frequently, for 15 minutes. Reduce the heat to medium-low and continue to cook, stirring frequently, until the rice is tender and the liquid has reduced to a thick sauce consistency—about 10 to 15 minutes. Stir almost constantly during the last 5 minutes of cooking to prevent scorching.

Turn off the heat and stir in the remaining 2 tablespoons rice milk and the vanilla extract. Cover and let stand 5 minutes, then transfer to individual dessert dishes and grate some fresh nutmeg onto each serving. Serve warm.

PEARS

Despite the apple's reputation as a super-food, the pear actually contains more pectin, which has been shown to tone the bowel and lower cholesterol levels. To select a good pear at the market, look for clear skin, unbruised flesh, and good color. A ripe pear will yield slightly when gently squeezed, just as an avocado does. Store unripe pears in a basket at room temperature and they will continue to ripen at home. Ripe pears should be eaten immediately or stored in the refrigerator for a day or two. If you are only familiar with Bartletts, be adventurous and try some of the other delicious varieties, such as the d'Anjou and Bosc.

Dried Apricot and Coconut Pudding

YIELD: 8 servings

1 ½ cups soy, rice, or nut milk

1 cup coconut milk

1 ½ cups coarsely chopped dried apricots

2 tablespoons maple syrup

1 tablespoon fresh-squeezed lemon juice

1 tablespoon pure vanilla extract

¼ teaspoon salt

2 tablespoons arrowroot powder

Place the soy milk and coconut milk in a saucepan and bring it to a boil, then pour it over the dried apricots in a heat-proof bowl. Cover the bowl and set aside in the refrigerator for 2 to 8 hours.

Place the apricots and their soaking liquid in a blender or food processor with the maple syrup, lemon juice, vanilla extract, and salt. Blend until smooth; small bits of apricot will be distributed throughout the mixture.

Transfer the mixture to a saucepan and heat over medium heat until simmering, whisking frequently. Dissolve the arrowroot powder in ¼ cup of cold water, then slowly pour it into the simmering mixture, stirring constantly. As soon as the mixture returns to a strong simmer, remove it from the heat and transfer it to 8 individual dessert dishes.

Chill until slightly thickened, at least one hour, before serving.

We have Ben Davis to thank for inspiring this delectable dessert. Dark, unsulfured dried apricots yield a pudding that has the color and taste of butterscotch. It's magical! If you prefer the hue and taste of fresh apricots, use the bright orange dried variety.

EACH SERVING PROVIDES

170 calories, 3 g protein, 7 g fat, 2 g dietary fiber, 27 g carbohydrates, 96 mg sodium, 0 mg cholesterol

Carob–Almond Pudding

YIELD: 6 servings

This rich and delicious pudding is a simple-to-prepare dinner party favorite. Whip it up the morning of the event, and you'll have one course out of the way. A mint sprig makes a nice garnish if you want a fancier presentation.

EACH SERVING PROVIDES

*168 calories, 2 g protein, 4 g fat,
2 g dietary fiber, 33 g carbohydrates,
138 mg sodium, 0 mg cholesterol*

⅓ cup raw slivered almonds, toasted (see page 10)

3 cups plain rice or soy milk

3 ½ tablespoons arrowroot powder

4 tablespoons unsweetened roasted carob powder

⅓ cup maple syrup

2 teaspoons almond extract

¼ teaspoon salt

Finely chop the toasted almonds and set them aside. Place ½ cup of the milk in a bowl and stir in the arrowroot powder until dissolved. Set aside.

In a saucepan over medium heat, whisk together the remaining 2 ½ cups of milk, carob powder, maple syrup, almond extract, and salt. Heat to boiling, then re-stir the arrowroot solution and whisk it into the pan. Bring the pudding back to a rapid simmer and cook no more than 1 minute.

Stir the chopped almonds into the pudding until well distributed, then pour it into 8 individual dessert dishes. Chill for a few hours before serving.

Chocolate–Cinnamon–Walnut Cake

YIELD: 12 servings

1 ½ cups unbleached white flour

3 tablespoons unsweetened cocoa
    powder

1 teaspoon baking soda

1 teaspoon ground cinnamon

½ teaspoon salt

1 cup organic granulated sugar

¼ cup canola oil

1 tablespoon distilled white vinegar

1 teaspoon pure vanilla extract

½ cup chopped walnuts

Serve this moist cake with vanilla tofu ice cream or a raspberry sorbet for a delightful finish to a formal meal. We also like to pack it in school lunches as a special snack.

EACH SERVING PROVIDES
*195 calories, 3 g protein, 8 g fat,
1 g dietary fiber, 30 g carbohydrates,
195 mg sodium, 0 mg cholesterol*

Preheat the oven to 350 degrees F. In a large bowl, sift together the flour, cocoa, baking soda, cinnamon, and salt. Stir in the sugar. Make a well in the center of the mixture, and stir in the oil, vinegar, and vanilla extract. Add 1 cup of cold water as you continue to stir. Beat until smooth, using an electric mixer, eggbeater, or wooden spoon. Fold in the nuts.

Pour the batter into an ungreased 8-inch or 9-inch square glass or ceramic baking dish, and place in the oven. Bake for 30 minutes, until a toothpick inserted in the center of the cake comes out clean. Cool on a rack for about 15 minutes, then cut into 12 squares while still in the baking dish. Transfer the squares to a cooling rack or serve warm.

Lemon–Poppy Seed Cake

YIELD: 12 servings

Serve this scrumptious cake as a snack with coffee or tea or as a lovely dessert with your favorite carob or chocolate ice "cream."

EACH SERVING PROVIDES
184 calories, 3 g protein, 6 g fat,
1 g dietary fiber, 30 g carbohydrates,
300 mg sodium, 0 mg cholesterol

1 ½ cups unbleached white flour

1 teaspoon baking soda

½ teaspoon salt

1 cup organic granulated sugar

¼ cup wheat germ

¼ cup canola oil

3 tablespoons fresh-squeezed
    lemon juice

1 teaspoon lemon extract

¼ cup poppy seeds

Zest of one lemon

Preheat the oven to 350 degrees F. In a large bowl, sift together the flour, baking soda, and salt. Stir in the sugar and wheat germ. Make a well in the center of the mixture and stir in the oil, lemon juice, and lemon extract. Add 1 cup of cold water as you continue to stir. Beat until smooth, using an electric mixer, eggbeater, or wooden spoon. Fold in the poppy seeds and lemon zest.

Pour the batter into an ungreased 8-inch or 9-inch square glass or ceramic baking dish, and place in the oven. Bake for 30 minutes, until a toothpick inserted in the center of the cake comes out clean. Cool on a rack for about 15 minutes, then cut into 12 squares while still in the baking dish. Transfer the squares to a cooling rack or serve warm.

Fabulous Fruit Crisp

YIELD: 8 servings

¼ cup canola oil

2 tablespoons fresh-squeezed
    lemon juice

3 pounds fresh apples or pears

1½ cups fresh or frozen blueber-
    ries, blackberries, or cranberries
    (see NOTE)

1 cup rolled oats

½ cup whole wheat flour

⅓ cup organic granulated sugar

1 teaspoon ground cinnamon

⅛ teaspoon salt

This crisp is a good fall or winter dessert, especially when served warm. It is delicious just as it comes from the oven, or you can dress it up with Creamy Vanilla Sauce (page 293) or Sweet Soy Cashew Topping (page 292). If you love nuts, combine some chopped walnuts, almonds, or pecans with the fruit mixture before adding the crumb topping.

EACH SERVING PROVIDES
*272 calories, 3 g protein, 8 g fat,
6 g dietary fiber, 50 g carbohydrates,
39 mg sodium, 0 mg cholesterol*

Rub a baking dish with 1 teaspoon of the oil. Set aside. Preheat the oven to 400 degrees F.

Place the lemon juice in a large bowl. Discard the cores of the apples or pears, and coarsely chop the fruit, tossing it with the lemon juice as you go.

Add the berries to the apples and toss to combine well. Transfer the mixture to the oiled baking dish, creating an even layer in which the berries are well distributed.

Place the rolled oats in a blender and grind to a coarse meal consistency. In a bowl, combine the ground oats, flour, sugar, cinnamon, and salt. Stir to combine well, then drizzle in the remaining oil about a tablespoon at a time, using your fingers to rub the oil into the dry ingredients until it is well incorporated and the mixture has a moist crumb consistency.

Distribute the oat mixture evenly over the fruit and shake the dish so some of the topping settles into the fruit. Bake for 40 to 45 minutes, until browned and bubbly.

NOTE: If using frozen berries, place them in a colander and rinse briefly under warm water to melt off any ice crystals before adding them to the dish.

Apple–Cranberry Pie with Butter–Free Crust

YIELD: 8 servings

Contrary to popular belief, you can achieve a lovely piecrust without using butter or short-ening. This classic pie makes delicious use of two of winter's most versatile fruits, and it is a recipe for happiness.

EACH SERVING PROVIDES

499 calories, 6 g protein, 27 g fat, 5 g dietary fiber, 61 g carbohydrates, 148 mg sodium, 0 mg cholesterol

The crust

2 ¼ cups unbleached white flour

Scant ½ teaspoon salt

1 tablespoon organic granulated sugar

½ cup plus 2 tablespoons canola oil

The filling

2 tablespoons fresh-squeezed lemon juice

8 cups peeled and sliced tart apples (about 4 large Granny Smith)

1 ½ cups fresh cranberries

1 cup coarsely chopped walnuts

2 teaspoons ground cinnamon

⅓ cup organic granulated sugar

¼ cup unbleached white flour

To make the crust: Sift the flour, salt, and sugar into a mixing bowl. Slowly drizzle in the oil, using your fingers to rub the flour into the oil. The mixture should have a coarse crumb consistency, studded with many small lumps of oil-saturated flour. Add 3 table-spoons of cold water, ½ tablespoon at a time, incorporating it by tossing the flour mixture around with your fingers. Add only enough water to make the mixture hold together in a loose ball. Wrap the ball of dough in waxed paper and set it aside in the refrig-erator to chill.

To make the filling: Place the lemon juice in a large bowl. Peel, core, and slice the apples, tossing them with the lemon juice as you go.

Add the cranberries and walnuts to the apples and toss to com-bine well. Sprinkle on the cinnamon, sugar, and flour, and toss again to coat everything evenly (this is best done with your hands). Set the filling aside, and retrieve the dough from the refrigerator.

Cover a cutting board or other flat work surface with a sheet of waxed paper and lightly dust the paper with flour. Separate the ball of dough into two pieces, one slightly larger than the other. Place the largest piece on the floured board, and use a rolling pin to roll the dough out into a thin circle about 2 inches larger in diameter than your pie dish. Pivot the paper as you roll the dough out to achieve a round, rather than oblong, shape. Carefully pick up the paper and use it to transfer the crust to the pie dish. Gently lay the crust into the dish, peel off and discard the paper, and arrange the crust so it sits snugly against the bottom and sides of the dish, over-hanging the rim by about ½ inch. If the crust breaks during this process, simply patch it with small bits of rolled out crust from the remaining dough ball.

Preheat the oven to 400 degrees F.

Place a clean sheet of wax paper on your cutting board and flour it. Roll out the other ball of dough so that it is slightly larger than the pie dish in diameter. Mound the filling into the pie dish, and cover it with the second crust, laying it carefully atop the mound. Again, if the crust breaks, patch it as best you can. Fold the overhanging margin of the bottom crust over the edge of the top crust and pinch them together to create a seal. Crimp the edges of the crust in a decorative pattern, if you wish. Use a sharp knife to make a few slits in the top of the pie, which will allow steam to escape and prevent the crust from ballooning up.

Bake the pie for 45 to 50 minutes, until the crust is nicely browned and the filling is bubbling. Cool slightly before serving.

Banana–Date Freeze

YIELD: 4 servings

Almost Instant

This very simple and light dessert is the essence of bananas. Serve it whenever you want a healthy snack or as the dessert course after an Indian-inspired meal. It's a snap!

EACH SERVING PROVIDES
*137 calories, 5 g protein, 2 g fat,
2 g dietary fiber, 27 g carbohydrates,
4 mg sodium, 0 mg cholesterol*

2 medium ripe bananas
¼ cup whole pitted dates, lightly packed

6 ounces firm silken tofu
¼ cup fresh-squeezed orange juice
1 tablespoon brown rice syrup

Peel the bananas, cut them into ½-inch slices, and place them in a glass jar or plastic bag. Freeze for several hours or up to 2 days. On the morning that you want to serve the dessert, chop the dates finely and place them in the blender, along with the frozen bananas, silken tofu, orange juice, and rice syrup. Purée until the mixture is smooth and glossy, with bits of date evenly distributed through it. Transfer the mixture to a ceramic or glass bowl and cover it with plastic wrap. Freeze for several hours, then use an ice cream scoop to serve. Use pretty dessert glasses, and garnish each serving with a sprig of mint, if you wish.

DATES

The date is an ancient food native to the Middle East. Some historians believe the date palm was the first tree to be cultivated by human beings at the dawn of agriculture. As fruits go, dates provide a healthy dose of potassium, iron, and phosphorus and are high in fiber. They also provide an intense sweet flavor in whole food form, so keep some on hand for yourself and the kids to satisfy that occasional sugar craving.

Sundae School

Some of our fondest childhood memories involve the ice cream parlor or a special birthday party. Vegan children don't have to miss out on such special dessert occasions. The abundant variety of nondairy frozen confections now available in natural food stores and supermarkets provides the perfect inspiration for a make-your-own-sundae event.

Gather together colorful bowls, straws, and long-handled spoons. Arrange them in a fanciful way on a paper-covered table, with fun napkins and seasonal party favors to help set the mood. Invite your favorite children and their favorite grown-ups. All will enjoy creating their own unique sundaes.

The necessary food supplies include: fresh fruits, flavored syrups, and chopped nuts, along with several varieties of frozen desserts. Carob chips and coconut flakes are popular sprinkles. Choose natural, nondairy chocolate, carob, or caramel syrups. Plain maple syrup and rice syrup also taste great as ice milk toppings. Another welcome offering is the Sweet Soy Cashew Topping on page 292. Cookies, such as vanilla wafers and gingersnaps, provide satisfying texture and flavor contrasts.

One pint of purchased sorbet, or soy or rice ice milk, will make 2 generous servings. Figure on at least ½ cup of chopped fresh fruit per person. Fruits that oxidize easily—like apples, pears, and bananas—should be left whole and cut as needed or chopped and tossed with lemon or lime juice. Plan on a tablespoon or two of chopped nuts per person—almonds, walnuts, and pecans are good choices.

No rules apply in building sundaes, but some of our favorite combinations include:

- Bananas with carob frozen dessert and chopped toasted almonds

- Vanilla frozen dessert with fresh sliced strawberries and lemon wafers

- Orange vanilla swirl sorbet, chocolate syrup, and cherries

- Peach sorbet with fresh blueberries and Sweet Soy Cashew Topping (page 292)

- Strawberry frozen dessert with pineapple chunks and coconut flakes

Grilled Fruit with Rum Glaze and Sweet Soy Cashew Topping

YIELD: 4 servings

This dessert will be a hit at your next backyard grilling party. Its presentation is elegant and thoroughly appetizing. You can grill the fruit early and hold it at room temperature until serving time. The glaze is best served warm.

EACH SERVING PROVIDES
373 calories, 7 g protein, 13 g fat, 4 g dietary fiber, 56 g carbohydrates, 8 mg sodium, 0 mg cholesterol

4 fresh green or black figs, barely ripe

2 fresh nectarines, barely ripe

4 1-inch slices fresh pineapple, peeled and cored

1 tablespoon canola oil

⅓ cup fresh-squeezed orange juice, strained

2 tablespoons rum

2 tablespoons maple syrup

1 teaspoon arrowroot powder

Fresh nutmeg for garnish

1 recipe Sweet Soy Cashew Topping (page 292)

Preheat the grill to medium-high.

Wash the figs and nectarines and dry them well. Discard the stems of the figs and slice them in half from top to bottom. Cut the nectarines in half from top to bottom and discard the pits. Rub or spray the cut figs, nectarines, and pineapple slices very lightly with oil. Place the fruit on the hot grill; skin side down for the nectarines and figs. Cook 2 minutes, then turn the fruit and cook an additional 2 minutes. (The grill should be hot enough to create dark slash marks on the fruit.)

Meanwhile, in a small saucepan, combine the orange juice, rum, maple syrup, and arrowroot powder. Whisk frequently as you bring the mixture to a simmer over medium heat. Simmer rapidly for 2 minutes, until slightly reduced.

Distribute the fruit among 4 dessert dishes. Drizzle some of the rum glaze over each portion and add a dollop of the topping. Serve immediately.

Oasis Orbs

YIELD: 24 orbs

½ cup shredded coconut

1 cup rolled oats

1 cup date pieces

¾ cup almond butter

¼ cup raw sesame seeds

2 teaspoons grated orange peel

⅓ fresh-squeezed orange juice

Place ¼ cup of the coconut on a plate and set aside.

Place the rolled oats in a heavy-bottomed skillet and toast for a few minutes, stirring constantly. When they begin to turn a darker shade of tan at the edges and emit a toasted aroma, transfer the oats to the bowl of a food processor. Process on high to pulverize them to a fine meal consistency.

Add the remaining ¼ cup coconut and the dates and process to finely chop them, then add the almond butter, sesame seeds, and orange peel. Add the orange juice and process until the ingredients come together to form a homogeneous mass. Add a bit more orange juice, if needed, to get the right thick and well-blended consistency. Don't add too much juice; you want the mixture to be fairly dry, not moist and mushy.

Use your hands to form the mixture into balls about 1 ½ inches in diameter, then roll the balls in the reserved shredded coconut. Place on a plate and chill for an hour or so before serving. They're also good, though a bit gooey, when eaten at room temperature.

Tad Toomay named this addictive high-nutrient snack. The finished orbs will stay fresh for a few days if well covered and stored in the refrigerator. If you don't have a food processor, you can combine the ingredients in a mixing bowl, kneading with your hands or stirring with a wooden spoon to achieve the right consistency. If you're planning to mix the ingredients this way, chop the dates very finely before you begin.

EACH SERVING PROVIDES

112 calories, 2 g protein, 7 g fat, 2 g dietary fiber, 12 g carbohydrates, 2 mg sodium, 0 mg cholesterol

Sweet Soy Cashew Topping

YIELD: 1 cup (about 6 servings)

This orange-laced topping is yummy on any fruit dessert or cooked cereal. It will keep up to a week in the refrigerator. If the mixture separates over time, stir it briskly to recombine the ingredients.

5 ounces firm tofu

½ cup raw unsalted cashew pieces

¼ cup fresh-squeezed orange juice, strained

¼ cup maple syrup

1 tablespoon pure vanilla extract

1 teaspoon fresh-squeezed lemon juice

Pinch of salt

EACH SERVING PROVIDES
*118 calories, 4 g protein, 6 g fat,
0 g dietary fiber, 13 g carbohydrates,
3 mg sodium, 0 mg cholesterol*

Dice the tofu into ½-inch pieces and wrap in a clean tea towel to absorb any excess moisture. Set aside until needed.

Finely chop the cashews in a blender or food processor, then add the orange juice in a thin stream while the motor is still running. Process for 30 seconds, then turn off the machine and scrape the sides and bottom of the blender to release the cashew "mud" back into the mixture. Add the tofu, maple syrup, vanilla extract, lemon juice, and salt. Blend at high speed until the mixture is very smooth and as thick as lightly whipped cream, about 1 full minute.

Chill for an hour or so before serving, if desired.

Creamy Vanilla Sauce

YIELD: ¾ cup, about 4 servings

6 ounces cultured soy "yogurt"

1 tablespoon maple syrup

1 teaspoon pure vanilla extract

In a bowl, whisk together the yogurt, maple syrup, and vanilla extract until smooth. Chill before serving, if desired.

Almost Instant

Nothing could be simpler than this deliciously smooth dessert or cereal topping. In a tightly closed container, it will keep in the refrigerator for up to a week.

EACH SERVING PROVIDES

45 calories, 1 g protein, 1 g fat,

1 g dietary fiber, 8 g carbohydrates,

6 mg sodium, 0 mg cholesterol

15

Frequently Used Homemade Ingredients

Steamed Brown Rice
Steamed Basmati Rice
Cooked Beans
Seasoned Bread Crumbs
Crostini
Pizza Crust
Pita Crisps
Tempeh Croutons
Tofu Chorizo "Sausage"
Baked Tofu
Salsa Fresca
Tomato Coulis

A well-stocked kitchen contains not only raw ingredients, but also items that can be made in advance to have on hand for convenient use in daily meal preparation. In this chapter, we provide recipes for some of the ingredients frequently called for in the pages of this book, and a few other basics you will come to rely on.

Of course, commercial versions of some of these foods are available—such as bread crumbs and salsa—but they often contain unwanted additives and will not deliver the best flavor. Remember the age-old gospel of cooking: Top-quality ingredients will always yield the best results.

Once you've experienced the great taste of these homemade foods, you'll agree that the minimal time needed to make them is well spent.

Steamed Brown Rice

YIELD: 4 servings

Brown rice is an important staple in the vegan diet. It is nutrient dense, provides a slow carbohydrate release for sustained energy, and is well-tolerated by just about everyone. We keep steamed brown rice on hand in the refrigerator to add satisfying texture and nutrition to soups, salads, burritos, and many other dishes. It also makes a great breakfast porridge when simmered in a little water with your favorite dried fruits and nuts.

EACH SERVING PROVIDES
108 calories, 3 g protein, 1 g fat,
2 g dietary fiber, 22 g carbohydrates,
49 mg sodium, 0 mg cholesterol

1 cup short- or long-grain brown rice, uncooked

⅛ teaspoon salt

Bring 2 cups of water to a boil in a medium saucepan over high heat. Stir in the rice and salt and return to a boil, then cover and reduce the heat to very low. Simmer for 45 minutes, then turn off the heat and allow the pot to stand without disturbing the lid for at least 5 minutes before serving.

Steamed Basmati Rice

YIELD: 4 servings

1 cup white or brown basmati rice,
　　uncooked

⅛ teaspoon salt

For a light and fluffy texture, wash the rice by placing it in a fine-mesh strainer and rinsing it for several seconds to wash off some of the starch that clings to the outside of the grains. Drain thoroughly.

　　Bring 2 cups of water to a boil in a medium saucepan over high heat. Stir in the rice and salt and return to a boil, then cover and reduce the heat to very low. Simmer for 45 minutes for brown basmati, 20 minutes for white, then turn off the heat and allow the pot to stand without disturbing the lid for at least 5 minutes before serving.

Another multi-purpose grain is fragrant basmati rice. It is available in both brown and white varieties. The brown will deliver more fiber and nutrients, but the white cooks quickly and has a fluffier quality. Either way, it makes a good side dish, especially with curries and other Asian dishes.

EACH SERVING PROVIDES
*103 calories, 2 g protein, 0 g fat,
0 g dietary fiber, 22 g carbohydrates,
45 mg sodium, 0 mg cholesterol*

Seasoned Fine Bread Crumbs

YIELD: 1 ½ cups

Make up a batch of bread crumbs whenever you have old, dry bread available. You will find many uses for them. You may also want to keep coarse bread crumbs on hand. These are made using the same process described below, but the bread is left in larger pieces.

EACH SERVING PROVIDES
113 calories, 4 g protein, 2 g fat, 1 g dietary fiber, 21 g carbohydrates, 234 mg sodium, 0 mg cholesterol

½ pound dry bread, broken into chunks

2 tablespoons Italian Seasoning (see page 310)

1 teaspoon granulated garlic

If the bread is not completely dried out, place the chunks on a baking sheet and put into a 250 degree F oven for an hour or so. You can also just leave it in the open air on the kitchen counter and wait until it air dries before processing into crumbs.

When you are ready to make the crumbs, place the dry bread in a food processor and process to a fine crumb consistency. If some of the bread remains in large chunks, pour the contents of the food processor into a medium-mesh strainer set over a bowl. The fine crumbs will fall through, leaving the larger pieces behind. Return the chunks to the food processor and proceed until all the bread is a fine crumb consistency. Place the crumbs back in the processor and add the herb blend and garlic. Process to combine. Bread crumbs will keep indefinitely in an airtight container at room temperature.

Crostini

YIELD: About 36 crostini (about 12 servings)

1 pound fresh unsliced baguette

Preheat the oven to 375 degrees F. Cut the baguette crosswise into ¼-inch slices. Arrange the slices in a single layer on a baking sheet and bake for about 8 to 10 minutes, until the bread is evenly browned and well crisped, but not rock-hard and dry. Use immediately, warm or at room temperature, or cool completely before storing in an airtight container at room temperature.

Prepare as needed to enjoy with spreads or other toppings. Unused crostini can be stored in an airtight container at room temperature for up to a few days.

EACH SERVING PROVIDES
104 calories, 3 g protein, 1 g fat, 1 g dietary fiber, 20 g carbohydrates, 230 mg sodium, 0 mg cholesterol

Pizza Crust

YIELD: 2 12-inch pizza crusts

Use bread flour or unbleached white flour for best results. The flour measure is given as a range, because the exact amount will vary depending on the day's humidity and other conditions. The temperature of the water used to start the yeast is import-ant—if it is too hot, it will kill the yeast; if it is too cold, the yeast will not be activated. A simple kitchen thermometer can be used to eliminate the guesswork. Be sure to check the date on packets of yeast, and use one that has not exceeded its shelf life.

¼ ounce active dry yeast (1 packet)

1 ½ cups lukewarm water (105 to 115 degrees F)

2 tablespoons plus ½ teaspoon olive oil

½ teaspoon salt

3 ½ to 4 cups cake or unbleached white flour

EACH SERVING PROVIDES
220 calories, 8 g protein, 1 g fat, 2 g dietary fiber, 44 g carbohydrates, 136 mg sodium, 0 mg cholesterol

Place the yeast in a large bowl and add the warm water. Stir with a wooden spoon to dissolve the yeast, then set it aside in a warm place until creamy in appearance, about 15 minutes. Stir in the 2 table-spoons of oil and the salt, then add 2 cups of flour. Stir to incor-porate, using a large wooden spoon. The mixture will be very sticky at this point. Add 1 more cup of the flour and continue to stir until the dough begins to form a ball. Turn out onto a lightly floured work surface and knead the dough until it is soft and smooth, about 10 minutes, adding the remaining flour as needed, a bit at a time, until the dough is no longer sticky. Too much flour will re-sult in a dry dough that can become a slightly tough crust, so don't add more flour than necessary.

Rub a large bowl with the remaining ½ teaspoon oil. Place the dough ball in the oiled bowl, turn it to coat the entire surface with oil, and cover the bowl with a clean tea towel. Place the bowl in a warm, draft-free place for the dough to rise until doubled in vol-ume, about 1 ½ hours. (An unlit gas oven or warm cupboard works well.) After it has risen, punch the dough down with your fist or fingertips to press out most of the air.

Place the dough on a lightly floured work surface and divide it into 2 balls of equal size. Working with 1 ball at a time, flatten it with your hands into a circle about 4 inches in diameter and 1 inch thick.

Begin working from the center, pressing the dough outward with the heels of your hands. If the dough sticks to your hands, sprinkle it lightly with flour. Keep pushing and stretching the dough in this fashion until you have a 12-inch round that is slightly thicker at the edge. (Alternatively, you may use a rolling pin to spread the dough into a 12-inch round.)

If you are making only 1 pizza, the remaining dough ball may be wrapped tightly in plastic and frozen for up to 3 months. Thaw the dough at room temperature for a few hours before rolling out as directed. When the dough is rolled out, proceed with the instructions provided with individual recipes.

If you want to cook the dough without a topping, drizzle a little olive oil on it, sprinkle with coarse salt, and bake until crisp at the edges and golden brown, about 10 to 12 minutes.

Pita Crisps

YIELD: 96 crisps (about 12 servings)

6 pita rounds
Canola or olive oil spray (optional)

Toasted pita triangles provide a nice crisp dipper for salsas and spreads. If you aren't going to use them immediately, allow them to cool, then store in an airtight container at room temperature for up to 2 days. If you have a non-aerosol oil spray bottle, you may spritz the chips with a little canola or olive oil before baking; however, they will be tasty and crisp without it. This same method can be used to make tortilla chips. Simply cut each tortilla into triangles before baking as directed below.

EACH SERVING PROVIDES
*85 calories, 3 g protein, 1 g fat,
2 g dietary fiber, 18 g carbohydrates,
170 mg sodium, 0 mg cholesterol*

Preheat a conventional or toaster oven to 350 degrees F. Cut each pita round into 8 triangles, as if cutting a pie. One piece at a time, slowly and carefully separate the two layers of bread. Each pita round will yield 16 thin triangles.

Place the pita triangles in a single layer, not touching each other. Spray very lightly with canola or olive oil, if desired.

Bake until lightly browned and crisp, about 10 to 12 minutes. To serve, place the crisps in a basket lined with a cloth napkin.

Tempeh Croutons

YIELD: About 8 servings

1 tablespoon canola oil

1 tablespoon vegetable stock

1½ teaspoons soy sauce

1½ teaspoons unseasoned rice
vinegar

1 teaspoon mild paprika

1 teaspoon granulated garlic

8 ounces soy tempeh

These yummy little morsels lend texture, flavor, and protein to leafy salads, creamy soups, or an appetizer buffet. Depending on the dimensions and thickness of the tempeh you purchase, this recipe yields about 60 to 80 ½-inch cubes.

Preheat a conventional or toaster oven to 375 degrees F. In a medium-sized bowl, mix the oil, stock, soy sauce, vinegar, paprika, and garlic until well combined. Cut the tempeh into ½-inch cubes and add to the bowl. Stir around until the tempeh pieces are thoroughly coated with the oil mixture.

Spread the tempeh cubes out on a baking sheet so that they are not touching each other. Bake for 20 minutes, turning the cubes every 5 minutes so they toast evenly.

Use immediately or cool completely, then store in a tightly covered container in the refrigerator for up to a week. The tempeh can be re-crisped, if desired, by baking at 375 degrees F for 5 minutes before serving.

EACH SERVING PROVIDES
*58 calories, 6 g protein, 3 g fat,
0 g dietary fiber, 1 g carbohydrates,
65 mg sodium, 0 mg cholesterol*

Tofu Chorizo "Sausage"

YIELD: 3 cups

Many people who have traveled in Mexico fondly recall the potent flavor of chorizo. This simple recipe will convince you that the flavor of chorizo is mostly in the seasoning, not in the pork traditionally used to make the spicy sausage. In this meatless version, ancho chilies, garlic, and an abundance of other strong seasonings create a mouthwatering intensity of flavor, and long cooking over high heat creates a satisfying chewy texture. Use this chorizo as a filling for tacos or enchiladas, or mix it with plain cooked rice for a delicious, warming treat.

EACH SERVING PROVIDES
*135 calories, 10 g protein, 9 g fat,
3 g dietary fiber, 9 g carbohydrates,
387 mg sodium, 0 mg cholesterol*

1 pound firm tofu

3 large dried ancho chilies

4 cloves garlic, coarsely chopped

1 tablespoon dried oregano

2 teaspoons mild paprika

1 ½ teaspoons cumin seeds

1 teaspoon salt

⅛ teaspoon dried red chili flakes

4 whole cloves

¼-inch piece cinnamon stick

2 tablespoons apple cider vinegar

2 tablespoons smooth peanut butter

1 ¼ cups vegetable stock

Cut the tofu into ½-inch-thick slices and place the slices on a clean tea towel on a flat surface. Cover with another clean tea towel and place a baking sheet or cutting board on top. Place a weight (a large can of tomatoes works well) on top of the baking sheet so the tofu is firmly pressed, but not mashed, between the towels. Allow the tofu to drain in this manner for at least an hour to remove most of its water.

Meanwhile, heat a cast-iron griddle or heavy-bottomed skillet over medium-high heat. Use your hands to tear the chilies into large pieces, discarding the stems and seeds. Place the chili pieces on a hot griddle and toast for 1 to 2 minutes, constantly pressing down on them with a metal spatula. They will blister a bit and begin to lighten in color. Turn them over and toast the other side briefly.

When the chilies are lightly toasted, place them in a food processor with the garlic, oregano, paprika, cumin seeds, salt, chili flakes, cloves, and cinnamon stick. Process until finely ground. Add the vinegar, peanut butter, and ¼ cup of the stock and blend until fairly smooth. Add the remaining 1 cup of stock and purée, then transfer the mixture to a heavy-bottomed skillet over medium-high heat.

Crumble the drained tofu into the skillet and bring to a simmer. Reduce the heat to medium-low and cook for about 20 minutes, frequently stirring and scraping the bottom and sides of the skillet with a metal spatula to incorporate any stuck bits of tofu back into the mixture.

The chorizo is done when the tofu has a fairly dry, crumbly consistency. Use immediately, store for up to a week in the refrigerator, or freeze for longer periods.

Baked Tofu

YIELD: 4 pieces

This recipe turns plain tofu into a tempting finger-food snack or sandwich ingredient. You can also add cubes to a green salad or stew or grate it into a bowl of hot brown rice. Once you discover how easy and delicious this is, you will no longer be tempted by expensive store-bought baked tofu.

EACH SERVING PROVIDES
143 calories, 11 g protein, 11 g fat, 0 g dietary fiber, 3 g carbohydrates, 517 mg sodium, 0 mg cholesterol

1 pound firm tofu

⅓ cup vegetable stock

2 tablespoons soy sauce

1 tablespoon dark sesame oil

1 teaspoon brown rice syrup

½ teaspoon granulated garlic

½ teaspoon ground ginger

½ teaspoon ground cumin

Rinse the tofu and, if necessary, cut it into 4 slabs that are about 1-inch thick. Place the tofu pieces on a clean, folded tea towel on a flat surface, like a cutting board or countertop. Cover with another clean, folded tea towel and lay a cutting board or other flat object on top. Place a moderate weight on the board (such as a large can of tomatoes) and leave to drain for about 30 minutes.

Meanwhile, in a baking dish just large enough to hold the tofu, stir together the stock, soy sauce, sesame oil, rice syrup, granulated garlic, ginger, and cumin. When the tofu has drained, place it in the marinade, cover the dish, and place in the refrigerator for a couple of hours. Turn the tofu pieces over midway through the marinating time.

Preheat a conventional or toaster oven to 400 degrees F. Place the baking dish in the oven, and cook for 30 minutes, then turn the tofu over and cook an additional 30 minutes. The liquid should be completely absorbed and the tofu should have a nice dark "crust."

Eat immediately, or store in the refrigerator and use over the course of a few days.

Salsa Fresca

YIELD: 5 cups

2½ pounds fresh tomatoes

1 can (7 ounces) whole green chilies

¼ cup fresh-squeezed lemon juice

1 medium onion, finely diced

⅓ cup minced fresh cilantro

3 cloves garlic, minced

⅛ teaspoon salt

A few grinds black pepper

Nothing beats the flavor and texture of homemade salsa. Make up a batch to serve at a party, or put some up for the pantry by packing in pint jars and processing according to standard canning procedures.

Blanch and peel the tomatoes. Coarsely chop them, drain off as much juice as possible, and set aside in a bowl. Drain the liquid from the canned green chilies. Finely chop them, and add to the tomatoes. Add the lemon juice to the tomato mixture, along with the onion, cilantro, garlic, salt, and pepper.

Though its flavor improves over time, this salsa can be enjoyed immediately. Leftovers will stay fresh for about 2 weeks if stored in a tightly closed container in the refrigerator.

EACH SERVING PROVIDES
9 calories, 0 g protein, 0 g fat,
1 g dietary fiber, 2 g carbohydrates,
24 mg sodium, 0 mg cholesterol

Magical Blends

For the freshest, tastiest, and most economical seasoning blends, make your own several times a year. Mixing up your own allows you to adjust the proportions according to your taste. Here are some of our favorite seasoning combinations, and some suggestions of dishes they enhance.

If you enjoy gardening, be sure to plant a few culinary herbs wherever you have a bit of space. Most herbs are forgiving of harsh conditions and won't require much tending. Rosemary is a perennial that will take root, grow large and lusty, and season your cooking for years to come. Thyme, oregano, and marjoram are other hardy species that may winter over and provide years of flavor. Tender, leafy herbs such as basil, cilantro, and parsley are annuals. For best results, buy small seedlings of these varieties, and plant them outdoors when the weather warms. Drying herbs is simply a matter of tying them in bundles and hanging them up in a warm spot out of direct sunlight. When the leaves are perfectly dry, rub them from the stems, and store in airtight jars in a cool, dark place.

If gardening isn't your thing, seek out a good bulk herb supplier for the best quality herbs. The larger natural food stores often sell bulk herbs, and dried herbs are also readily available by mail-order.

The fragrance and flavor of dried herbs do diminish with age. Most dried herbs and herb blends should be replaced in your pantry about every 4 months. To check for potency, simply remove the lid and take a sniff. If the aroma is musty or nonexistent, discard the herb.

The instructions for making these blends is the same in every case. Simply toss the ingredients together and store in a tightly closed jar in a cool and dark place.

ITALIAN SEASONING

Stir together. Use for soups, tomato sauces, salad dressings, and marinades

1 teaspoon dried basil	2 teaspoons dried parsley
2 teaspoons dried oregano	1 teaspoon dried rosemary

HERBES DE PROVENCE

Stir together. Use for bean stews, salad dressing, stir-fries, and potato dishes

1 teaspoon fennel seed, finely crushed	1 teaspoon dried rosemary
2 teaspoons dried oregano	1 teaspoon dried tarragon
2 teaspoons dried thyme	½ teaspoon ground sage
1 teaspoon dried lavender flowers	

CURRY BLEND

Stir together. Use for vegetable stir-fries, soups and stews, rice, and tofu dishes

1 tablespoon ground ginger

1 tablespoon ground coriander

2 teaspoons ground turmeric

2 teaspoons ground cumin

1 teaspoon ground cinnamon

1 teaspoon ground cloves

1 teaspoon cayenne pepper

CHINESE FIVE-SPICE POWDER

Stir together. Use for vegetable stir-fries, cakes, cookies, and fruit salad dressing

Equal parts, ground:

Anise seed

Dried licorice root

Dried ginger

Cinnamon

Cloves

SWEET SPICE BLEND

Stir together. Use for cakes, cookies, sweet potatoes, and winter squashes

1 teaspoon ground ginger

1 teaspoon ground cinnamon

1 teaspoon ground nutmeg

½ teaspoon ground cloves

GOMASIO

Grind together. Use as table condiment in place of salt

1 tablespoon sea salt

1 cup raw brown sesame seeds

SPICY SEAWEED CONDIMENT

Grind together. Use as table condiment in place of salt

4 tablespoons dried dulse flakes

3 tablespoons whole flax seeds

3 tablespoons raw brown sesame seeds

1 teaspoon dried red chili flakes

Tomato Coulis

YIELD: 2 cups

Make this quick sauce during tomato season and keep it on hand in the refrigerator. It's great on pasta, polenta, and cooked grains. If desired, you can prepare a larger batch and freeze it in pint jars or put it up following standard canning procedures.

EACH SERVING PROVIDES

70 calories, 2 g protein, 4 g fat, 2 g dietary fiber, 9 g carbohydrates, 82 mg sodium, 0 mg cholesterol

3 pounds fresh pear tomatoes

2 tablespoons olive oil

2 cloves garlic, minced

1 fresh lemon wedge

1 tablespoon dried oregano

¼ teaspoon salt

A few grinds black pepper

Blanch, peel, and seed the tomatoes (see page 5), and chop them coarsely. Heat the oil in a heavy-bottomed skillet, then add the garlic and stir and sauté for about a minute. Add the tomatoes, lemon, oregano, salt, and pepper. Cook over medium-high heat, stirring frequently, about 5 minutes. The tomatoes will break apart and liquefy a bit. Simmer about 10 more minutes over low heat, until a thick sauce consistency is achieved.

TOMATOES

An antioxidant called lycopene is being studied for its anticancer properties, and tomatoes are the main source of lycopene in the American diet. Other bright red foods—such as ruby grapefruit and watermelon—also contain the substance. Some studies suggest that lycopene is easier to assimilate when consumed in cooked tomato preparations, like tomato sauce.

Appendix: Nutrition Fundamentals

Food is the body's fuel, and it should come as no surprise that some foods provide better fuel than others. To a great degree, the foods you eat determine your physical and mental energy levels, so if you care about being positive and productive, you should pay careful attention to how you nourish yourself. Becoming familiar with the nutritional building blocks of good health can help guide your food choices. Here, we offer some information about the basic nutrients and their functions.

CARBOHYDRATES

Simple sugars, also called refined carbohydrates, enter the bloodstream quickly; different sugars do so at different rates. Plain white table sugar, for instance, is solid sucrose, and it enters the bloodstream very quickly, creating a "sugar rush" that overworks your metabolic processes. Complex carbohydrates—whole grains, for example—are metabolized more slowly, so they can help you sustain a high energy level between meals. They also provide fiber, which contributes to good digestion and elimination.

PROTEIN

Protein plays an essential role in building and repairing all the body's tissues. Most people think of meat as the only source of protein; however, many plant foods—notably grains, beans, and nuts—provide amino acids, which are the building blocks of protein. When a variety of these foods is eaten daily, the amino acids combine to form complete proteins.

FATS

For some people, eating an extremely lowfat diet is a recipe for disease, not health. Fats perform a number of essential functions in the body, such as lubrication and nutrient transport. Perhaps it makes better sense to pay attention to the *quality* of the oils you consume, than to obsess about the *quantity*. The fats derived from plant sources are monounsaturated and polyunsaturated, and they do not pose the same threat to heart health as the saturated fats in meat and dairy products.

But not all vegetable oils are created equal. Research indicates that olive and canola oils, which are highly monounsaturated, may be the healthiest oils of all because they oxidize slowly. Highly polyunsaturated vegetable oils, which are more prone to oxidation, can create "free radicals," the marauding molecules that appear to play a role in cancer development. For this reason, our recipes almost exclusively call for olive and canola oils.

FIBER

Grains, beans, vegetables, and fruits provide plenty of insoluble fiber, also called "roughage." Roughage helps sweep toxins out of the intestines and keeps the digestive system functioning efficiently. When you have adequate dietary fiber, your body processes and absorbs nutrients better, so your vitality increases. A sensible vegan diet is high in fiber, which is one of its many important benefits.

VITAMINS AND MINERALS

Below we discuss some of the main functions that known vitamins and minerals perform in your body. We also indicate good vegan sources of each nutrient. Vitamin and mineral supplements are widely available, but most experts agree that if you eat a varied and balanced diet—including lots of fresh, unprocessed foods—supplements are not usually necessary to maintain good health. Eating whole, natural foods generally ensures that you get the vitamins, minerals, and fiber you need, along with other health-promoting substances that may still be undiscovered.

A great deal of nutritional research has been done on a group of food components known as antioxidants. Antioxidants neutralize the unhealthy effects of oxygen-hungry cells known as "free radicals," which are implicated in the development of cancer, cardiovascular disease, and cataracts, to name just a few dread diseases. Notable antioxidants include vitamins C, E, and A (made by the body from beta carotene), and selenium, a trace mineral. Many other compounds present in whole, natural foods also have antioxidant powers. all the more reason to eat a wide variety of high-quality foods.

The following vitamins and minerals are some of the most important health-promoters. Fortunately, they are plentiful in a diverse natural foods diet.

Vitamin A

This antioxidant is important in preventing heart disease, cataracts, and macular degeneration. Like the other antioxidants, it wards off cancer by neutralizing free radicals. The body is able to synthesize vitamin A when given a sufficient quantity of certain carotenes, notably beta-carotene. Provitamin A carotenes are plentiful in dark leafy greens and yellow-orange vegetables like sweet potatoes, carrots, and winter squash.

Vitamin B1 (Thiamin)

Thiamin plays an important role in metabolism, helping cells convert carbohydrates into energy. It also plays an important role in heart function and is necessary for the maintenance of healthy brain and nerve cells. Deficiencies most notably cause fatigue, weakness, and nerve damage. Whole grains (especially wheat germ), dried beans, and peanuts are good sources.

Vitamin B2 (Riboflavin)

Like other components of the B-complex, riboflavin helps convert carbohydrates into energy. In conjunction with other B vitamins, it is essential for production of red blood cells and inhibits dry, cracked skin. Important sources are nuts, green leafy vegetables, and legumes.

Vitamin B3 (Niacin)

Niacin is important in the conversion of food into energy. It is instrumental in maintaining normal functioning of the skin, nerves, and digestive system. Eat foods such as nuts, legumes, and enriched breads and cereals to ensure adequate intake.

Vitamin B6

Vitamin B6 helps maintain normal brain and immune function and plays a role in the formation of red blood cells. The best dietary sources for vegans are nuts, beans, bananas, avocados, sweet potatoes, and whole grains.

Vitamin B12

As with other B-complex vitamins, B12 aids in the formation of red blood cells and helps to maintain a healthy central nervous system.

Since the primary dietary source for B12 is animal foods, vegans must be careful to get sufficient amounts of this vitamin. Some nutritionists believe that miso and other fermented foods—as well as wheat grass, barley green, blue-green algae, sea vegetables, and some nutritional yeasts—provide enough of this vitamin. However, it is often recommended that vegans take a B12 supplement.

Vitamin B5 (Pantothenic acid)

"Pantothenic" means widespread, and this vitamin is so named because it is found in all live plant and animal tissues. Consuming a wide variety of whole grains, legumes, and vegetables will ensure adequate intake.

Biotin

Another B-complex vitamin, biotin is essential for the metabolism of proteins and carbohydrates. Consuming a wide variety of whole grains, legumes, and vegetables will ensure adequate intake, to supplement what is manufactured in the intestine.

Folacin

Folacin, or folic acid, acts in conjunction with B12 to produce red blood cells. It is important in the synthesis of DNA, which controls heredity and tissue growth. Folacin is plentiful in many foods, including dark green leafy vegetables, asparagus, avocados, green peas, wheat germ, broccoli, citrus fruits, beans and other legumes, and whole grains. Since folic acid is essential for a healthy fetus, pregnant women should be very careful to get enough. Some women choose to take a supplement while pregnant. We recommend you discuss the issue with your prenatal health care provider.

Vitamin C

Many studies have been done on vitamin C and the role it plays in promoting health. It is known to contribute to healthy gums and teeth, aid in iron absorption, maintain the connective tissue known as collagen, and speed our healing from a cold or flu. Enjoy the many sources that nature provides, such as citrus fruits, strawberries, tomatoes, broccoli, greens, sweet potatoes, red bell peppers, papaya, and cantaloupe.

Vitamin E

This vitamin is renowned for its antioxidant properties, as it helps neutralize free radicals (unstable oxygen molecules). In protecting tissues from the damage of oxidation, it can prevent cancer and slow the aging process. Vitamin E also aids in the formation of red blood cells and in the utilization of vitamin K. Research shows that it helps prevent cardiovascular disease by reducing the harmful effects of LDL cholesterol and by preventing blood clots. The best sources are vegetable oils, wheat germ, nuts, seeds, olives, asparagus, spinach, and other leafy green vegetables.

Vitamin K

Though somewhat overlooked, this vitamin plays an important role in blood clotting and maintaining strong bones, which is especially important as you age. Healthy bacteria in the body's intestines manufacture about 80 percent of the vitamin K that you need, but the rest comes from your diet. Taking antibiotics may cause a deficiency, as these drugs destroy healthy—as well as infectious—bacteria. Good dietary sources of vitamin K are kale, cabbage, broccoli, spinach and other leafy greens, soybeans, and vegetable oils.

Calcium

Throughout our lives, bones constantly absorb and release calcium. It is critically important that children and young adults consume adequate amounts of calcium during their formative years to ensure that peak bone mass is achieved.

As we age, calcium intake continues to be important in maintaining strong bones that are resistant to fractures and osteoporosis. Good vegan calcium sources include dark green leafy vegetables, broccoli, and tofu.

Iron

Iron plays an essential role in carrying oxygen to the blood and muscles. People at risk for iron deficiencies are menstruating women, pregnant women, endurance athletes, infants, and children. This list also includes vegans, since the highest concentrations of dietary iron are found in animal foods. Good vegan sources are peas, beans, nuts, dried fruits, leafy green vegetables, and calcium-fortified whole grain cereals. Another way to increase your iron intake is to cook in cast-iron pots, especially when preparing high-acid foods such as tomatoes.

Magnesium

Magnesium is the second most prevalent mineral in our bodies, indicating its importance in maintaining good health. Its power to prevent heart disease and kidney stones is widely accepted by medical experts. Low levels of the mineral are also associated with cancer, insomnia, and menstrual problems. Good dietary sources of magnesium include sea kelp (kombu), what bran and germ, tofu, and most nuts and seeds.

Potassium

Potassium is the most prevalent mineral in our bodies and the most important dietary electrolyte. It plays innumerable functions, including conversion of blood sugar to glycogen, which is used by muscles during exercise. Hence, the earliest signs of a potassium deficiency are often fatigue and muscle weakness. Good sources of potassium include potatoes, avocados, lime beans, tomatoes, and bananas.

Selenium

This important mineral has potent antioxidant action, protecting against cancer, cardiovascular disease, cataracts, and other free radical-associated damage. Good dietary sources include wheat germ, brazil nuts, wheat bran, and oats.

Sodium

Sodium helps to regulate blood pressure and water balance in the body, but as important as it is in maintaining health, there are many warnings against ingesting too much. A major concern is that sodium elevates blood pressure in some people, setting the stage for strokes. Try to wean yourself from the salt shaker, relying instead on the sodium that occurs naturally in foods and the small amount you add during cooking. For a lower-sodium table condiment, try our Gomasio (page 311) or Spicy Seaweed Condiment (page 311).

Zinc

An adequate level of zinc in the blood is essential for strong immunity, proper gland function, and healthy skin. Studies have shown zinc supplementation to be effective in controlling acne and in treating prostate problems. Zinc is present in good measure in pumpkins seeds and other nuts, as well as many whole grains and legumes.

Glossary of Specialty Ingredients

Adzuki beans These small, oval, reddish beans have been enjoyed in Asia for thousands of years. They have a distinctive nutty flavor and retain their texture well when cooked. Look for dried adzuki beans at Asian markets and natural food stores.

Arrowroot powder Ground from the tuber of a starchy tropical plant, this fine white powder is primarily used as a thickening agent for sauces. It is available at natural food stores and some supermarkets, and is sometimes sold as arrowroot "flour." Dissolve it in cold water before adding it to a hot liquid. In the proper proportion, it will thicken the liquid almost immediately. Overcooking can turn it gummy, so add it to a dish very near the end of the cooking time.

Arugula Deep green in color, this cruciferous vegetable is rich in beta-carotene and high in vitamin C. The small, flat leaves resemble dandelion greens in shape and have a distinct peppery taste. Arugula is also known as rocket or roquette. It is easy to grow in the garden and is widely available in produce markets.

Balsamic vinegar An invention of the Italian province of Modena, this vinegar is uniquely rich, dense, and mellow. True balsamic vinegar is made according to ancient techniques and aged ten to fifty years in wooden barrels before bottling. Its unique flavor has no substitute.

Basmati rice This aromatic rice is grown in India and Pakistan and is available in white and brown varieties. Its fragrance is rather nutlike while it is cooking, yet its flavor is almost buttery. Basmati is lower in starch than other long-grain rices, so its cooked consistency is light and fluffy. White basmati can be found in most grocery stores; the brown variety is available at natural food stores.

Brown rice syrup Made from brown rice, water, and grain enzymes, this syrup has a consistency similar to that of honey, but a much less intense sweetness. It is available at natural food stores.

Bulgur wheat Bulgur is produced from whole wheat kernels that are steam-cooked, then dried and cracked into a coarse, medium, or fine grain. Because of the initial steaming process, bulgur requires considerably less cooking time than cracked wheat.

Calamata olives These succulent purple-black olives (sometimes spelled "kalamata") are native to Greece They have an intense, piquant, and distinctly bitter flavor.

Cannellini beans Also known as white kidney beans, cannellinis are mildly nutty in flavor and hold their texture well. They are a popular ingredient in Tuscan cooking. They may be purchased dried or canned at Italian groceries and some supermarkets and natural food stores.

Chili oil Oil in which hot chilies have been steeped, added to recipes in small amounts as a spicy flavoring agent

Cilantro The fresh leaves of the coriander plant, this distinctive herb—quite common in Mexican and many Asian cuisines—is often sold as Chinese parsley. It is widely available in American supermarkets.

Couscous Couscous traces its roots to northern Africa. Made from pre-cooked semolina wheat, the tiny grains of couscous are added to boiling water or stock, which they quickly absorb. The result is tender, light, and fluffy—more similar in texture to a grain than to other types of semolina pasta.

Crostini This Italian work refers to crunchy oven-baked or grilled toasts, which may be eaten with a variety of savory toppings. (See our recipe on page 301.)

Daikon radish Large, white radish commonly used in Japanese cuisine

Dark sesame oil This thick, brownish oil is very aromatic and is used more as a flavoring than as a cooking oil. Look for it in any Asian grocery store or a well-stocked supermarket.

Dried tomatoes Dried tomatoes have a intense flavor and a chewy texture. Different varieties are available—the driest ones can be extremely tough and should be reconstituted before using. Place them in a small bowl and cover with hot water for 5 to 30 minutes, or heat in a microwave for about a minute. Drain, reserving the liquid for soup stock, if desired.

Dry oil-cured black olives These pungent, wrinkled black olives lend a distinctive bitter flavor to Italian-inspired dishes. They are available in gourmet food stores or in the delicatessen case at Italian groceries.

Epazote Epazote is a leafy, aromatic herb used in traditional Mexican dishes. Mexican markets, both north and south of the border, usually carry the fresh herb, which is the preferred form for cooking.

Fennel Fresh fennel bears some resemblance to celery, with overlappng layers of thin stalks attached to a base. In the case of fennel, however, the base is a much rounder, slightly flattened bulb. Fennel's foliage is feathery and is a nice addition to salads or soups. Fennel has a pronounced licorice flavor, mellowing to a delectable sweetness when cooked. It is widely used in Italian cooking and sometimes sold at the market as sweet anise or called by its Italian name, *finocchio*.

Kasha Kasha is roasted, hulled buckwheat kernels that have been cracked into coarse, medium, or fine grains. This grain has a strong, earthy flavor that combines well with the flavors of Eastern Europe, where it originated. It is widely available in natural food stores and some supermarkets.

Lentils This category of legumes includes many varieties. In this book, we use the small green lentils sometimes called French or "du Puy" lentils; the widely available brown lentils most familiar to American cooks; and red lentils, favored in classic Middle Eastern preparations. Seek out the less common types at the natural food store, gourmet shops, or ethnic specialty food stores.

Miso Some types of this fermented soybean paste are intensely salty, others have a mellower, sweeter flavor. All contain beneficial organisms that can aid digestion. Dissolve a little miso in water and add it to enrich a soup or sauce at the end of the cooking time, as too much heat will destroy the "live" cultures. We usually use mild light-colored miso, which is less salty than the darker varieties. If your regular supermarket doesn't carry miso, purchase it at a natural food store or Asian grocery. (Read our discussion of soy on page 20 for more information.)

Organic granulated sugar There are many forms of granulated sugar available at natural food stores. We look for "organic" on the label so we can be assured no bone meal or questionable chemical agents were used during processing. Organic granulated sugar is made from the dried juice of organically grown sugar cane; it is unbleached and minimally processed and is used as a replacement for regular granulated sugar on a cup-for-cup basis

Orzo Orzo is a rice-shaped semolina pasta that hails from Greece. Like other pastas, it cooks in lots of water and is drained before being added to other ingredients. It is available wherever a wide variety of pasta is sold.

Parchment paper This heat-proof paper is used for classic meal-in-a-pouch preparations called by the French term "en papillote." It is sold at supermarkets, usually displayed alongside aluminum foil and other standard kitchen wraps.

Pastina Tiny dried pasta shapes, such as stars, most often cooked in soup

Pickled jalapeños Although pickled jalapeños are milder than the fresh peppers, they are still hot, so handle them accordingly. The seeds may be removed to reduce their spicy bite. The pickling process adds a pleasant, piquant note to the peppers. Look for them in Mexican markets or well-stocked supermarkets.

Pine nuts Pine nuts are seeds harvested from the cones of the stone pine, common in the Mediterranean region. These small oval nuts have a creamy color and texture, and a unique rich flavor. They are often toasted to intensify their flavor. Look for them at natural food stores or Italian specialty markets.

Polenta Polenta, a staple food in parts of Italy, is dried corn ground into a medium-grain meal. Some markets sell a product labeled "polenta," but if you can't find it, American cornmeal will do the trick. Cooking polenta requires boiling it in a large volume of stock or water and stirring vigorously and frequently. The resulting mixture has a thick porridge texture and deliciously creamy taste. As it cools, polenta's leftovers can be sliced and reheated by pan-frying or grilling.

Porcini mushrooms Another special favorite of Italian cooks, the porcini is a prized field mushroom with a delicious, rich flavor. Also sold by its botanical name, *boletus edulus,* the porcini is difficult to find in its fresh form, and expensive even in peak season. Fortunately, dried porcini are more readily available and lend an intense depth of flavor to soups and sauces. Look for fresh porcini at a well-stocked produce market. You may be able to find dried porcini in the larger grocery stores, or seek them out at an Italian specialty market.

Portobello mushrooms These large mushrooms are tender little criminis all grown up. They can measure 4 to 6 inches across and have a good solid texture. They are particularly delicious grilled and make excellent "burgers." Portobello mushrooms are widely available in standard supermarkets and Italian specialty shops.

Quinoa Quinoa is usually considered a grain but is technically the seed of a vegetable species. It cooks like a grain, however, and has similar uses. Quinoa is a nutritional powerhouse, packed with important minerals and very high in protein. It is readily available at natural food stores.

Radicchio A member of the chicory family, radicchio adds a unique, mildly bitter accent to salads and other dishes. Though different colors are cultivated, the most common variety in American markets is mottled purple and white. It is sold in small heads in the produce section of specialty markets and large grocery stores.

Rice milk A non-dairy liquid available in various flavors, rice milk is a good alternative to dairy milk, especially for people who don't enjoy or are allergic to soy milk. It is available at natural food stores and some supermarkets.

Serrano chilies These moderately hot peppers popular in Mexican and Southwest cooking are smaller and longer than jalapeños. Their color can range from glossy green to reddish. For a milder taste, cut them in half lengthwise and scrape out their seeds with a teaspoon.

Sesame tahini Tahini is made from hulled raw or unhulled toasted sesame seeds that are simply ground into a paste. The resulting spread has an earthy sesame flavor and is similar in texture to smooth peanut butter. Most natural food stores carry it, as do Asian specialty markets.

Shiitake mushrooms The shiitake (*pasania cupidata*) is increasingly available in fresh form, as well as dried, at well-stocked supermarkets and Asian grocery stores. These rich and chewy mushrooms combine well with many seasonings, especially those of the Far East.

Soba Soba is the thin Japanese noodle typically containing buckwheat flour but also sometimes made with yam flour or flavored with green tea. The price can vary a lot from brand to brand. Soba is usually available at natural food stores, but for the best selection, try an Asian market.

Soy mayonnaise This eggless emulsion made from tofu has a spreadable consistency similar to standard mayonnaise. It is readily available at well-stocked supermarkets and natural food stores. Sample different brands to discover your favorite.

Soy milk Soy beans are soaked in water, pureed, cooked, and pressed to create this rich milk-like liquid. It actually provides more protein than cow's milk and is suitable for many of the same uses. The different brands of soy milk vary in thickness and taste, so taste several and decide which one you like. Plain soy milk will have more culinary uses than the flavored varieties. (Read our discussion of soy on page 20 for more information.)

Tempeh A native of Indonesia, tempeh is produced by fermenting whole soybeans, sometimes in combination with grains. It is a high-protein food with a chewy texture and nutty flavor. Tempeh is often tolerated by people who have trouble digesting non-fermented soy foods like tofu and soy milk. It is widely available at natural food stores. (Read our discussion of soy on page 20 for more information.)

Tofu Tofu, a high-protein food used extensively in the cuisines of Asia, is made from soy milk that has been coagulated to form curds. Tofu's blandness makes it very versatile, as it readily takes on flavors. Tofu comes in various textures, from soft and silky to dense and chewy. Buy it at a natural food store or supermarket. (Read our discussion of soy on page 20 for more information.)

Tomatillos These firm, lime-green fruits, about the size and shape of a standard cherry tomato, grow inside a paper husk which is discarded before cooking. It has a fresh, tart flavor essential to many traditional Mexican dishes, particularly sauces. Well-stocked supermarkets may carry fresh tomatillos in season; otherwise, look for them at a Mexican specialty market. Canned tomatillos are often available when fresh ones are not.

Index

International Conversion Chart

These are not exact equivalents: they have been slightly rounded to make measuring easier.

Liquid Measurements

American	Imperial	Metric	Australian
2 tablespoons (1 oz.)	1 fl. oz.	30ml	1 tablespoon
1/4 cup (2 oz.)	2 fl. oz.	60 ml	2 tablespoons
1/3 cup (3 oz.)	3 fl. oz.	80 ml	1/4 cup
1/2 cup (4 oz.)	4 fl. oz.	125 ml	1/3 cup
2/3 cup (5 oz.)	5 fl. oz.	165 ml	1/2 cup
3/4 cup (6 oz.)	6 fl. oz.	185 ml	2/3 cup
1 cup (8 oz.)	8 fl. oz.	250 ml	3/4 cup

Spoon Measurements

American	Metric
1/4 teaspoon	1 ml
1/2 teaspoon	2 ml
1 teaspoon	5 ml
1 tablespoon	15 ml

Weights

US/UK	Metric
1 oz.	30 grams (g)
2 oz.	60 g
4 oz. (1/4 lb)	125 g
5 oz. (1/3 lb)	155 g
6 oz.	185 g
7 oz.	220 g
8 oz. (1/2 lb)	250 g
10 oz.	315 g
12 oz. (3/4 lb)	375 g
14 oz.	440 g
16 oz. (1 lb)	500 g
2 lbs	1 kg

Oven Temperatures

Farenheit	Centigrade	Gas
250	120	1/2
300	150	2
325	160	3
350	180	4
375	190	5
400	200	6
450	230	8